THE DIVORCED
MOTHER

THE DIVORCED
MOTHER

A Guide to Readjustment by Carol Mindey

McGRAW-HILL BOOK COMPANY

New York St. Louis San Francisco London Sydney
Toronto Mexico Panama

Acknowledgement is made to the following sources for permission to use material already published:

Lasser, J. K. and Sylvia Porter. *Managing Your Money*. New York: Holt, Rinehart and Winston, 1961. Reprinted by permission of Sylvia Porter.

Nathaniel Branden "The Psychology of Pleasure," in *The Virtue of Selfishness* by Ayn Rand, New York: Grove Press, 1949. Reprinted by permission of Mr. Branden.
Nathaniel Branden, "The Concept of Mental Health," *The Objectivist,* February, 1967. Reprinted by permission of Mr. Branden.

Question-and-answer material from the *Playboy* interview with Ayn Rand reprinted by kind permission of *Playboy* magazine.

Library of Congress Catalog Card Number: 75–80972

First Edition   42405

for

H. M. E.

mentor and friend.

Preface

THIS book is primarily addressed to the divorcee or potential divorcee with children. I hope to communicate to her that most of the anguish, anxiety, disillusionment, and sense of failure that accompany divorce in our culture today is unnecessary and can be avoided. The two basic themes of this book are:

1. The act of divorce usually solves nothing for an individual. You may sincerely believe you are getting rid of your biggest problem—your mate—only to discover your biggest problem has always been *you*.

2. Successful divorce requires rational preparation.

I lived as a divorcee for almost six years. My marriage failure was the greatest personal tragedy of my life; yet my divorce gave me the opportunity to grow as a woman and to have a way of life more suited to my values, desires, and needs.

My own need for explicit information—for facts, suggestions, indeed for *help*—during the chaotic period in which I struggled to handle my new independence and vastly increased responsibilities was what led me to write this book. It began as a twenty-four-page article I showed to my psychotherapist a year or so after being separated from my husband. (I began therapy six months after filing for divorce.) The psychologist was aware of my ambition to be a writer as well as a fulfilled, self-sufficient, and sane individual. He also realized I was still timid about taking the necessary steps to have what I wanted. After he read my first efforts, he suggested I expand the article into a book.

I went home and thought about it. I doubted then that I had the self-discipline for such a venture; I even suspected he was giving me therapeutic busy-work. But I began to read everything I could find pertaining to divorce and the practical and psychological problems facing young mothers like myself. I decided to write this book.

For three or four months I worked like mad—reading, writing, talking to male and female divorcés, writing some more, then rewriting. I evaluated what I had produced, then put it aside, realizing I was too emotional, still too subjective (often still bitter), perhaps not well-educated enough to express myself clearly. After a year I picked up my manuscript once more, became reinspired, and began again. I kept thinking of the many women with children who are divorced every year—almost a quarter of a million of us with many problems in common, all across the country in small towns, big cities, in suburbs—such a huge and varied audience! Could I say something necessary and helpful to each of these mothers?

In my readings about divorce, I also read about love, sex, men, and women. I recognized my need for more formal education after reading Simone de Beauvoir's perceptive book, *The Second Sex*. At this point I enrolled full-time in a local university and continued my education after being away from school for fourteen years—I have been a full- or part-time student ever since. My return to school meant reorganizing my life: I had to limit my working hours, cut my expenses, curtail my social life, and schedule my classes to suit the schedules of my sons. (I'll never forget my older son's question the day I went to take the entrance exam: "What do you want to be when you grow up, Mom?")

Had I waited another year or two, I undoubtedly would have written a different kind of book about divorce. However, it was clear to me the book could not wait. Each time I talked to another divorcee (or potential divorcee) who was struggling with the new and seemingly impossible demands of her situation, I wished I had a copy of my book to hand her.

Although most of this book deals specifically with the problems confronting the divorced mother, I believe it will also be of value to the man who is divorced or is contemplating divorce. One chapter is specifically directed to the male divorcé, and parts of other chapters (about children, legal problems, and so on) are intended for him as well. Other individuals interested in marriage problems and family life in America may also find the book of interest.

Forgive me if some of what I say at times seems overemotional.

I have lived divorce. What I say comes from my mind, my heart, my former agonies, and my new and joyful discoveries. I have learned that although divorce is difficult, one's situation need not be impossible because of it.

Acknowledgments

MY DEEPEST thanks to the following for their help: Dr. Roger Callahan, who encouraged me to write this book; attorney Herb Eiges, for his help, advice and encouragement, and assistance with the fifth chapter; Leon Jaroff, science editor of *Time* magazine, for his help and advice; Dr. Alvin Rose, my social psychology professor at Wayne University, for help in obtaining special reading materials as well as his enthusiastic encouragement of my project; Jay McCormick of Wayne University for his succinct and excellent advice; attorneys Phil Penberthy, for help in obtaining special reading materials as well as comments on Chapter 5, and attorney Henry Baskin, for special information for Chapter 5; Fenton Calhoun, for his encouragement and help.

My thanks to my dear friends Doranne Crable and the late Shirley Carlyon, for their help with reading and editing the manuscript; also special thanks to John D. Hilberry and Bob Sundmacher, for their invaluable help with certain sections of the book. My thanks also to Cleo Abuin, Marilyn Kershenbaum, Shirley Templin, and Cathy Volante for their suggestions and insights about various sections of the book. My sincerest thanks to the many other men and women who gave me their personal stories, opinions, and criticisms.

My thanks also to psychologist and philosopher Nathaniel Branden for permission to use material obtained at various lectures, as well as Dr. Roger Callahan for special material for Chapter 8.

And a most special thanks to my sons, Christopher and David, for their help, love, and patience during the living and writing of this book, as well my husband, Wayne Franson, who endured with us the hardest part.

Contents

Foreword

HERE at last is a much needed, down-to-earth book full of practical help for people contemplating divorce. But there is more. Mrs. Mindey's excellent book is an omnibus of advice and aid for people encountering marital problems. There is help offered ranging from how to find and choose a marriage counselor, how to deal with problems with neighbors, to tips on running a household.

This book also offers potential help to those who are *considering* marriage. There is enough rational stimulation provided to allow one to anticipate certain problems before they arise and perhaps prevent some divorces by discouraging some marriages that should never occur in the first place. Too, Mrs. Mindey's book may help some readers to be more conservative about having children until there is a fair certainty of having a successful marriage.

But life and marriage are much more than running a household or getting on with the neighbors. Central to marriage, of course, is romance. Writers in psychology have devoted little attention to the important subject of romantic love. There is an excellent discussion of this in the book, which counselors and therapists would be well advised to read. It includes some of the profoundly important and insightful ideas of the brilliant psychologist Nathaniel Branden. It is extremely valuable to have this material available.

Mrs. Mindey's work is backed by substantial scholarship and bibliographic research. But this is no mere dry citation of facts. The author has a lively style and she draws freely and engagingly from her personal experiences.

An important major theme of the book is the fact that personal psychological problems are not dealt with or solved by switching marital partners any more than they are by a change of climate. Because there are so many excellent concrete points in the area of coping and dealing with marital and psychological problems, many counselors who encourage bibliotherapy for their patients will want them to read this book in order to improve the efficiency of the counseling. The book should stimulate thinking and expand the range of awareness and sensitivity to problem areas and may thereby improve the introspective efforts of patients.

ROGER J. CALLAHAN, PH.D.

[*Dr. Callahan is a psychotherapist, and a marriage and family counselor in private practise in New York City.*]

THE DIVORCED MOTHER

Chapter 1

Mothers and Divorce

OUR tremendous divorce rate—a current total of almost one million men and women and at least 600,000 children personally involved in homes breaking up every year—is the result of many factors. I am not going to study these factors in this book, although I will refer to them from time to time. Other writers have studied divorce and its effects on society; there is a reading list at the end of the book for those who want such information. What I am most interested in is what actually happens to the divorcee with children—and how she can best adjust to single life again and make a happy home for her children after the shock of divorce. Can she possibly avoid divorce—not only for the sake of her children, but for her own sake? It does not seem to matter much who instigates the divorce; there is a period of shock and anguish most divorced persons suffer and somehow endure. If we are going to break up our marriages at such an alarming rate, we must try to change our lives (and our children's) in a more rational way. Those who are not divorced feel lucky and somehow untouched by all this. But if they examine their innermost thoughts, they will learn that they feel threatened every time they hear of a friend or relative getting divorced. They may say "It can't happen to us," but it can. I was one of those who believed her marriage would never be ended by divorce.

I became interested in the possibility of rational divorce shortly after the breakup of my own marriage. I am not a doctor, sociologist, psychiatrist, psychologist, lawyer, or other kind of expert. I am simply a thirty-seven-year-old woman who married at twenty, divorced at twenty-nine, and remarried at thirty-six. I managed the lives of three human beings for six years—mine and my twelve-and thirteen-year-old sons'. As I look back now on my years as a divorcee, I see I could have been much happier and much more productive—had I known what was ahead of me and been prepared for it.

Divorcees who have children still at home are neither fish nor fowl: we are still in a sense "married"—we must keep house for our children and take care of them, yet we are now significantly alone and often want and need to be able to function as single adults in many of our new social, professional, and romantic relationships.

We are too often not at all prepared for the step we have taken (or that has been thrust upon us) and find ourselves overwhelmed by our old emotional problems in addition to the burden of new and frightening practical and psychological problems.

This book has been painful to write. I have been forced to think about many things I would like to erase and completely forget. But I have learned that as a divorcee one can only face the future in a healthy way by understanding the past. The divorcee must understand the forces and factors that led her to the mate and the life she chose: she must see that the pattern for her often-neurotic choice of a mate and her own neurotic behavior during her marriage actually began early in her childhood.

With three kinds of sight she can prepare herself and her children for a happy, productive future. What I believe and know about divorce has evolved from these three kinds of sight:

1. *Hindsight.* I reviewed each stage of my life and my relationships with the key people in my life. I thought about my goals and aspirations before marriage and how I had allowed myself to be sidetracked. I thought about the point at which I became aware that my marriage was in distress and would probably not last unless drastic changes were made. I considered the years in which I tried unsuccessfully to do something about my unhappiness in marriage. I thought about the steps that led me to a lawyer's office. And I examined my years as a divorcee.

2. *Insight.* I scrutinized as closely as possible my own emotions and personality with the help of psychotherapy and an objective

method of introspection. I learned to think about myself in a detached way by imagining what I would tell another woman who had the same problems, and I then tried very hard to take my own advice by not making exceptions for myself. I learned to assess my fears, problems, hopes; to observe myself as an individual who was not functioning the way she would like to; to test new ways of thinking and acting. I learned that the responsibility for my future actions was now mine alone. I realized that I was a victim of my past—I had not chosen my early environment, genes, or training—but that I did not have to allow factors over which I had had no control to devil me for the rest of my life. I learned to change myself gradually whenever I discovered a character defect or a self-defeating personality trait. After almost a year of psychotherapy I continued to be my own therapist, reindoctrinating myself with the healthy concepts I had learned in psychotherapy, catching myself when I goofed and not being too embarrassed to go back for a session with the psychologist when I ran into a problem I could not understand and solve. I learned to retrain myself to be more productive, rational, and happy. I learned that the growth of the human personality need never stop: with continuous insight and effort, one *can* create a new soul.

3. *Foresight*. After I understood why my past was the way it was, I also understood the forces that had shaped my personality and why I had functioned as I had. I was then able to choose a goal, focus on it, and redirect my thinking and actions. I learned to plan for my future and the future of my sons in an efficient, realistic, and constructive way, keeping in mind at all times who I am and what my talents, inclinations, and limitations are. I was able to see my sons as individuals with marvelous potential, not as remnants of a personal disaster.

A divorcee needs these three kinds of sight or she will be blind to what actually led her to her poor marriage choice and eventual divorce. She must understand clearly how and why it all happened or she will not be able to make necessary changes in her life and personality. She will be ineffectual as the guardian and counselor of her children and she will be frustrated by failure to make realistic plans for the future.

This book is not a panacea for the problems of divorce. An act so final and serious as the breaking up of a family brings with it immense practical and psychological problems for each member of that family. Since I have been focused on the subject of divorce—not just my own divorce, but the causes and effects of divorce—I have observed a great deal of avoidable waste, waste of human effort and emotions and time, and a waste of hard-earned money. Many of the costly mistakes commonly made by the uninformed divorced mother or father can be avoided. The woman who is not yet divorced but seriously considering it would do well to think clearly about what lies ahead of her and her children. Divorced persons of both sexes owe it to themselves and their children to come out of the experience as unharmed as possible.

Had I been aware of these matters when I filed for divorce, I could undoubtedly have saved myself much acute mental and physical suffering, as well as several thousand dollars spent on medical bills, impulsive and unnecessary purchases, and lost income. My children certainly would have been spared some of their suffering, and I probably would be closer today to the goals I set for myself. But eight years ago I was desperate and concentrated on one thing: getting out of an unhappy marriage as quickly as possible.

Several months after filing for divorce I went to the library to find some books that might tell me what to expect as a divorcee. The books told me how terrible divorce was, how it would damage my children emotionally, what a national disaster our zooming divorce rate had become, how immature and neurotic we Americans were because we could not all stay married until "death us do part." But there was no concrete advice for *me*—not a word about how I should handle the numerous practical and psychological problems facing me and my children. In fact, what I found was so negative and full of despair that I was thrown into panic. What had I done to myself and my sons? I had no desire to have my husband back—we had just failed at a reconciliation attempt and I was in the throes of what I describe elsewhere in the book as the divorcee syndrome.

My health was not very good. I had insomnia, the beginnings of a serious skin disturbance (anathema to my part-time career as a model), and I had developed an ulcer from the tensions of the last year of my unhappy marriage. My children, who were then in the first grade and kindergarten, had begun to show signs of disturbance as a result of the tensions before their father left, but I was too distracted to know how to help them. The best I could do was to continue to cook and keep house for them, but they did not have much of an in-focus mother during those months. Was there no hope for us?

Fortunately, my anxiety became so acute that I was forced to seek help. I was intelligent enough to see that my illnesses were psychosomatic—that they were psychological, not organic, in origin. I had not been a sickly person most of my life and these new ailments were preventing me from functioning fully. (I will discuss elsewhere in the book the value and necessity of some kind of psychotherapy for the divorcee. I learned that neurosis can be cured.)

While writing this book, I have thought about all the different kinds of information that would be most useful to a divorced mother. What are some of the things *I* should have known? I have doubtless overlooked some of the problems facing many divorced mothers with unique backgrounds, values, and needs. I have nevertheless made general statements about our problems, and in some cases I have given both general and specific advice. Each woman will have to find what suits her in these pages. I believe newly divorced mothers have these things in common:

1. We have the need and desire to be loved, yet we do not always know how to get or give love, share it with others, and keep it alive and growing. The ability to earn and keep love—genuine, healthy, mature love—can be learned. The divorcee may discover that through painful trial and error, but with help she can improve her ability to love and be loving.

2. We care about and love our children, but too often we are so burdened by our own fears and problems that we have little energy or time left to love our sons and daughters in a mature, constructive way.

I will also discuss what can be done to repair and preserve a marriage. One need not hastily discard a rapidly deteriorating marriage —there is a sane way to evaluate just what it is that is wrong with the marriage and the individuals in it. There are ways to solve the many problems we face as husbands and wives, and I advocate a method of problem-solving based on accurate perception of the facts of reality. Married couples who decide to stay together "for the sake of the children" and then continue to mistreat one another verbally and physically make a grave mistake. No doubt, they decide to stay in the unhealthy marriage for themselves, not their children, because if they had their children's best interests at heart, they would either change their destructive treatment of one another and learn to live happily, or dissolve the marriage and try to live as happy individuals, each giving the children his best. There is overwhelming evidence that children who live in homes split by emotional divorce are generally worse off than children whose parents separate and obtain a legal divorce. In any case, *I am never suggesting that there is any better way to rear children than in a home with two mature, sane, reasonable adults who love one another and their children.* If the choice is between having the children live with both parents when the parents are consistently miserable and neurotic together or with one parent who can behave in a more reasonable way, I believe that the children fare better with the one happy, rational parent. (How the court decides who gets custody of the children is another problem I discuss later.)

Of the 500,000 couples who are divorced every year (and the rate increases as our population increases), 60 per cent are parents, which means that this year about a quarter of a million women will face the overwhelming problems of being divorced mothers. The average divorcee is often naïve and totally unprepared for what is ahead of her. The frustrations and new problems unleashed by the ending of her marriage may compel her to marry the first available and willing man who happens along. Or she may begin a series of seriously self-defeating actions that may prevent her from being the right woman when the right man *does* come along.

She learns quickly that not many satisfactory choices are available. Her new role as breadwinner and double-duty parent will exhaust her. She will resent having to sacrifice so much to have her freedom; she may not be able to accept the never-ending, undeniable responsibility that comes with her freedom. The plethora of dull housekeeping chores, the constant needs and demands of her children, her desire to be socially and romantically active, her anxieties about money and her future will cause stress and tension such as she never imagined possible. She will be maligned, scorned, guilty, overworked, tired. The stigma of divorce will (at first) weigh heavily upon her until at last she forces herself to not give a damn what others say or think. She may even become destructively rebellious in her newfound independence. Sometimes she gives in to the stress of her new situation and falls apart completely.

How then can the divorcee become that unique, productive, happily integrated individual she believes she can be and wants to be? Though she may desire marriage again, she suspects that she needs some time to think, to change, to find herself. But the immediate practical problems of rearing children with no man around will cause conflict. She will be torn about leaving her preschool children so she can go to work. She will worry about leaving her older children—who need her more than ever now in a different way—to go to work or on dates. She may be afraid to marry again, not trusting her judgment. Or she may impulsively marry a man who (though he looks nothing like her earlier mate) is her former husband's psychological twin, and there she is again, with the same old problems.

How can she avoid trapping herself? No matter what she may think about herself, she will continually run into those who mock her efforts, criticize her, tell her to go back to her husband, to stay home with her children, to get married again, to get a job, to move in with her parents. Some old-fashioned types will project to her the attitude that marriage is strictly a "woman's job" and, because she is a divorcee, she failed at her job and is therefore worthless. The outdated notion that women are inferior, subordinate—indeed "the second sex"—is still deeply imbued in our culture and will continue to be for some time in spite of the emancipation of women (although education, increased job equality, the fact that child-bearing is now a matter of choice for most women and not an accidental burden hopefully will lead to true equality of the sexes for subsequent generations). The divorcee will discover a negative attitude toward her because she presents a threat—to wives who may believe she is after their husbands, and to husbands who may fear she will encourage their wives to get divorces too!

The divorcee must develop a strong back and a thick skin (and often a hard head) if she is to survive. She must learn to see things as they are, to develop her self-esteem, and to have good reasons to believe in herself and her new choices. She *can* lead a sane, productive, and happy life, but only if she plans every aspect of her life and her children's lives carefully and realistically.

The decision to divorce can be the beginning of facing reality, of recognizing and reaching for one's true human potential. However, the decision must not be made without calm consideration. Why do you want a divorce? What is your real problem? What is the real problem between you and your spouse? The answer is probably not to be found in any of the legal grounds a lawyer would discuss with you. The only true grounds for divorce are *conflicting values*. If you are neurotic, you are not even certain what your values are. I hold that mental cruelty, desertion, adultery, alcoholism, violence, and the many other legal grounds for divorce are inadequate and wholly unsatisfactory ways of saying "We do not value the same things; we each have a different style of life and are therefore incompatible." But first you must determine what your values are and what you would like your style of life to be. By *style of life* I mean more than the material things we surround ourselves with; I mean one's philosophy; one's idea of what is valuable, ethical, and moral; one's attitude toward work, play, love, recreation, art, and so on.

Remember that it will be difficult to find acceptance as a divorcee with children in a society that is still basically Judeo-Christian and middle-class. Marriage brings social acceptance for many. A wedding band seems to say "I am worthwhile. Someone wanted me." Unfortunately, for many a divorce decree spells failure and frustration. The divorced are often suspect; the individual who remains unmarried for a long period after his divorce often prompts others to think "Doesn't anyone want you?" or "What's wrong with you— why can't you put up with another human being?" Marriage is the "in" thing to do in many circles—it encourages consumerism and supports and promotes "the American Way of Life"; most divorced people may have little left over for luxuries after stretching their reduced, often meager incomes to cover basic necessities. They may begin to feel like seedy, underprivileged outcasts and may indulge in self-pity because of their poor financial position and outlook.

If you are divorced after much thought and soul-searching and a genuine attempt to save your marriage, you need not feel guilty or apologetic. You will know you have done the right thing for the right reason. But if you are angry, frustrated, impulsive, and irrational, you are almost certain to reap a harvest of despair.

Perhaps you have tried the existing methods of trying to save your marriage and have discovered there is no marriage to save. Then you must prepare for a divorce in a rational way. You must start now to build a new self to take into a new life. You must allow yourself plenty of time to expand, to develop, to *become*. You must avoid rushing into or being pressured into an unsatisfactory second marriage.

Divorcees are often idealistic about love. If we are not too neurotic, if we have not been too brutally wounded (in childhood as well as in love relationships and marriage), we can believe in love and ourselves enough to try again (and again and again and again, in some cases). We must mend not only our broken hearts; we must somehow mend our broken lives and take care that we do not break other hearts and lives in the process.

We must work diligently to see that our children are not warped or maimed by our failures and mistakes. We must live in the present, building workable, reasonable values so that we may live sanely whether we remarry or remain single.

We must face practical problems that are often our psychological undoing; we must solve our personal difficulties with the inadequate tools available—it is unfortunate that there are not enough good marriage counselors and psychotherapists available to re-educate us all to be happy lovers and good parents. We are stuck with our country's archaic and irrational divorce laws and must somehow retain our human dignity as we use these primitive tools to untie ourselves from the bonds of marriage. We must make wise decisions about our new family roles and responsibilities, our new sexual and romantic needs. We must develop new and sensible relationships with our former husbands because they are the fathers of our children and our children need their fathers. And we must develop our potential as human beings.

The marriage habit is hard to break. Don't let breaking the habit break *you*.

Chapter 2

Can You Avoid Divorce?

An open letter to husbands and wives
with divorce on their minds

YOUR marriage is sick and you know it. Because you do not know how to make it well, you have decided to kill it. What weapon can you use? You've tried nagging, blaming, violence, noncommunication, impotence, frigidity, infidelity, indifference. You want to put it away for good now. The ultimate weapon: *divorce.*

Stop! If you are unhappy in your marriage, there are concrete reasons for your distress. Do you know them? Are you able to see objectively what the problems are and what is causing them? How stable are you? Are you clear-headed enough right now to assess accurately the condition of your marriage? Personal problems can be solved by asking clear questions, assembling evidence, judging the possible consequences, and trying to verify in practice what has been concluded from the evidence. Irrational persons fail at problem-solving in marriage because of distortion, self-deception, defense mechanisms, and rationalizations. Because they are unable to estimate probabilities they may adopt fatalistic or superstitious solutions.

Divorce is about as final as you can get. You are saying "There is no hope for us." Are you certain? Do you have a clear idea of the ramifications and repercussions of divorce? How many divorced persons do you know? Did divorce solve their problems? At the present time, more than six million Americans are divorced or separated; approximately 50 per cent of divorced persons are the chil-

12

dren of marriages which ended in divorce. Divorce breeds divorce. But you'll have little or no peace unless you go about this the right way. There *is* a right, reasonable way to end a marriage. You should first get an estimate of how sick it actually is. If you owned a basically good house with a leaky roof and an old furnace, would you burn down the house? No. You'd repair the roof and get a new furnace. An ailing marriage can be like such a house—basically good but in need of repair. Sometimes all a marriage needs is some investment to make it valuable again. Ask yourself and one another clear questions about your marriage: what did you each bring into it, what are you giving to it now, where is the evidence that he is entirely wrong or that you are entirely wrong; what are the consequences for you both if you divorce? What about your children?

Your first move before doing anything destructive or final should be to see a skilled psychotherapist or marriage counselor—together or separately. Psychiatrist Edmund Bergler says in *Divorce Won't Help:* ". . . neurotic conflicts in marriage should be treated psychiatrically and not in divorce courts." Both spouses should be treated, because if only one of them were changed, the "neurotic balance" would be endangered. Neurosis is curable. The neurotic lacks the ability to work, to love tenderly and with normal potency, to have normal social contacts and interests, and to enjoy hobbies. Does that sound like one or both of you?

Another consideration. Perhaps you are not psychologically sick. It is possible your marriage problems are caused by something organic and quite beyond your emotional control. There is a connection between mental and physical health. If your mate is "driving you out of your mind," your marriage problems may be caused or aggravated by the physical problems one or both of you are having. There are certain periods in a woman's life which can be quite stressful and emotionally upsetting: pregnancy, the months immediately after childbirth, menopause. Some women become upset and physically uncomfortable each month with premenstrual tension. A trip to the doctor's office for an examination, some pills or an injection can save much grief. Women have other physical problems not tied to their reproductive systems. Men have ailments peculiar to their sex, as well as high blood pressure, heart trouble, ulcers, and other problems. Perhaps what is making one or both of you hard to live with is organic and not psychological in origin.

You should both have complete physical examinations by a competent physician. You must also get an accurate evaluation of the state of your marriage before doing anything about ending it.

A trained professional who regularly deals with these problems can help you assess what is wrong and can teach you a method of solving problems together. Divorce *can* be avoided if you get the right kind of assistance, and the cost of counseling or psychotherapy is much less than the cost of a hasty divorce. (See pages 33 and 208 for ways of finding a psychotherapist or a marriage counselor.)

Most marriage counselors agree that the following underlying factors are present in most unsatisfactory marriages (from an article in *Redbook*):

1. *Unsound reasons.* Many persons marry early to avoid loneliness or to find security or prestige.

2. *Unrealistic expectations.* "And they lived happily ever after" is the last line of many fairy tales, but marriage is not a fairy tale. We must stop being so addicted to fairy-tale endings. We need to recognize the stresses that can occur in any normal marriage and know how to handle them.

3. *Pressures and stresses contemporary society imposes.* We often expect more than is humanly possible from our mates. A woman is expected to be an enlightened and stimulating companion to her husband, a charming hostess and good homemaker, an attractive and exciting sex partner, a patient and understanding mother, and hold a job outside the home for some portion of her marriage. A man is expected to be an ideal and compassionate companion, a wise father, active in community affairs, a good provider so his family can have creature comforts, a thoughtful virile lover, and handy and generally helpful around the house. We are all expected to be mobile enough to pack up and move when a promotion or job transfer comes along.

4. *Inability to "ride the waves."* Some of the ordinary life problems such as money, health, children, housing, in-laws, jobs, and the like overwhelm many couples. Each begins to blame the other for situations that may not be either partner's fault.

According to marriage counselors, the problem expressed most often by husbands and wives in trouble is *We can't communicate.* There can be no mutual problem-solving in a marriage without communication and a healthy interaction between husband and wife. A skilled marriage counselor or psychotherapist can listen objectively to both sides and teach couples to reach one another—perhaps for the first time in their married lives! You must remember that your partner is not a mind-reader; no matter how long you have lived together it is necessary and important to talk things over when there are difficulties. If you have trouble verbalizing what is bothering you, write it down. Give your mate a letter that describes and explains your upset feelings. If matters are touchy and delicate between you, have your spouse reply in writing until you are both able to talk face to face. I cannot stress enough how important this is, to let one another know what you are thinking and what is really disturbing you. If writing it all out seems easier and less painful than talking, do so. Perhaps when you see your own complaints in writing you will understand yourself much better, too. The process of writing it out will force you to slow down and become calm. You cannot shout on paper or punch someone in the mouth. You may even discover that many of your complaints are groundless, or are matters you bring on yourself. It's worth a try. I would also suggest that you write a letter to *yourself* about what you think divorce would do in your case.

To sum it up: talk, talk, talk. If you cannot talk, then write. But somehow, *communicate.*

TO HUSBANDS

These next few pages are intended for *husbands.* I shall review some common problems women have with their husbands. Marriage has a meaning considerably different for a woman than it does for a man. Although today's woman has many more opportunities for self-fulfillment than did her mother, she still usually looks for her greatest satisfactions in marriage and parenthood. Sometimes a woman mistakenly believes that once she is married, she will indeed "live happily ever after." She may need more from the marriage (and her children) than the man does because she has so few outside interests. What can you do to improve life for your wife? It is not enough to supply her with security and material comforts. She perhaps seems restless and unhappy to you and you wonder, as Freud did, "What is it that women want?"

Does your wife have some talent or ability she had to set aside to manage your home and children? Is there a reasonable way she can work toward a goal of her own? Can you cooperate with her, and get your children to be more cooperative and less demanding? Could you possibly cook dinner once a week, or could some of the older children take over more of the chores? Do you resent any time your wife spends away from home doing something which matters only to her? Do you like having her tied down or would you prefer a less exhausted, more stimulating companion? You have your work; if things are not going well at home, you can justify longer working hours, your nights out, your weekends or weeks spent fishing, golfing, hunting, and so on. What does she have besides work that never seems to be done? Could you possibly help her organize your household more efficiently?

Your wife may have more gadgets to help her do her job, but she also has greater responsibility and more awareness of what her life could ideally be. Are you blocking her from doing what vitally interests her? She wants to do more, know more, see more, and *be* more. If she thinks being your wife is preventing her from living fully, she may consider divorcing you. You have the opportunity to help her have this fuller life—without divorce—and you can both benefit. Perhaps in your struggle to keep her in the home you have avoided taking *your* place in the home. Why can't you both have *both*—a good home life and a stimulating life outside the home?

If you never agree about how your time should be spent, about what your individual responsibilities are, it is time to take inventory of yourselves, your marriage, and your life style. You can have a rich, full life together, but you will have to clear away the debris of generations and generations of silly thinking about what man is and what woman is. We are human beings first. As humans, we have human natures that cannot be ignored, regardless of sex. Males and females have both similar and different capacities and needs—we must not overlook our similarities or exaggerate our differences. We each have the need to achieve, to love, to have the approval of others around us, and to have our own identities. It is not enough for a woman to be known as Jack's wife or Debbie's mother. Your wife gave up her name when she married you. Did she give up her identity too?

When she is unhappy, do you buy her another gadget? Do you

you? Are you pampered and humored like a small boy? This is a
dangerous attitude for both husband and wife because it turns married life into a game. It is true that in marriage at times one partner
needs more comforting and understanding than the other, but this
should be done with a spirit of benevolent and loving generosity
rather than in a condescending or supercilious way of "humoring"
the partner who is behaving immaturely.

Another expert who studied the problem of the battle of the
sexes (Ashley Montagu in *The Natural Superiority of Women*) has
this to say:

> ... the male's drive in work and achievement may actually be the con-
> sequence of his recognition of his biological inferiority * with respect to
> the female's creative capacity to conceive and create human beings. One
> of the ways in which the male may compensate for this biological inferi-
> ority is by work and achievement.... Hence, the great opposition to
> women when they begin to enter into "competition" with men in earning
> a living. Married men, in particular, frequently object to their wives
> working; they consider it, somehow, a reflection upon themselves. They
> fear it will be said that they are unable to support their family.

Is part of your marriage problem the ancient and erroneously
founded battle of the sexes? Do you believe that women are indeed
inferior and should be subordinate?

As women observe the culture that has been formed largely by
males, they often do not like what they see. Perhaps you and your
wife could start on your marriage problems by helping one another
get rid of your irrational beliefs—this would be far more constructive
and profitable for you both than divorce.

Another book about the problem women are facing today has this
to say:

Women will never learn to give of themselves until they are psychologi-

---

* Montagu regards females as biologically superior because they live
longer and have greater stamina than males; they endure starvation,
exposure, fatigue, shock, illness better than men; the female is constitu-
tionally stronger than the male, and only muscularly less powerful; there
are thirty serious disorders found more frequently in males than in females;
in every age range, more males die than females; men have a higher suicide
rate, there are many more of them in mental institutions, and they break
more easily under emotional strain than do women; women do not fight or
commit acts of violence against others as often as men do; more boys than
girls have behavior problems—a 4-to-1 ratio; in school performance, girls
outdo boys; the suicide ratio is ten males to three females, which would
indicate that women appear to value life more than men do.

realize that aside from wanting her own identity, she i
want more of *you*—sharing common interests, talking abo
tant things together, sharing your joys and sorrows? Do
your family will enjoy the new swimming pool you bought
never home to enjoy it with them? *Things* are poor subst
action, for achievements, for shared love.

Do you share similar values? Do you have the same i
what love is? Have you fallen out of love, and has your
suffered? Do you think it is impossible to find your way bac
another's good graces?

What is ahead for you after divorce? You will lose you
and the comfort and service you have become accustomed
will lose your children—most of their companionship,
some of their respect and affection; you will lose money—chi
port will continue until the last child is eighteen, and son
child support and alimony take one-third to one-half of your i
(consider too that you will have little or no say about ho
money is to be spent); sometimes you lose friends after a di
and your career can sometimes be adversely affected by a di

As women become more independent and self-assertive,
want and expect more from life, marriage, and their husban
their deepest needs are not being met, they may mistakenly tu
divorce as a solution to their problems as human beings. Many
lusioned and disappointed wives show their rejection of male va
codes, rules, and regulations by obtaining divorce. These wo
feel they are being held back from life's joys by husbands who
ther care enough about them nor understand them. Not all of t
divorcing women are neurotic—many of them can have happy
ond marriages. However, the neurotic woman may unconscio
choose a man who will dominate or degrade her, undermine
efforts, and who may be threatened by her talents and competer
Such a person is constantly frustrated in the marriage and deci
she can be happier on her own.

Dr. Bergler takes the position in *Divorce Won't Help* that the
tire husband-wife relationship in our culture is based on a coloss
bluff—the bluff of male superiority—and that the typical woma
intuitively does not take her husband too seriously because she kno
he is at best a "grown-up baby." Does your wife feel this way abo

cally secure and emotionally self-sufficient—confident that the integrity of the personality has been preserved in the pursuit of self-defining adult activity.

The quotation was from *The Love Fraud* by Edith de Rham, which discusses the fraud imposed upon women in general through the popularization of the notion that *being* is as satisfactory as *doing* and that love is a valid substitute for action.

In the past, women often resigned themselves to thinking they were handicapped by the role Nature handed them. Most men have assigned us the role of inferiors and we have generally accepted the role without much challenge. But today there are many women who demonstrate daily that we who choose to be active rather than passive are *not* neurotic or in competition with men. It is not so that if men are this, women are that. There are active men and active women, just as there are passive men and passive women.

I am not suggesting that women must give up parenthood in order to have other meaningful work. It is quite possible for women to have both the joys of parenthood and the rewards of their own productive work, but one's time must be valued and carefully planned; while a woman has preschool children, she can continue her studies on a part-time basis or work part-time in her chosen field. (More than 60 per cent of all part-time workers are women.)

The working wife needs an understanding husband, and she herself must be sure she does not get her own values confused: she must put first things *first,* and her children's needs are immediate until they become reasonably independent (some children reach the stage of relative independence by the time they are in the second or third grade).

If your wife has been restless, scrappy, not especially interested in you or your sex life together but has not yet threatened you with divorce, do not be complacent. There is trouble coming, but you *can* avoid it. Talk to her—find out what is really disturbing her, encourage her to fulfill herself in a way that will benefit you both (and your children). If she has a goal of her own, she will not be so insistent on pushing you ahead in your career. Many wives try to force their husbands to move faster in their jobs because their entire identities are tied up with the husband's prestige and position. Encourage her to use her mind, to develop herself and her capabilities. If you fight her, she may abandon you in her struggle toward her own self-esteem.

If she *has* threatened you with divorce, moves into the guest room (or goes home to mother), and says she needs and is getting professional help, *pay attention.* If you love her, forget your prejudices and your concepts (which may be based on false premises). Go with her to the marriage counselor or psychotherapist. (One-third to one-half of the marriages headed for divorce are saved when the couples obtain professional help.) If, after counseling or therapy, you decide to divorce, you will know you have explored the possibilities of repairing your marriage. The divorce will be far less painful for you and the entire family if you both rationally decide it is the best solution.

Men somehow think there is something unmanly about saying "Things are going poorly and I need help." To be able to say "I am in trouble and I do not know what to do" is not cowardly. Facing reality takes courage, and facing our own inadequacies with a willingness to do something about them takes special courage. The coward wants to escape, to avoid conflict and unpleasantness, and fears or resists change.

Most women actually do not want to be divorced. What they do want is a significant change for the better in the marriage. A woman may be crying "Wolf!" to shock an indifferent husband into action. This is a dangerous game and both could lose. A man has the right to avoid the break-up of his marriage, but he must be aware of what it is his wife wants. All her threats are undoubtedly intended to get action from you: she wants to know that you *do* value her, that you do care about the marriage and your life together. Perhaps she is too distressed to approach the problem in a logical way. Don't condemn her because she is upset. She has much at stake, and so do you.

If you find it extremely difficult to live with your wife during this period, you may find Dr. Albert Ellis' *How to Live with a Neurotic* helpful.

Perhaps your wife screams at you—"Get out. You're driving me crazy." No matter whom she blames for her misery, sometimes it is better for an agitated couple to separate until things calm down. When I was in group therapy six years ago, there was a couple threatening violence to each other at each session. The therapist recommended that they separate temporarily until they calmed down enough to assess reality with greater equanimity. There was no telling whether or not they had a marriage to save; they were very hostile and antagonistic and both out of control. After a few months apart they gained greater understanding of themselves and their marriage problems and were able to live together again and work on some of their problems.

One of the first places the trouble shows up in an unhappy marriage is in the sex relationship. It is beyond the scope of this book to give detailed descriptions of the psychological problems which can cause sex problems, but I can say this much: A woman cannot surrender herself sexually to a man she fears or hates. Your wife must trust and respect you and feel proud of your relationship or you may both have serious sex problems. (In the last chapter I discuss the essentials of a good romantic love relationship.) A woman must feel that the act of love is one of her own choice, not *duty*. Women today are becoming less and less sexually inhibited and they want more from their love relationships with their husbands. Not just greater and more frequent orgasms, but the profound and beautiful feeling that can come only from loving and being loved. If you have somehow lost your way sexually, you may need to rebuild your marriage relationship carefully so that you can fully enjoy together a good emotional and physical relationship. This can never be achieved by force. Many women head for the divorce courts because their physical relationships with their husbands have become dull, painful, or repugnant. You may need to be completely re-educated so that you can become a better husband and lover. Unfortunately, you will not find all the information you need for this in the marriage manuals. Romantic love is much more than physical technique.

If your wife constantly baffles you, it is possible you do not understand women at all. We are tied to our reproductive systems and our husbands must be aware of the changes that continually take place in us because of hormones. How much do you know about premenstrual tension? If your wife is impossible to live with a week before her menstrual period, do you blame her and tell her it is all in her mind? Did you know that 79 to 84 per cent of all crimes committed by women occur during, or in the week before, their periods? Did you know that her irritable moods can be controlled with pills?

If your wife is dieting to be more slim and attractive for you, did you know that she could develop temporary neurotic or even psychotic symptoms because she is not getting enough sugar in her diet? I am not suggesting that you can solve your problems by giving her sugar (although a box of candy now and then might be helpful). I am emphasizing these physical differences because many men still do not understand the physiology of women. Unfortunately, many women do not understand their physiology either.

If you are genuinely interested in knowing and understanding your wife, read some of the books on the following reading list. Here are just a few to start you. Your book store or library no doubt has many new books on the "woman problem." Pick up one of your wife's magazines and see just what it is that women care about most: husbands, home, children, social problems, personal problems. We women also share many concerns and problems with you, but unfortunately many of us remain strangers all our lives because we cut ourselves off from one another's worlds.

The books written for women about the problems modern women must face would be better read by men than women. For women to read them is almost a waste of time—we *know* how difficult it is to be women in the twentieth century. We live the difficulty every day. We may try too hard to be all things to all people, thereby neglecting ourselves. In neglecting ourselves we often neglect the men we love.

Women and Sometimes Men by Florida-Scott Maxwell
The Second Sex by Simone de Beauvoir
The Feminine Mystique by Betty Friedan
Gift From the Sea by Anne Morrow Lindbergh
The Love Fraud by Edith de Rham
Why Young Mothers Feel Trapped, a *Redbook* documentary edited by Robert Stein
Special for Women by George Lefferts, adapted from a television series
The Natural Superiority of Women, by Ashley Montagu

Max Lerner discusses "The Ordeal of the American Woman" in his *America as a Civilization,* in Chapter 8. If you read the books on the foregoing list, you will have a good start toward understanding the "woman problem" and if you decide to make a project out of this and read everything you can find on the subject, you may decide your wife is not so bad after all, that she shares similar problems with millions of other women, and that you might do well to stand by her—even help her.

Divorce creates special problems for the man with minor children. Their mother will undoubtedly have custody, and the father will be allowed to visit them perhaps as often as several times weekly, every weekend, or as seldom as once a month or even once a year, depending on the circumstances of the divorce and the kind of relationship he has with his former wife.

I have seen a sad thing happen far too often: some men who love their children deeply are denied the right and opportunity to be true fathers to their children after divorce. The former wife, if she is vindictive, may use the situation to get even with her former husband for his divorcing her or for the years she felt she wasted, suffering him and the marriage. Even a once quite reasonable woman may do all she can to cut a father off from his children; the man may retaliate by sending child support checks or alimony late or not at all. If the mother is disagreeable about visits and fosters an attitude of hostility in her children toward their father, the father (if he is weak) may eventually lose interest in his children and give in to her neurotic wishes. He may fade away altogether to avoid the conflict and bitterness that taint the visits. It takes a strong, emotionally mature man to keep a close, healthy relationship with his children after divorce. A man must objectively understand that his children need him, regardless of what their mother says. He should not make an effort to win them away from her (unless she is very sick and he decides to get custody), but he should give them constant evidence of his love and care for them by being available, responsible, and interested. This is difficult to do at a distance. Sometimes a man's children will be thoroughly indoctrinated against him by their mother and members of her family. He must be very careful about how he goes about earning and keeping his children's love— he must not bribe them or use emotional blackmail against their mother. No matter how much the mother objects to his visits or the gifts he sends, he must at all times keep in mind what is objectively necessary and important and right for his children. And he must also try to communicate with his former wife in a reasonable way.

Sometimes a divorced father may have to turn down job transfers and promotions because he does not want to move away from his children. He may have thought when he got his divorce that he would at last have freedom, but he sadly learns that there is a tremendous lack of freedom coming out of all this freedom!

Something else to consider: as a divorced father you will not have much say about your children's education unless you have an agreeable working relationship with your ex-wife.

The father-child relationship that develops after divorce is unfortunately for many men and their children quite artificial; they have "dates" with their children and become either "good-time Charlies" or Boy-Scout leaders. Having a constructive, rewarding parental influence after divorce takes more work and effort than a man may be willing or able to expend.

What about summer vacations? Perhaps after divorce you decide you want to see your children for your annual vacation because it is the only opportunity you have for an extended visit with them. What about much-needed time for yourself? If you were still married you would think nothing of taking off for two weeks with your wife and leaving your kids with a housekeeper or relative. Could you do that as a divorced father and not feel guilty?

Something else: all those "Sundays with the kids" may get to be a chore after a while. How many times can you go bowling, to the zoo, the museums, the circus, children's plays, and the like? You may soon weary of having to contrive activities for each visit. The man with sons can take them fishing or hunting or to various sporting events, such as baseball and hockey games, and races, but what about the man who has daughters? How can he plan his time with girls? It may be somewhat easier after a man remarries, but suppose his second wife has children of her own? When would he be able to work in those infrequent but so precious and necessary moments alone with this or that child?

I am not suggesting that a man stay married only for the sake of his children. An unhappily married man should nevertheless consider repairing the marriage and staying in it for his own sake. If he values his children, he will want to do all he can to be a continuous constructive force in their lives. He can *best* accomplish this by having a good relationship with their mother, preferably in marriage to her.

Therefore, if you have children and are seriously considering divorce, think about these issues. You will have to work twice as hard at being a father after divorce. Are you up to it? You will discover that you miss a casual relationship with your children. You will wonder if perhaps there was something you could have done to save the marriage. If you can avoid divorce, *do so*. If you cannot, be prepared for the life ahead of you, and help your wife and children prepare themselves for what is ahead of them also.

TO THE WOMAN CONSIDERING DIVORCE

Most of this book is directed to you and discusses many of the problems you may face as a divorced woman with children. As you decide whether divorce is your answer, make yourself aware of the risks involved.

I would not want to dissuade any woman from the worthy goals of having romantic love and a good marriage; if it is possible to have those goals with the man you are presently married to, it makes more sense than getting divorced to reach the same goals. Did you know that as a divorcee with children your statistical chances for remarriage are not very good? Only two of three divorced mothers remarry. Are you prepared to live the next thirty or forty years without a mate? You may have to struggle alone for many years; what if you become seriously ill—who will look after you and your children? Are you being realistic about the enormous task ahead of you as a divorced mother?

Do you think you will receive plenty of money from your former husband? Do you know that most ex-husbands (even the nicest ones) actually hate to send that weekly or monthly check, and that you will undoubtedly spend many years haggling with your children's father about child-support payments (and perhaps alimony for yourself), extra money for summer camp, music lessons, education, and so on?

Do you realize that you will not be accepted with open arms in many social groups—an extra woman at a party is not considered the blessing an extra man is. Do you realize that your life as a divorced mother may be about two or three times as exhausting as your present routine?

Consider these questions:

OCCUPATIONAL: Are you psychologically prepared to take a full-time job?

Are you trained for a job?

Do you have a reliable housekeeper or baby-sitter?

Are you physically and emotionally strong enough to manage both home and outside work without the help of a husband?

FINANCIAL: Do you have enough money of your own to cover an emergency?

Does your husband earn enough to support two households?

Do you manage money wisely?

Will your children be seriously deprived materially after a divorce?

PARENTAL: Are you confident you can rear your child or children alone? (You may be one of those one in three divorcees who does not remarry.)

How much of an active role in your children's lives is your husband willing to fill after divorce? (He may run away to punish you for rejecting him.)

SOCIAL: Are you equipped to attract eligible men?

Are you aware of how few eligible men are seriously interested in a divorcee with children?

Are you willing to make an entirely new set of friends if necessary?

Are you flexible enough to change your way of life (for better or worse) for yourself and your children?

If your husband asks for a divorce, what should you do? There is no way to force a man to love and respect you. You can force him to stay legally married to you, but such a marriage will exist on paper only. Some vengeful wives refuse to consent to a divorce even though they know there has been no marriage for years. If you are fighting a divorce, what is your *real* motive?

Can you stall your husband if he seeks a divorce? Of course. An attorney can use many legal means to prolong divorce proceedings: you can contest indefinitely (when the case comes up, if your husband has no legal grounds, divorce is denied); you can demand an exorbitant property and financial settlement. You may end up with money and no man.

If you wish to win your husband back, what can you do? If you have been indifferent and disinterested for years and he has now fallen in love with another woman, you may have had it. Can you possibly get him to love you more than the other woman, or delay things until he loses interest in her? If you really want to hold him, do you think you can do it by force and by being spiteful?

Make an objective evaluation of yourself. Have you been a good companion, friend, lover, mother? Are you a competent home-maker? What do you have to offer? There is no denying that being physically appealing helps any romantic relationship: are you sexually desirable? Have you offered less than he has offered and demanded more than any man could give?

Is your husband susceptible to extra-marital affairs and is he having a fling now? The problems of the promiscuous man (married or single) have often been glossed over with the excuse that men need variety. If your husband is chronically unfaithful, he has a severe personality problem and needs help. If you want to stand by him while he gets straightened around, you may be able to save your marriage. Some women threaten divorce whenever a husband errs. Be sure this is not a sick game you two have learned to play.

If you have been a dud as a wife and your husband is seriously considering divorce, you will have to make an all-out effort to be of greater value to him. What is it he wants in a wife? Can you give it to him? Occasionally a man will ask for a divorce as a means to shock a dull, apathetic woman into action, but I think women use the threat of divorce much more than men do; if he's asking, he's undoubtedly serious about it.

Again, I would suggest seeing a marriage counselor or a psychotherapist to get help with your personal problem. Whether you stay married or end up divorced, you will gain greater insight and have a clearer idea of what you want and how to get it. If you wish to see a lawyer to learn what your rights are, do so, but be cautious. Do not make any decision about divorce while you are upset or hurt. Confusing American divorce laws vary from state to state and are all too often inadequate for the realities of modern marriage and divorce. You will need the best legal advice you can get, and you will need to evaluate the situation carefully. Chapter 5, "Divorce and the

Law," gives suggestions about how to find a competent attorney and which questions are crucial to you.

Remember that couples who rush into divorce without adequate counseling may be too falsely proud to drop the suit after papers are filed. There usually have been bitter words, ugly scenes, sometimes friends and relatives have been told too much (or have seen too much) and the couple must "save face" by going ahead with a divorce neither of them actually may want. Perhaps they are hoping someone will stop them before it is too late. But no one will stop them.

You must take the responsibility for your own actions. You must stay in control of your emotions and thoughts. If you are served with divorce papers (a woman rarely is, but if it happens, be prepared), see a good lawyer. You can contest a divorce if you sincerely love your husband and want to stay married. It may take a long time to win him back, but if you have children and if you believe there is something worth saving, it is worth a try. A number of states have conciliation courts that assist couples to repair marriages.

Forget about false pride now; there is too much at stake for you to attempt to hurt your husband just because he has hurt you. Take your time and make a decision based on reality.

Perhaps you will learn you would be better off divorced. If that is the case, face it. Divorce can give you a second chance, but only if you're ready for it. You will eventually get used to the loneliness. After the first feelings of euphoria and relief fade away, you will be able to face the reality of your new existence as a divorced mother.

For myself, I chose to get out of a sick marriage. I was not at all prepared for what was ahead of me. It appears now I had the same delusion I did when I was twenty ("I'll get married and live happily ever after"), except at twenty-nine I thought "I'll get divorced and live happily ever after."

Is that what you are thinking? If your marriage is sick and you're willing to stay in it without demanding and working on changes and improvements, ask *why*. Do you feel you are undeserving of anything better than what you now have?

For better or for worse, you married. If you divorce, will it be for better or for worse?

FOR BOTH HUSBANDS AND WIVES

Suppose you have both had complete physical examinations and determine there is nothing organically wrong, and one or both of you go through some form of counseling or therapy. You decide to divorce because your values conflict and you are no longer in love. Perhaps deciding to divorce is the most realistic decision you've made in years. If your mate is a chronic alcoholic, philanderer, gambler, criminal, or the like, or an individual who is otherwise unable and unwilling to face reality, you do have the right to leave this mate, provided you have given him enough warnings and enough time to change. If you have undergone the painful but worthwhile process of psychotherapy and your mate has not (refusing all the while to recognize his or her serious emotional problems), you are entitled to an existence without such a mate. It is difficult if not impossible to lead a reasonable, productive life with a seriously disturbed husband or wife. No sane individual should be expected to make such a sacrifice for another human being.

Your decision to go on alone will meet with much resistance. If you are certain you have tried to assist your partner in working on and solving your individual and mutual problems and your partner neurotically refuses to do anything constructive, you are justified in seeking a divorce. You need not be a prisoner of love or of hate.

If two persons are psychologically healthy, and share similar values, they certainly have a much better chance of staying happily married than do two persons who are not psychologically healthy and have conflicting values. Of course there must also be a physical attraction, but can you love a person whose style of living you disapprove of? A mentally healthy person will not endure or participate in "mental cruelty" and other neurotic interactions in marriage. An individual with sound values, a good estimate of himself, pride and self-esteem will not tolerate poor treatment from any other individual, nor will he contribute to another individual's neurotic behavior. The sane, sound person will do everything possible to avoid and eliminate neurotic behavior on the part of others.

Love and marriage should be taken more seriously—we should be better prepared for both. Alfred Adler says in his book *What Life Should Mean to You* that man is faced with three problems:

... how to find an occupation which will enable us to survive under the limitations set by the nature of the earth; how to find a position among our fellows so that we may cooperate and share the benefits of cooperation; how to accommodate ourselves to the fact that we live in two sexes and that the continuance and furtherance of mankind depends upon our love-life.

IF YOU KNOW SOMEONE WHO IS HEADED FOR DIVORCE: Too often bewildered relatives and friends stand by mutely, watching a couple they love mutilate the bonds of matrimony. Yet a wise adult would not permit a young child to carry a destructive tantrum to its conclusion lest the child be harmed. Wise friends and relatives must at times involve themselves in someone else's business—they must intervene and even contravene.

Can you in good conscience stand by and watch a human being you value destroy himself and possibly others? Do you have a right to say "You are making a mistake"? You have a moral obligation to yourself and the troubled individual (providing the person is important to you—we should certainly not go tapping at our neighbors' doors every time they do something we think is bad for them). If you are mature and respected by the person you want to advise, it is likely you will be listened to.

I recently talked with an older woman who told me of an experience which validates this. Her married son had told her that his marriage was headed for divorce, as he was involved with an older woman who had given him a superiority complex, making him feel that his wife had failed him. The mother finally decided to intervene. She wrote him a letter explaining why she believed he was on the wrong path, and suggesting that he and his wife seek professional help for their marriage. After much work, expense, and time, the marriage was saved, thanks to the initial influence of the mother.

Chapter 3

The Predivorce Period

H*elp—my husband walked out on me . . ."*
Every year several million husbands walk out on their wives. Some of these men vanish completely and do not turn up ever again, in spite of the efforts of police, relatives, detectives, missing-persons bureaus, and other agencies. After seven years (in most states) a deserted wife is automatically granted a divorce. Some of the husbands come back (sometimes as soon as the next day) to face their problems; some of the couples are able to save their marriages. Some of the men come back, only to leave again, and eventually divorce their wives or are divorced by them.

What should the woman with children do if her husband walks out on her? I can sum it up in four words: *Stay calm—get help.* If the marriage has become troubled enough for a husband to leave his wife, there is the added problem of one or both of them using the desertion as the final step to end the marriage. When they are under emotional pressure they must hold off making decisions they will regret later. A deserted wife can feel many different emotions—panic, anger, hatred, extreme hurt, rejection. Sometimes she is glad and relieved when he is gone.

The woman whose husband deserts his family must be aware that he is having serious problems with himself as well as with her. Perhaps he is not running away from her and their children, but actually from himself and his life situation. He may be having job diffi-

31

culties, health and emotional problems, or perhaps he is heavily in debt. Perhaps he has found another woman. Whatever his reasons for leaving, the deserted wife must keep in mind that most of these problems can be solved. This is a crisis in their marriage and must be dealt with calmly—a bad decision now may seriously alter the lives of family members for many years to come.

Some choices available to the deserted wife:

1. Wait until your husband returns, taking no action of you own in the meantime.

2. While waiting for him to return seek help for yourself (and perhaps your children).

3. If you are calm enough, evaluate the situation yourself. Ask yourself why he left; do you want him back; what do you think you can do to improve yourself and your relationship with him, and so on.

4. You can leave too (go home to your mother, for example).

5. File for divorce immediately to get even, shock him, hurt him, or threaten him.

The last choice leads to disaster. Never use divorce as a threat or a weapon. If you rush to a lawyer while you are distressed and upset, it is quite possible you will have your husband served with divorce papers before you have carefully reviewed the situation. A lawyer may ask you several times if there is any hope of reconciliation and he may even recommend counseling, but if you are in a huff you will repeatedly say "What I really want is a divorce—let's get this over with." After a man has been tracked down and served papers, it is usually immensely difficult for either partner to make the move toward reconciliation. Pride gets in the way and neither will budge. Too often a marriage that might have worked ends abruptly. Do put off any final decision until you have had good professional counseling. It is of course a good idea to find out what your legal rights are and what might be ahead for you and your children in the event of a divorce. If you decide to see a lawyer to get facts and information, list your questions and take notes while you are in his office. It is too easy to forget or later misinterpret what a lawyer said. If you cannot afford the services of a lawyer, check your phone directory for the number of a local Legal Aid Bureau.

The deserted wife faces the danger of going to pieces (becomes acutely anxious and unable to function at all) or becoming severely depressed. If she is the kind of woman who worries about what others say and think, she will suffer loss of face when friends and neighbors learn her husband walked out. However, when a husband walks out, it is not always so final as a woman may think. He may need a breathing spell, a chance to go away and think things over. Often he discovers that he misses his wife and children so much that he cannot bear to be away. Sometimes, however, he is so relieved to be away from tension and hostility that he will not come back unless she promises to change her behavior. She must realize that he cannot be forced to come back, and if he makes certain demands, she will have to meet them or be willing to compromise. She must try to accept him when he comes back and be willing to make a real effort to settle their problems. There are trained experts to turn to now, persons who can give the necessary assistance to help solve the immediate practical and psychological problems brought about by desertion.

Here are some suggestions about how to handle things temporarily. Much will depend upon the woman's financial situation. The deserted wife of a man who has been out of work for several months will need something different from the wife whose successful executive husband left her for a fling with another woman. In most instances, women with children will want their husbands back and will be willing to work at improving the marriage.

For the woman who is strapped financially, there are places to go for free or low-cost help. Each city, county, and state varies in the kinds of services it offers persons in distress. It is possible you will not know where to go, who to call, or even what to look for in the yellow pages of your phone directory. Contact any of the following for help. You are sure to get a good lead to the right kind of individual and family counseling services available.

1. *A psychologist or a certified marriage counselor.* Beware of getting someone who is not adequately trained and who does not have proper credentials. "Selecting a Psychotherapist" on page 208 will help you choose a good therapist.

2. *Your family doctor.* He will know of the public agencies that could help you, or he may be able to recommend a psychiatrist, social worker, psychologist, or marriage counselor.

3. *Your children's school.* Ask for a conference with the principal of the school or a visiting teacher or school psychologist. Most

schools have specially trained individuals on their staff either full or part-time to assist parents and children in trouble. If your trouble at home has been of long duration, it is likely that your child's teachers have been aware of it. Remember that the teachers and principal and others at your child's school are trained professionals—they know other trained professionals who can help you. Do not be embarrassed to ask for assistance. Your tax money pays their salaries and you have a right to whatever services are available.

4. *Your church.* If you are religious and a churchgoer, you may be more comfortable seeking help through your church. Many priests, rabbis, and ministers are specially trained to do some family counseling. Your religious adviser may be able to help or may direct you to someone else. There may be real (though sometimes temporary) comfort in prayer and increased church attendance in time of stress and confusion; meditation is good not only for the soul but also for the mind. Do not confuse prayer or increased attendance at religious services with *thought and action,* however. There is a danger of accepting your suffering with meekness and resignation instead of actively helping yourself. Religion used as a permanent means to evade reality does more harm than good.

5. *Your local college or university.* Ask for the Sociology or Psychology department and state your problem briefly, for example: "I am an unemployed mother with three small children and my husband has deserted us. Can you tell me where I can get help for myself and my children?" You may get no help at all, but there is no harm in trying. It is quite possible that you will be put in touch with a professor who can refer you to just the social agency you need.

6. *Your local newspaper.* Ask or write for information about family aid. Perhaps a writer or an editor of the woman's section could help you. Remember, these trained professionals are likely to know where someone in your situation can get assistance.

Because many public service agencies have waiting lists, you may have to wait several months for an appointment. If this happens and your need is immediate and urgent, you may have to pay for help. If you are too broke to pay for the counseling you need, you should consider making an investment in yourself. If necessary, get a job to pay for your counseling, or borrow the money from a friend, relative, or your local bank. Most psychotherapists are willing to arrange reasonable terms with their patients—they realize that when a person is in emotional trouble, lack of money prevents him from seeking and getting the right kind of help. Once a person who has been troubled gets his life straightened out, money is usually less of a problem and paying back a loan is not so difficult.

You may be temporarily relieved after discussing your marriage problems with your mother or sister or best friend but, more than likely, after you have unburdened yourself there will be little or no constructive advice to follow, and the problems loom just as darkly as they did in the beginning. If you choose a confidante who is not wise or objective, you may be led into doing something you will later regret. When you feel you hate your husband or when you want to be vindicated of guilt or blame for his actions, you may actually *like* hearing "We always said your husband was a no-good bum"—but this is not constructive or objective. Perhaps you need to be told what you have done wrong also, but it is hard to take criticism from friends or close relatives. I am not suggesting that you must never talk to a friend or relative about your problems. You must choose someone who is wise, honest, and objective. A well-trained professional counselor will not take sides the way your mother or best friend might and will help you establish and understand what the problems are and teach you methods of solving them.

If your children are old enough to ask, they will want to know where their father is. Try not to run him down, no matter how hurt you are now. You will have to keep your family together during this crisis and you must make it possible for your children to love and respect their father. You might say "Daddy and I have been having some trouble [they are probably aware of this fact] and he went away because he is upset and unhappy. Don't think he left because of you. And try not to worry—I am doing all I can to help fix things up."

With time, patience, and the proper help, you will learn whether or not there is a marriage to save. You will make matters more difficult than they need be if you turn the situation into a catastrophe.

Suppose you want to find your husband and get him to return. How can you best go about this? Here again a person who regularly deals with such problems can advise you on the best course to follow. Should you call the police to help locate your runaway husband? That depends on his emotional and physical state when he left. If he was drunk, ill, or seriously emotionally disturbed, you want to be certain he does not harm himself or others. It is difficult to say how a husband would feel about being brought home to his wife and children in a police car; it may be the wrong action in many cases, yet in some cases it might be just the thing to shock him into facing reality. You will have to evaluate this. If you cannot decide what to do, call a wise person you know and trust, such as an older male relative who might know where to find him, a close family friend, or your family doctor. You cannot force your husband to come back. If he is completely out of control, you must take steps to prevent him from harming himself or others.

When some men and women become emotionally upset, they go out of focus to the degree that they can do serious (sometimes fatal) damage to other human beings. Violence never solved a human problem, but persons who are feeling upset and destructive and base their actions on uncontrollable feelings must be stopped and helped. If your husband has a violent temper that flares up regularly, perhaps you are afraid to have him return. If you suspect he might harm himself or another human being, call the police. We have all read about or heard of husbands and wives who kill one another (or try) when they are having marital problems.* If you are married to a violent man, you must face the fact that he has a serious problem and needs help. In order to see that he gets that help, you must remain calm and not antagonize him.

You must guard against being impulsive now. This is not the time to be careless about spending money or running around with friends where you can be seen "living it up" in public. You may want to strike back at your husband for leaving you, but any punishment you try to inflict on him is sure to backfire. Keep in mind that suspicious and upset husbands sometimes do strange things to those they love; if your husband thinks you are interested in another man, he may use violence against you, even if you are innocent. And if you *are* interested in another man and have been seeing him secretly, remember too that outraged husbands who desert their wives can turn up unexpectedly and harm their wives (and sometimes the wife's lover and anyone else who may happen to be around).

Keep track of your expenses. If you have never handled the fam-

* The marriage quarrel is the single biggest cause of murder, according to the National Crime Commission Report to the President in 1967.

ily money, you may have trouble managing the finances, particularly if you must live indefinitely on a reduced income. If your husband left no money for you, and if you do not have access to a savings or checking account, you may have to take a job or seek welfare. Do not be too embarrassed to discuss your financial problems with someone who can help you. Do not run up a lot of debts. Your husband is required by law to pay for certain necessities such as household items, rent, utilities, medical expenses, shoes and clothing for the children, but you must have ready cash in hand for groceries and other necessities.

If you really believe your marriage is going to end in divorce, it is particularly unwise to spend large amounts now on unnecessary items. Buy only what you and your children need—if the marriage is legally dissolved and your husband cannot pay the bills, you may be required later to pay for all or half of what you charge now. Do not abuse the privileges and protection granted you by the law.

To summarize what you can do in the event your husband leaves you:

1. Do not panic.

2. Talk your problems over with a trained professional, and get regular psychotherapy if it is recommended.

3. Watch your spending, and do keep records of your expenses while your husband is gone.

4. Help your children face the situation by:
   a. not running down their father.
   b. giving them assurance of your love and concern for them and your concern for their dad.

5. Do not "run wild" socially as a way of distracting yourself or getting even with your husband.

IF YOU AND YOUR HUSBAND ARE WAITING FOR A DIVORCE

A couple whose divorce is pending may elect to stay together until the divorce is final. If they have mutually decided this because they're trying to sell a home or make other living arrangements, and agree they have come to the end of their marriage, they need not be bitter or ugly to one another while they work out these final details. However, staying together after divorce proceedings are started can be one of the most tension-producing arrangements possible.

For many couples, a Bill of Complaint is a declaration of war. It may be better to separate immediately than stay together and risk having the relationship deteriorate further. For some couples, there may be an improved chance for reconciliation if they separate. However, if your spouse has fallen in love with someone else, it may be too late. If you do continue living together, and you want to make an all-out attempt to win him back, you will have to correct the faults he's complained about. You can't expect to win if you don't change.

Occasionally one hears of a man who wants to divorce his wife but refuses to move out until the divorce is final. This adds insult to injury. If he stays and uses financial necessity as his excuse, he has no business getting divorced—he can't afford it.

I recently heard of a complicated case. The man asked for a divorce after bringing his girlfriend home to meet his wife and three children. The wife, shocked and upset, resisted the idea of divorce for almost a year. He persisted and she went away for the summer with the children. While she was gone, her husband started divorce proceedings. During their vacation she met a kind widower who also had children. Romance bloomed, all the children became friends, and by the end of the summer she wanted to be divorced. She returned home in the fall and told her husband she was willing to go through with it. He became upset when he learned she cared for another man, refused to move out of the home, and made life miserable. He upset a holiday dinner by accusing her of adultery, beat her in front of their children, and finally she was forced to move out to protect herself and the children. (Her divorce went through. She is now happily married and living in another state with her new husband and all their children.)

If your husband files for divorce, decides to stay around until the divorce is final, and you cannot move away, here are some suggestions:

1. Be circumspect in your social activities. If you begin dating and appear to be having a good time, he may make your life unbearable. Don't flaunt your activities. If you decide you wish to be divorced too after he has filed, don't talk about it too much or he

may change his mind and decide to delay things. Some men seem to be motivated more by a desire to punish their wives than to be free of an unhappy marital situation.

2. Sleep in separate rooms.

3. Keep track of household expenses. See to it that he pays the necessary bills. If you work, you'll have to pay for your own entertainment and extras. Save as much as possible.

4. Don't talk against him to the children. Realize that he may be upset and not be in control. He may drink heavily and come home violent, looking for the opportunity to make a scene. If he regularly becomes dangerously abusive to you and your children, call your attorney for advice. There is no need to live in fear.

5. Do not provoke him. Keep your distance, be civil, and realize it will soon be over.

It is difficult to force a man to move out of his own home if he does not choose to. You would have to prove that he has harmed you physically (the threat is not enough). Check with an attorney on this point if it becomes necessary.

Chapter 4

What Every
Divorcee Needs

THE life of a divorcee with children is a most complicated one. In order to adjust to her new problems, a woman must make careful preparations to ease the transition from married mother to divorced mother. If you have thought the matter over carefully and have concluded that you and your husband do not share similar values, have no love left between you, and have no other valid reasons for staying together, your next step will be to see a lawyer to file for divorce. Before you do so, remember that you need to get ready for your new life as a single parent. Because divorce is painful, many women try to avoid thinking about it as much as possible and may allow themselves to be catapulted into an action they will later regret. If your husband demands a divorce and you realize there is no way to regain his love or hold him, you are entitled to some time to prepare yourself. A woman must be (or be prepared to be) independent before she is divorced. Self-sufficiency and emotional and financial independence are primaries for every divorcee. Without them a woman may flounder indefinitely or be forced in desperation to contract another bad marriage because she cannot go on alone.

There is a painful and long period of readjustment, of introspection, of finding one's way again. A woman with most of the practical problems solved beforehand seems to have less trauma and anguish after a divorce. American women have been conditioned to think of marriage as their most important goal. A woman who has failed at marriage (no matter who instigates the divorce) is likely to think of herself as worthless for a while. Therefore, project into your future. Think about the kind of life you and your children will live, and try to plan and prepare for it while you are still married. Don't be so completely out of focus that you can concentrate only on being rid of your husband.

Be aware that money is likely to be your biggest problem. Most divorced women get less money than they need and most divorced men must pay more than they can afford. The average woman does not get important alimony; sometimes she receives a token payment of ten or twenty dollars a week. Often the woman who can work receives nothing. The wife who has been totally dependent all during the marriage may receive some alimony, but usually not as much as she could earn herself. A woman has a choice: she can remain a "dependent" and require and obtain alimony, taking her chances that she will receive enough to live on, or she can prepare herself for independence and support herself after divorce. Child support and alimony are not one and the same. Child support is based on a man's income and lasts until the last child is eighteen. It is usually not enough to cover all of a child's needs, and it certainly does not include payment for the time a mother must spend with a child, thus making herself unavailable for other work. If your children are teenagers, the child support will last just a few years. If and when your former husband remarries, he will undoubtedly try to have the child support (and/or alimony) payments reduced. This money from her former husband is not something a woman can always count on.

The divorcee will also be cut off from any of the financial benefits of widowhood (if she remarries a man who is also divorced, it is quite possible that he will be so financially burdened that he will be unable to provide adequate life insurance for her and any children they may have together). In most divorce settlements the alimony then is either negligible or nil, unless the woman is divorcing a wealthy man. Even then she may not receive alimony if her husband can prove she was the "guilty" party (sexually indiscriminate)— wealthy men have the means to hire detectives to spy on adulterous wives; see Chapter 5. If there are children and you are an average couple with an average income (the median annual wage for the full-time working man is $6497, for the full-time working wife it is $3859), you probably will not receive enough child support to maintain your family's former living standard.

The following would be most helpful for the divorced mother:

1. *A sense of humor.* If you do not have the ability to laugh—at yourself, at your children, at the flooded basement, at the cracked plaster, at the overdue bills, at life—many days will be filled with tears. In those horrid months before my separation, I misplaced my sense of humor. Nothing was funny. I learned to laugh again when I got tired of being anxious, grim, and depressed so much of the time.

Your children are a marvelous source of fun and humor. They will appreciate your efforts to see the humor in things, and because they are still unsophisticated (and not cynical) they can laugh at simple things—such as your pretending to be a broken record. During the first year after my divorce, I used a trick to keep myself from crying when things got too grim. Sometimes I would be totally exhausted and missing something I felt I'd never had: the love of a sane, kind, strong male. I would stand at the kitchen sink and sing corny love songs—off key—to amuse myself. After two or three bars of "I Love You Truly" or "Indian Love Call" my sons and I would be laughing.

Read funny books. If your children are old enough, read to them from any one of S. J. Perelman's books; though they are not for children, the books are such delightful nonsense that anyone can appreciate them. Listen to your children's jokes and riddles, and tell them jokes too. You will have to work at this if you are not used to being funny and laughing at things.

Friends rescued me by sending funny cartoons, newspaper clippings, cards, and the like. It's a good idea to stay in close touch with your humorous, optimistic friends. Even though you may feel like completely withdrawing from the social scene, don't. My friends saved me many times by making me laugh.

If you have the space and the patience, having pets around helps one's sense of humor. We've always had a dog or a cat and my sons and I have enjoyed our animals' antics.

Life is rather empty without romantic love—imagine how empty it would be without laughter!

Okay. Stop laughing long enough to get

2. *A job*. This is essential. If you are well established in a good position, you will be secure financially, and financial security will help you gain emotional security. No one pays housewives what they are worth; I recently read a report that estimated the average wife and mother's services are worth $8994.52 annually. After your divorce you will have just as many chores, plus the additional burden of the work your husband did. You may be doing almost $9000 worth of work at home, but no one will pay you for it. So get a job!

If you are an employed and well-trained professional, you have a definite advantage over the woman who has stayed home for ten or twenty years. She may receive alimony because she is helpless and "dependent," but you will have the advantage of absorption in useful work. You will be more in touch with reality, you will have necessary and enjoyable contact with others, and you will have greater self-esteem than the stay-at-home woman. Betty Friedan expounded on the "problem that has no name" in her book *The Feminine Mystique*—which explained why most women regularly get depressed when they do not do useful, productive work outside the home.

Any mother with small children (and a past history of "cabin fever") has days she wishes she could go off in the morning to a stimulating or even a dull job. This is not to suggest that the divorcee with infants or preschoolers abandon them immediately for a career. Many women can arrange to work part-time until the children are in school. Perhaps you can set your own hours, or work at home, or do some kind of free-lance work. There are several helpful books written for the working mother, among them:

The Case for the Working Mother by Dorothy W. Cotton and *So You Want To Be a Working Mother* by Lois Benjamin.

Whatever your situation, whatever the ages of your children, some kind of work (for which you are paid) is necessary. Your job will give you a reason to have a schedule and to stay well-groomed and attractive, interested in something besides your own problems, and stimulated and stimulating. The lonely divorcee without productive work and contact with others will have too much time for self-pity and self-blame. To be cut off from other adults is demoralizing. Consider too that an excellent way to meet your future husband is on the job.

Incidentally, employment agencies and employers request information about one's marital status; if you are in the midst of a divorce, your application might be put in the inactive file. Some cautious or conservative employers do not wish to hire individuals who have marriage and emotional problems. However, the owner of a large employment agency told me that widows and women who are already divorced usually make much better employees than married women because women on their own are "hungry" and more willing to work hard. Do try to find your job while you are still married, if possible, so that you can learn to organize your life around a job.

3. *Good health.* See your doctor for a complete physical examination. Take care of any major or minor health problems which may intensify after a divorce; it is better to have surgery done (if you need it) while there is still a man around to drag out the trash and do other heavy work. Most of the divorcees I know have experienced one or more of the following problems during and after their divorces: insomnia, stomach and digestive problems, high blood pressure, alcoholism, severe and frequent headaches, extreme fatigue, dizziness, anxiety or depression to the degree that they could not function at all, acne, eczema, warts and other skin disorders, and other real or psychosomatic ailments. Functional problems can be just as painful as organic ones. Do not endanger your health with little rest, too much alcohol and smoking, too much worry and anxiety, and other bad habits. Be certain your health and hospitalization insurance covers you adequately, and maintain it after the divorce. And, be sure you have

4. *Good teeth.* Dental work often hurts; it's expensive and time-consuming. Be smart enough to see your dentist every six months whether or not you're getting divorced. If you require any dental work, major or minor, don't put it off. At the time I considered divorce, I procrastinated about seeing the dentist. My irrationality cost me more than $700 in dental bills after I was divorced. Don't feel guilty about having your teeth fixed or your appendix removed. Your husband is legally responsible for these matters. Does this sound too calculating?

I am not suggesting you buy a fur jacket or a new convertible. And speaking of convertibles, let's consider the matter of transportation. You'll need a

5. *Reliable car.* Indispensable, unless you live near the subway, ride a bike, like to walk a lot, or roller-skate. If you cannot drive, learn to do so *now*. If you have a used car, keep it in good repair. I was stuck with an eight-year-old heap I was able to trade for $50 after my divorce on a $2000 new compact car. I wish now I had been farsighted enough to have purchased a new car *before* filing for divorce. I had a difficult time getting an automobile loan without a co-signer. (See the section on finances for information about credit and credit ratings.) In most two-car families, the wife is awarded the second or older car in the property settlement (after all, the woman usually gets the home and everything in it). The courts figure the husband needs the newer, better car to drive to and from work.

6. *An education.* If you have not worked for several years or ever, you must be either retrained or trained for a job. Long before you actually see a lawyer, you might want to attend night school or college during the day, or get a specific kind of vocational training. Your education will increase your chances for good employment and stimulate your thinking. You'll meet new people you may want to have as friends after you are divorced. If you have always been one of the thirty-five million American women who have been stay-at-home housewives, perhaps it is time for you to re-evaluate what you intend to do with yourself and your time. Technology makes housekeeping a part-time job for those who want to use every device and service available. Our nation is short of nurses, teachers, social workers, psychiatrists, psychologists, medical technicians, not to mention the large shortages in professions largely ignored by women. This may be your opportunity to change every aspect of your life for the better. As you become more and more involved in the world around you, you may discover you demand less and less from your husband and your marriage. You may even decide to stay married. Some women become quite frustrated and unhappy in their marriages because they expect more from their husbands than the poor overworked rat-racers can deliver. If a woman has meaningful work of her own, she may become more understanding of her husband's career problems—when she stops being "just a housewife." Because she will not be using up all her energies on frustration and resentment, she will be able to develop her own talents and abilities.

Most urban areas have excellent programs for the older woman returning to school. For example, the older housewives in Great Neck, N.Y., can take courses in the "World of Work for Women" and "Career Planning for Women" to help them prepare for working again as well as organize their homes and their time. Oakland University in Rochester, Michigan, offers special courses and educational programs for older women. It is not unusual to find many women over thirty on college campuses working on their bachelor's and master's degrees (the ratio is one in three females getting bachelor's and master's degrees, and one in ten working on a doctorate).

Because the "trapped housewife" has become a figure of such great national interest and alarm, there is new emphasis on how women can combine homemaking and a career. The YWCA has a program designed to train women for many different kinds of jobs. If you do not care to return to school for formal training, call your local Y to see what you are now equipped to do, or what you can be trained for.

The Y also offers courses of great help to the woman on her own: Practical Tips on Household Electricity; Law for the Ladies; Making Home Repairs; Know Your Automobile; Understanding Your Emotions and Attitudes (an introduction to group therapy); Furniture Repair and Refinishing; Income Tax Clinic; Investing for Growth and Income; How to Buy or Sell Your Home; Discovering and Using Your Aptitudes. The Chicago Y, for instance, offers more than 450 courses to men and women. One can even go on a guided tour of Europe, slim down in an exercise class, learn to drive, or enroll in a secretarial institute. The courses range from $18 to $35 for ten to twelve weeks.

7. *A bank account.* You should have your own money, no matter what your marital status. A bank account in your own name will give you independence and a feeling of security. Pick the method of saving that is best for you and stick to it. After your divorce you'll need money for legal fees, new clothing, new furniture and equipment for a new place if you move, possible medical expenses, and many other things. There is always the possibility that you will not receive your child-support or alimony checks regularly, and you will need an emergency fund to cover several months' living expenses. The worst possible way to begin your life as a divorcee is to be financially insecure. Be prepared. Before I married, my mother (who was of the old "keep it in the sugar bowl" school) advised me

to keep my own bank account. I ignored her advice and pooled my savings with my husband's. After we paid cash for his new car, our wedding expenses, and a honeymoon in Florida, I was left without ten dollars of my own. I worked full-time for three years before my sons were born, stayed home for about four years when I was pregnant and the children were little, then worked part-time for several years as a model. All during the marriage I had no knowledge of our exact financial position. I had to ask for money when I needed it.

It is unnecessary and degrading for a woman to beg, plead, bribe, cajole, plot, plan, cry—and often even sneak—when she needs money. A wife should *never* put herself in the position of a child asking for "treat money." I do not blame my former husband for my ignorance about our money—I willingly let him control things. I thought then he could handle it better because he was an accountant when we married, and also more thrifty than I. It was a relief then to turn the responsibility over to someone else, but this laxity caused me much trouble later. When I filed for divorce, I did not have my own bank account, though I had earned thousands of dollars as a working wife. I wish now I had been better prepared for my years as a divorcee. They have been expensive in more than one way. I did manage to earn enough money for one year's psychotherapy, years of college work, music lessons for myself and my children, a used grand piano, a flute, a cornet, drums and a guitar, various vacations for us all and several weekend trips for myself, two new cars, clothing when I needed it, a fur coat, and many medical expenses for myself, as well as those dental bills and my own living expenses.

8. *The ability to take over.* This will be of interest and help to the woman who intends to keep the family home after her divorce. I am aware that there are some rare women who are competent enough to do their own work and a man's work too, but there are too many of us who think it is charming and adorable to know nothing about plumbing, fuse boxes, income tax, insurance, and so on. I am ashamed to admit I was once one of these darling women. My six-year-old son had to show me where the fuse box was a month after his father moved out. I would have lit candles and called the electrician, but my alert son saved the day as well as fifteen dollars for an electrician's services.

If you are anticipating divorce but your husband still lives at home, ask him to show you how to maintain your home and property. You should know all this anyhow, just as a man should be able to cook a meal for himself or wash a load of clothing in an emergency. Not knowing about fuse boxes, septic tanks, and income tax is just plain irresponsible.

Let's start with *your basement*. How much do you know about all the equipment down there? This requires a long list. Take a pad and pencil with you, a flashlight, and go downstairs.

The furnace. Does it need a filter change regularly? How often and what size? Does it need an annual cleaning? Is it gas or oil or coal? Does it have a switch for manual and automatic control? Would you know who to call for service? Is it an old fussy furnace or a new one that will not give you problems? If you have coal and must stoke the furnace and remove ashes, perhaps you ought to have it converted to gas or have a new one put in. Incidentally, if your furnace will not start, you may have a blown fuse.

The hot water heater. Do you know how to regulate the temperature control? Does the heater need draining or cleaning? Is there anything special you should know about the pilot light?

Water softener. Do you know how to operate it?

Water pipes. Do you know how to turn off the water pressure; can you tell the difference between the hot and cold water turn-off? Can you replace a washer in a leaky faucet?

Storm windows and screens. Where are they stored and what special care do they require?

Plumbing. Do you know what a plunger is and how to use it? Do you have a good drain cleaner (Rooto, Draino, Chloroben, are some of the trade names)? If the toilet bowl was clogged, would you know what to do? (I managed to get an apple core out of the toilet one day with a wire coat hanger, but that doesn't always work.) Do you have the name and number of a reliable plumber?

Fuse box. Learn to replace a burned-out fuse, learn to remove the main fuse, and keep your new fuses in a handy spot.

Tools. If they are stored in the basement, look them over. Do you know how to use various kinds of wrenches and screwdrivers? Could you handle an electric drill without harming yourself? Learn to identify and use tools. (One of my own biggest problems is keeping my own tools away from my sons—they invariably borrow a hammer or a wrench from me, then leave it outdoors to be rained on, snowed on, or insulted by some roving animal.)

Meters. Do you know where the electric meter is; the gas meter, the water meter?

Other things you may need to know about are: an incinerator, a water pump, a well, a septic tank. Swimming pools are a special problem; not being the owner of one, I don't know the first thing about them. If you have a pool, make it your business to learn how to fill, drain, clean, and purify your pool.

Check anything else in your basement that you cannot operate (such as a dehumidifier), and learn to operate and maintain all the equipment in your home.

Appliances. If you have a washer and dryer in the basement, learn to do minor repairs so you need not run up exorbitant service bills when a hose or a drain is plugged. Use appliances according to the manufacturer's directions and have them cleaned regularly. Do not overload your washer and be sure to clean the lint trap regularly in your dryer. Stoves and refrigerators and dishwashers are not too difficult for a woman to maintain. Never move a heavy appliance by yourself. With all the problems you'll be having, the last thing you need is a wrenched back.

Lawn and yard care. How often does your lawn need fertilizer and weed killer? What brand and what formula? What kind of grass do you have—merion blue, red fescue, bent? You'll need to know these things when you go to your local hardware store or nursery for supplies. Can you trim shrubs, trees, evergreens? Do you know their names? What about flowers, bulbs, annuals, roses? Can you handle electric trimmers, clippers, edgers, and the like? What about the power mower? I could not start our second-hand rusty power mower and no man on the block could either. I was determined not to ask my former husband for help, so I traded the mower in for a small daffodil-yellow reel-type mower my sons could operate.

Electricity. Be sure to turn it off before starting any electrical repairs. Learn to fix plugs, cords, and don't overload the circuits. Call an electrician for serious problems; this is simply too dangerous to tinker with.

Painting, plastering, wallpapering. Learn to use the appropriate tools. Acquaint yourself with spackling paste—this comes in a can or a tube for minor repairs to cracked plaster. If you do any painting, be certain you clean the brushes properly and that you use the right kind of paint for whatever type of surface you're working on. Spend an hour or two in the hardware store just learning about the stock. It's a fascinating place, and it's worth your while to get on friendly terms with the owner or manager. People who work in hardware stores are generally quite helpful and pleasant.

Children's toys, bicycles, and so on. Bikes, it seems, need repairing about once a month. Learn to adjust seats, handlebars, to fix bent or broken spokes, slipped chains, and similar problems. Teach your children, or have their father teach them, to repair their own equipment when possible.

Some other matters you'll have to acquaint yourself with are: preparing your income tax, balancing your checkbook, buying and selling stock, buying insurance, maintaining a good credit rating. Further discussion can be found in Chapter 7. Also learn to give your automobile proper attention and maintenance.

It is beyond the scope of this book to teach you in detail to prepare your income tax, buy insurance, or repair and maintain household equipment, but I wanted to point out the multitude of things you'll have to look after when your husband is gone. It will be to your advantage to be self-sufficient enough to take over completely. You may have a male relative, neighbor, or friend who can help with some of these practical issues or teach you to handle them yourself. The more you can handle alone, the more independent you will be, and the less you will need to spend on repairs and services. At times you will require the services of a professional, but with proper instruction the average woman can handle many of these things if she has the time and energy.

Don't let something like a wiggly doorknob throw you! I dissolved into tears the first time I had to clean the basement after the drains backed up. My husband had handled it when it happened every nine months or so, and I never even had to go in the basement. Since my divorce I've called the plumber seven times and cleaned up most of the mess myself. It is an ugly, smelly job (most of the jobs around the house that a man traditionally does *are,* you will learn) but I got used to it.

I had a husband who could repair anything; he even built things. I was completely inept when it came to anything mechanical, but I could do "woman's work" better and faster than most. I have learned to repair the garbage disposal, my sewing machine, plugs, cords, and lamps; I can unplug the toilet, paint, hang wallpaper, hang drapes and pictures, and do all the other things mentioned. But I was usually short of time and often completely out of energy.

A talented divorcee I know had a lovely swimming pool which became too much to maintain, so she had it filled with dirt one fall and planted cattails in it!

Let's review everything so far. Got your *sense of humor?* You'll need it as you drive to *your job* every day in your *reliable car* in a traffic jam coming and going, after getting up at 6 A.M. or so to fold some laundry, cook breakfast, shovel the walk, carry out the trash (unless you have a remarkable housekeeper). If you work a thirty-five- or forty-hour week, consider you need an hour each day to get washed, dressed, made up, combed and sprayed, and prepare and eat breakfast. You must also have a few relaxed moments to talk to your children. After you leave, count on thirty minutes to an hour in traffic, unless you work very close to home. You'll get back by about 6 P.M. to prepare dinner, clean up, talk to your children, help them with homework, and so on. Then the children must have a bath, and perhaps a story or some conversation before bedtime. By 8:30 or 9 P.M. you are ready to relax—or collapse, depending upon your stamina. Perhaps you want to continue your *education* and decide to attend classes two evenings a week. You can expect to do about two hours of homework for each hour spent in class. You must also get seven or eight hours of sleep at night because of the increased demands on your life. You want to stay in *good health.* Don't get too overtired and anxious or you'll wear out your *good teeth* by grinding them in your sleep at night, or gnashing them during the day. Of course you have a *bank account* and you are hoping to increase it regularly. Ah, but at least you have *the ability to take over!* Look at those fine muscles you've developed and those strong, calloused hands! You look rather healthy and tan (or is it windburn?) from being on a ladder all weekend painting the outside of your house.

I don't know of any divorcee with children who has been able to work full-time, manage her household well, guide her children and have enough relaxed time available to spend with them, have a hobby or attend school, and maintain a decent social life (I mean husband-hunt) for any length of time without collapsing from mental, physical, and emotional exhaustion. If any woman can manage all the foregoing for more than one year, she is indeed a unique human being. She will either scare most men away or have them chasing her like mad because they want someone like her to run their lives.

Modern family life is a complex process. The ideal way to manage it is with two very capable adults sharing the pleasure as well as the work. After reading this you may realize your husband is actually indispensable and you really can't live without him. Maybe you'll forget all this business about getting a divorce.

Chapter 5

Divorce and the Law

THE most important man in your life, if you decide to leave your husband, is your attorney. Choose him carefully. You probably know little about grounds for divorce, alimony and child support, child custody, property settlement, court conciliation services, and divorce law in general. Find an attorney who specializes in divorce and family law and who will give your case the special attention you need. An attorney friend of mine confided that most lawyers handle divorce cases quite perfunctorily—much like they would handle any other civil suit. You owe it to yourself and your children to find an attorney who will consider the best interests of your entire family—even your husband's best interests. Some attorneys can cause a more serious rift between husband and wife than is necessary, hindering future interaction between ex-spouses and their children.

Probably your biggest problem is that you know little or nothing about the law. You may find yourself turning to your attorney for spiritual and emotional guidance as well as legal counsel, but he is undoubtedly going to be very busy. He may recommend that you get marriage counseling or therapy, and make a referral. Sometimes it's difficult for a lawyer to say to a client "I think it is in your best interests to have psychotherapy or marriage counseling." Some clients are overemotional and may respond poorly to such a suggestion, taking it as an insult. If you have an attorney who takes the trouble to make a referral to a therapist, get the help he recommends.

How can you determine if you have a truly broken marriage? Here are some considerations suggested by an attorney who is also a sociologist:

1. Your life together cannot be effectively carried out.

2. The welfare of the spouse or of the children is in real present or imminent danger.

3. The parties have earnestly but unsuccessfully tried to resolve their differences.

4. The courts, agencies, and professionals have done all they can to help the couple.

5. The state of affairs is such that the situation or the parties can never be changed or improved; the parties can never live together in a reasonable or workable relationship. (My own added consideration: you are definitely no longer in love.) If your spouse refuses to seek help, there should be nothing to stop *you* from getting it.

If counseling fails and divorce seems the only remedy, you must establish that you have legal grounds for divorce. You may simply have a dead marriage and no legal ground to get out of it. You may be shocked to find yourself exaggerating or telling an out-and-out lie to untie your matrimonial bonds. Unfortunately, many unhappy couples are forced into this. I heard about a psychologist who wished to divorce his wife because he no longer loved her—he told an attorney friend that he was going into court without grounds and planned to say to the judge "I want a divorce but I have no legal ground. I simply do not wish to be married to my wife any more." His friend advised him that this would not work and that he needed a legal ground or would have to manufacture one. "Incompatibility" or being out of love is not enough. But if your spouse does not contest the case and you obtain your divorce by default, your charges of "extreme and repeated" cruelty are often sufficient.

The existing archaic divorce laws have a basically destructive effect on the divorcing couple, because one must be the plaintiff and one the defendant, which means that one party is "innocent" and one is "guilty"—the innocent party is "awarded" the divorce and may receive recompense for suffering in the form of property, money, or otherwise.

Because of the remnants of chivalry in our society, men usually step aside and permit the wife to obtain the Judgment of Divorce. It seems kinder that the man stands "guilty" of the acts of mental cruelty and it appears that about three-quarters of all divorces are granted to women. Women are granted special protection under the law because they are still considered the weaker sex. If you file for divorce and the court awards you the divorce decree because *legally* your husband has been guilty of a "marital misdemeanor," realize that it is quite likely much of the fault for the marriage failure has also been yours.

Many members of the legal profession and other professions are working to have our divorce laws revised because they see the evidence of what the concepts of fault and guilt have done to many divorced couples and their children. A woman who has custody of the children and has been granted a divorce on the ground of her husband's cruelty may start to believe that she was entirely innocent of any fault in the marriage. She may degrade the children's father to them, claiming that the failure of the marriage was all his fault. She might even show them that statement in the divorce judgment if she's foolish or vicious.

The way the present laws are, a woman who has been a poor wife can have the upper hand in divorcing a man of substantial wealth. Suppose she has not been civil to him for years; suppose the intimacies and pleasures of marriage stopped long ago and he has now fallen in love with another woman. He asks his wife for a divorce and she discovers that under our confused and sometimes unfair laws she can make him pay and pay and pay for his freedom.

I know of the sad case of an overworked, unhappy wife and mother of seven children (the youngest is sixteen) who wants to leave her husband. She has no legal grounds for divorce—this is simply a dead marriage. She had worked in and out of the home for twelve years or so and had contributed much to the family's support. Her husband earns about $18,000 a year but is in heavy debt because of poor management and business failures. This woman was told that she had no guarantee of being awarded alimony, because she was able to work and had worked during more than half of their married life, that it was unlikely she would receive any property or money—not even half the equity in their remortgaged home because her husband would be entitled to sell the home and use the money to settle his debts. Because she was seeking the divorce, had no real legal grounds, and he wanted to stay married, he had the upper hand. They are still officially married.

Our laws seem diabolically designed to promote and foster such inequities. Know what the facts are, and somehow, with your attorney and spouse, work out the most reasonable and equitable solution. If there is property to divide, be fair about it. If your husband wants to leave you, do not punish him financially or emotionally. Do keep in mind that you must support yourself and perhaps contribute to the support of your children after he leaves, that you and your ex-husband will still be the parents of your children, and that you must be reasonable for the welfare of your children.

The state of Hawaii has tried to alleviate some of the hostility that exists between spouses after a divorce. As a public service, divorced individuals receive a brochure listing social agencies and organizations that can help with family problems after divorce. The title of the brochure is "You Are Still Parents." It would be constructive for each divorced parent to remember that fact.

The United States legal system is based on English common law, which presupposes adversaries in court cases. Our divorce laws treat divorcing couples as adversaries. If two persons have decided to have a friendly divorce, they may be shocked when they learn this is impossible under our system. The confused array of grounds for divorce spring from many laws of the Roman Catholic Church, deeply embedded in what is actually a civil affair. If you really think there is a separation of Church and State, you may be angered when you try to get a divorce. You are not that free to decide your fate because of laws made centuries ago.

The State is a party to your marriage, and only the State has the power to sever your marriage. We have made marriage public and monogamous. In ancient Rome, marriages could be dissolved by mutual assent; today this is considered collusion and is illegal.

Each state preserves its right to have jurisdiction over the marriages of the persons domiciled there. It would be more constructive to have a uniform national marriage and divorce code.

According to the February 11, 1966, issue of *Time,* our present divorce laws are "... out of touch with the changing realities of modern society, and most of them tend to embitter spouses, neglect the welfare of the children, prevent reconciliation and produce a large measure of hypocrisy, double-dealing and perjury." We desperately need more humane laws.

DO YOU HAVE LEGAL GROUNDS FOR DIVORCE?

Your attorney will help you determine if you have legal grounds for divorce or annulment in your state. Adultery is ground for divorce in every state; cruelty in all states but Virginia and North Carolina; desertion in every state but North Carolina. Other grounds include alcoholism, impotence, felony conviction, nonsupport, insanity, pregnancy at marriage, bigamy, separation, indignities, drug addiction, violence, fraudulent contract, incompatibility.

To quote from *American Jurisprudence*: "It is said that the moral, social, economic, and physical differences which distinguish the sexes and divide them into natural classes justify differences and inequalities in the legislative treatment of them in the matter of statutory provisions as to grounds for divorce."

Remember that if you are expecting men and women to be treated equally in the eyes of the law. Sometimes this attitude works in your favor, but much of the time it can work against you as a woman.

Adultery is charged in about 5 per cent of all divorces, and mental or physical *cruelty* is the ground in most divorces. A single act of adultery is enough to maintain a divorce action and may be proved by circumstantial evidence; a witness is always necessary to prove adultery (the testimony of detectives and other paid investigators is treated like other testimony in divorce cases). If a husband charges his wife in or out of court with adultery and cannot prove it, his wife may be entitled to a divorce and alimony on grounds of mental cruelty.

Cruelty is conduct endangering the life, limb, or health of the complaining spouse, or creating a reasonable apprehension of such injury. To distinguish between physical and mental cruelty: physical cruelty is conduct that actually or apparently endangers the health or safety of the other spouse; one need not be assaulted—a threat is enough, if there is a witness. Mental cruelty is any act that threatens to injure the mental health of the complainant. One would need the advice of an attorney to determine if there actually has been mental cruelty. What you may consider mental cruelty may not hold up in court. In determining what is and is not cruelty, the training, intelligence, sensitivity, and cultural level of the offended party is taken into consideration. The courts normally assume the wife is more sensitive than the husband.

Refusal of one spouse to speak to the other for a long period of time has been held, in connection with other circumstances, to constitute cruelty. One husband did not speak to his wife while they lived under the same roof for three months; this was considered "cruel and inhuman" treatment and she was granted a divorce. If one partner has a venereal disease and knowingly transmits it to his or her spouse, this can be cruelty and ground for divorce. One single, atrocious violent act that endangers the plaintiff's life may be ground for divorce. Generally, however, cruelty must be repeated and consistent. Cruel conduct provoked by the conduct of the plaintiff does not, as a rule, authorize a divorce. However, if your spouse was insane at the time you filed your Bill of Complaint, legal cruelty is not present; in fact, insanity is sometimes a defense in a divorce case.

Indignities that can be attributed to irritability caused by illness are not a ground for divorce. Personal indignities, in order to be a ground, must render the plaintiff's condition intolerable and his or her life burdensome; if they were caused by a spouse's insanity, they are not a ground for divorce (a wife who is being treated for emotional disturbance is not considered responsible for the verbal abuse she inflicts on her husband).

Desertion is the voluntary separation of one spouse from the other without the intention of returning. Separation by mutual consent does not constitute desertion. Regular refusal to have intercourse, for no good reason, can be considered willful desertion. When a spouse decides to occupy a separate bedroom and refuses to have sexual intercourse, if not for a health reason this can be construed as willful desertion. If a spouse joins a religious sect that professes to believe the relation of husband and wife is unlawful, divorce may be granted on refusal to cohabit. The rules differ for men and women. A wife who has deserted her husband has not only the right, but also the duty to go home, and she need not first secure his permission to return. A wife must accept a bona fide offer of reconciliation from her deserting husband or she has no ground. A man may be entitled to a divorce if his wife refuses to follow him to another state after he has changed jobs; the husband generally has the right to establish the residence of the family.

Suppose your husband has been absent more than seven years. In order to end your marriage legally, you must have your missing husband declared dead by a court. You may be entitled to file for divorce on the ground of desertion after the statutory period for desertion elapses, from eighteen months to seven years, according to your state's laws. About 20 per cent of all divorces are granted for desertion, which has often been called "the poor man's divorce." In 1962, more than nine million women and children were affected by the estrangement of the fathers. Public money granted for support of deserted families in 1960 came to $800,000,000 (about one quarter of deserted families applies for public aid).

What about the man who deserts? He may have a personality problem he expresses by running away. He may be described by his wife as an irresponsible criminal: He is in real need of professional help, and most of the time so is his wife. His side must be heard; if he can be found, the chances for reconciliation are fairly good.

A wife can be justified in leaving her husband if some act on his part forced her to do so. This is known as constructive desertion and is not a legal ground for divorce.

SELECTING AN ATTORNEY

Do not use your husband's attorney unless you agree to terms in advance and the attorney represents just one of you. You can simplify your divorce if you wish to do it this way, and avoid the cost of a second attorney. This may work with a couple in agreement on the terms of their divorce. An attorney can go to jail or be disbarred for representing both parties.

It is advisable for the wife to have her own attorney, expert on divorce. The decisions made now will undoubtedly affect the rest of your and your children's lives. You will probably need the services of an attorney again after the divorce, in cases of nonsupport or if your former husband's income rises considerably and you would like to have the original financial agreement modified, or if something happens that seriously impairs your ability to work and you later require alimony or additional child support. There may also be problems about visitation and custody.

According to an attorney friend of mine, a good attorney is honest, thorough, alert, resourceful, a good speaker, a good negotiator, mature, and discreet. If you do not know of a good divorce lawyer, ask friends or relatives to recommend one, or call the local bar association for names of three or four attorneys who specialize in divorce. Call for appointments and choose the one you like best after an initial consultation.

After you have selected an attorney and have had your first conference, he will tell you if you have sufficient evidence to win in the event your case is contested, although about 90 per cent of all divorces are uncontested.

The cost of a divorce can range from several hundred dollars to $25,000 or more and is divided into legal fees and court expenses. Your attorney will require a retainer, usually one-third of the fee. The fee is dependent upon how complicated your case is, how much time your lawyer must spend in conferences and on paper work, and—if the case is contested—how long the trial is likely to last. Court costs in an uncontested divorce run about $100 or less.

If you wish to start divorce proceedings or defend yourself in the event your husband starts divorce proceedings but have no funds of your own to hire an attorney, your attorney may be able to get your fee from your husband. If your husband's attorney refuses to have the fee paid, the judge who hears the case may award a fee to your attorney. Women are usually given a break here because, if they are not wage-earners, they often do not have means at their disposal.

If, after starting proceedings you decide your attorney is not doing a good job, you may dismiss him after paying him for his time and paper work and employ another attorney. The second attorney will then obtain whatever papers have been prepared and filed, and start on your case.

QUESTIONS YOUR LAWYER WILL ASK YOU

As you tell your attorney your story, he will ask questions about the way your husband has treated you and your children, the general nature of your life together, and the last time you had sexual intercourse. (Continuing to cohabit with your husband after filing for divorce can be construed as condonation of his wrongful behavior and may eliminate your ground for divorce.)

Your lawyer will ask where you live, where your husband lives, what his income and occupation are, how much insurance he has, how much property you both own, your net worth, the date and place of your marriage, how long you both have lived in the state, the date you left him or he left you, the reason for the divorce, the names and ages of your minor children, and whether you think your husband will contest the divorce. He may also ask for your husband's social security number, and your and his next of kin. Your attorney will also ask about your physical and mental health, if there is a possibility of reconciliation, if you are employed or trained to work, and whether this is your first, second, or third marriage. Be honest and as accurate as possible.

He will also ask you to prepare a list of your living expenses, showing how much you need for food, shelter, clothing, medical and dental expenses, and the like for yourself and your children. He may also ask what your earnings are, if you are employed.

HOW TO SUE FOR DIVORCE

A Bill of Complaint is the legal means by which divorce proceedings are begun—it is a formal legal statement prepared by the plaintiff's attorney (the complaining party is called the plaintiff) requesting that marriage be dissolved by a decree or judgment of divorce. The Bill of Complaint is then served upon the defendant along with a summons. A divorce is based on grounds that existed before the Bill of Complaint is filed. The plaintiff and the plaintiff's attorney are required to sign the Bill of Complaint.

Here is a recent note from an attorney regarding the Bill of Complaint:

Under revised rules [in Michigan], in starting divorce cases, we do not spell out in detailed specifics the items of extreme and repeated cruelty. We merely allege in the Complaint that the plaintiff says that the defendant is guilty of such cruelty and unless the defendant demands a list of specifics, we don't include them in the Complaint. The reason is obvious. Many suits are started when the parties are not at all certain that a divorce is going to be the ultimate result of the action. Yet, when the defendant is served with the Complaint, he is hurt and angry and finds fault and damns the plaintiff and her attorney for the "untrue" "vicious" allegations. The charges made against the husband plus the coldness of the legal language undoubtedly (in the past) damaged the chances of reconciliation. It was in the hope that this further aggravation of the defendant would be alleviated that the new rules were promulgated.

If your husband becomes so upset after receiving a Bill of Complaint that you expect violence from him, you can get an *ex parte* restraining order against him if he threatens you or your children. This is a temporary order granted on the basis of plaintiff's sworn complaint, stating grounds for fear, threats, and the like. In general, in case of molestation or interference pending litigation, either party can seek an injunction, but only if there has been harm or threat of harm, and if the judge in his discretion thinks it wise or necessary.

Supposing *you* are served with a Bill of Complaint? What can you do? Many defendants do not fight the case, but let plaintiff proceed and win by default. Following are some legal defenses to divorce: nonproof of grounds asserted, collusion, connivance, condonation, recrimination, insanity, countersuit.

Nonproof. Charges in a divorce action generally must be proved. For instance, the defense of condonation must be proved by the party asserting it; inferences may be drawn from evidence of the surrounding circumstances. To get sufficient evidence, testimony of a paid private detective or other investigator is admissible. Courts have an aversion to calling children as witnesses; however, when necessary, the important factor is the child's intelligence rather than his age. The testimony of a child of tender years * is carefully weighed.

Collusion is an agreement between husband and wife to obtain or facilitate the obtaining of a divorce by having the accused spouse commit, or appear to commit, or be falsely represented in court as having committed an act that constitutes a ground for divorce or to suppress or refrain from presenting evidence that would prove or tend to prove a defense to the action for divorce. Collusion involves an agreement of the two spouses.

Connivance is a corrupt consenting of one spouse to the conduct of the other to which complaint is afterward made and is limited to the ground of adultery (the husband, for instance, would prearrange adultery for his wife, then try to divorce her on that ground). The theory of connivance is that the defendant has been "framed" by the plaintiff and the latter is not entitled to a divorce; the one seeking relief must come into court with "clean hands"—he or she must be blameless.

Condonation is the forgiveness of a marital offense on condition

* Up to age seven.

that it will not be repeated. If the ground for divorce has been condoned by the plaintiff, the ground is thereby eliminated. A single act of intercourse after a divorce action is not always evidence of condonation. However, if the partner is well aware of a cause for divorce and has started suit, yet continues to cohabit, this may be construed as condonation. The aggrieved spouse must forgive the offender and restore him or her to all marital rights, including sexual relations.

A marriage counselor who was not thoroughly acquainted with divorce law was trying to save the marriage of a couple who had not had intercourse for several months. The wife was advised by the counselor to cohabit with her husband again. She had already filed for divorce on the ground of extreme mental and physical cruelty. Her husband was a seriously disturbed man, and it was in this woman's best interests to be divorced from him. By resuming marital relations she lost her ground for divorce and had to start all over again with a new suit when her husband pleaded condonation as a defense. If you are seeing a marriage counselor, be sure he knows something about divorce law!

Recrimination is the doctrine that where both husband and wife are equally at fault, a divorce cannot be granted. He who comes to court must do so with "clean hands." In many jurisdictions, recrimination is an absolute bar to the granting of a divorce.

Insanity can be a defense, when the insanity caused the wrongful conduct. A divorce cannot be authorized because of acts committed by one who was incapable of understanding their nature or of restraining himself.

Countersuit. A Bill of Complaint may be answered by a countersuit (cross bill or counterclaim) denying generally or specifically the alleged misconduct or ground for divorce. With the filing of an answer, the case becomes contested. By filing an answer, you say "I deny plaintiff's right to have the relief he seeks." If you file a cross complaint, you are virtually saying "I am the one who has grounds for divorce—deny plaintiff's claim for relief and grant me the divorce on my cross complaint." If your spouse gives *you* a ground for divorce after serving you with a Bill of Complaint, you may counterfile. WARNING: If you have filed for divorce, make sure your behavior after filing of the papers does not offer grounds for a countersuit from your spouse.

A *doctrine of comparative rectitude* applies in some states: the principle that where both parties are guilty of misconduct for which a divorce may be granted, the court will grant a divorce to the one who is less at fault.

Cooling-off period before trial. Some states provide for a delay of six months or more between commission of the offense and the filing of the complaint; some states require a delay between filing of complaint or serving of divorce papers and the date of the trial. This is to give the parties time for reflection, so they may possibly effect a reconciliation. Another purpose of the cooling-off period is to prevent fraud and collusion and to allow the defendant a reasonable time to prepare his defense.

Ask your attorney about conciliation services in your state. In some states either party or an attorney may apply to the divorce court for the assistance of the conciliation commissioner, or the court may refer the case to the commissioner (often done where there are children).

How long will your divorce take? That depends upon the state in which you live; the type of divorce; the number of minor children you have; how long it will take to get your case on the court calendar; how quickly you and your spouse can agree about property settlement, child support, custody, alimony, and similar matters. Your divorce can be over in a month or two if there are no children, or it may take several years. A defendant usually has twenty days after he is served to decide if he cares to hire an attorney and contest the case.

Something should be said here about detectives and spying. Electronic spying by suspicious spouses can often produce very damaging evidence in divorce suits. Where there are large amounts of property and money involved, a vindictive husband or wife may stop at nothing to win money, property, custody of the children, and the satisfaction of exposing a "guilty" mate. Private detectives have been used for years by jealous husbands. Now fantastic electronic equipment makes detecting and spying much easier. The practice of wiretapping and electronic snooping has become so widespread in this country that it has become one of the trickiest and stickiest legal problems even in divorce cases.

An estranged or suspected wife must be on the lookout not only for bugged telephones but also for such items as fountain pens, wrist watches, FM transmitters that fit into a cigarette case, plastic olives with built-in transmitting devices and a toothpick antenna that can carry a conversation 100 feet. Be careful. If you are planning a rendezvous with your husband's best friend, check the olive in your martini. It may be bugged!

While you're at it, check those picture frames in your bedroom. If you are having romantic meetings when your husband is out of town, or intimate phone conversations, everything you say and do may be recorded. Don't worry about Big Brother watching you—it's your about-to-be-ex-husband you have to worry about. That picture frame can contain a hidden transmitter that will operate for 200 hours on a built-in battery. These inexpensive, easy-to-install snooping devices can be purchased with no questions asked by anyone with a penchant for playing master spy. The government has been spying on citizens for years as an aid to law enforcement. The problem of private citizens spying on other private citizens is relatively new; the dangers to individual rights and privacy are frightening.

Some states have outlawed telephone wiretapping, but some permit it under court order. Better check with your attorney to see if any unfavorable evidence obtained in this way is admissible in court in your state. To be safe, don't do anything you know you shouldn't be doing until you are legally free!

Some alternatives to divorce. When an individual cannot get an absolute divorce or does not wish to do so, there are other legal alternatives. An *annulment,* a legal proceeding declaring that a marriage never lawfully existed and declares it void from the beginning, may be obtained in some cases. Ask your attorney about this. Until recently adultery was the only ground for divorce in the state of New York and many individuals therefore resorted to annulment.

Separate maintenance, a civil proceeding instituted by the wife, awarding her alimony without obtaining a divorce. The wife may want this instead of divorce because of religion. She must prove that she was not at fault in breaking up the marriage.

Legal separation. The husband must support his wife and children if she has obtained the legal separation; when he obtains it, he is considered the "innocent" party and does not have to support the wife, but must support their children. The wife may not change her name, and neither party can remarry. The advantages of a legal separation are time to adjust to the idea of divorce, an opportunity for reconciliation, and accordance with certain religious beliefs. If the man and wife have sex relations during the legal separation, their separation is terminated.

Residence for divorce: Most states require one year's residence before filing except the following:

Idaho and Nevada: 6 weeks
Wyoming: 60 days
Arkansas, Utah: 90 days
Florida, Georgia, Maine, North Carolina, Oklahoma: 6 months
Delaware, Hawaii, New Jersey, Rhode Island, Wisconsin: 2 years
Connecticut: 3 years
Massachusetts: 5 years

In many states there is no waiting period before both parties can remarry. In Alabama, West Virginia, and Oregon, however, both plaintiff and defendant must wait sixty days; in Arizona, Iowa, Texas, and Wisconsin both parties must wait one year. The waiting period is 10 days in the District of Columbia, thirty days in Kansas, three months in Utah, six months in Minnesota and Oklahoma. In some states an attorney can lengthen the waiting period. Several states may penalize the defendant alone by making him or her wait before remarrying: in Vermont the waiting period is two years; in New York, three years, and in Virginia, six months.

The difference between alimony and child support is something every potential divorcee should know and understand. Alimony is an allowance to the wife for her support and maintenance and the husband is ordered by the court to pay this where there exists between the spouses a legal separation or a divorce. The function of alimony is to provide support for the wife, not compensation for the wrong and injury a wife has suffered because of her husband's misconduct. There are two kinds of alimony and child support: temporary and permanent. Child support is for the support and maintenance of minor children. A father is legally required to pay child support until his children reach legal age.

The amount of alimony and or child support is based on the husband's ability to pay as well as on the needs of the wife and children. Too many women think they can "take a man for all he's worth" after a divorce. You may be awarded approximately one-third to one-half of your husband's net income (actually, it is nearer one-fourth to one-third). Newspaper accounts of divorces among the wealthy have given the average woman mistaken notions about alimony and property settlements.

Temporary alimony is paid to the wife by the husband while the divorce is pending, for her maintenance and support; the wife is entitled to support during litigation unless she has sufficient means to support herself. The matter of temporary alimony is within the discretion of the court. Important are the parties' needs and abilities; considered are one's station in life and the accustomed style of living. Temporary alimony is not always the same amount as permanent alimony (and does not usually exceed one-third of the husband's income). It is frequently stressed that the wife is entitled to the same economic advantages and standard of living after separation as she would have enjoyed had the parties continued living together.

The court may deny temporary alimony to a wife who is guilty of marital misconduct; if her guilt is established sufficiently at an informal hearing—if she fails to deny the accusations of misconduct or her guilt is shown by judgments in criminal or civil proceedings or by her confession in writing or stated orally to husband and others. Regarding suit money and counsel fees, the same rules which govern allowance of temporary alimony apply here. Sometimes if a wife has hired a detective to investigate her husband's marital wrong-doings, and she is awarded the divorce, her husband may be required to pay detective fees.

This is from a schedule for 1968 from the Friend of the Court in Wayne County, Michigan: The recommended amount for support of minor children, pending litigation, to be paid weekly by a man who earns between $101 and $105 net per week is: $17 for one child, $32 for two children, $40 for three children, $44 for four children, $48 for five children, and $52 for six or more children. If you think about these figures, it seems unfair that a woman should receive approximately the same amount for six children that her husband gets for himself alone. Six growing children eat almost six times as much as does one man, they wear out six pairs of shoes six times as fast, they get six times as sick, and so on. There is not much logic in any of this, but this is what you will be faced with as a divorcee. Some hardship is imposed on everyone in these situations. But, isn't a man entitled to at least half of his own income?

Permanent alimony. The amount of permanent alimony and the way it is paid is determined by the circumstances of the parties at the time of the original divorce trial: the financial condition of both parties; the capacity of each to earn money; the age, health, and general physical condition of each; their social standing; and their conduct or misconduct, length of time they cohabited in marriage, and the expense of maintaining their children. However, it is not the policy of the law to give the wife a perpetual lien on her divorced husband's future income if she has the ability to earn a living. But her lack of property, coupled with her inability to earn a living, may require an allowance of permanent alimony. If your children are preschool age, you may receive alimony until you are able to work or until you complete special training you may require to be employable. Permanent alimony does not last *permanently* and can be terminated for a number of reasons that will be discussed later.

It is an almost universal rule that permanent alimony will be denied to a wife who is guilty of adultery. Usually no alimony is allowed to the wife who has abandoned her husband without legal justification, to the wife who has been consistently guilty of lewd or lascivious conduct and drunkenness, or to a wife who is serving a prison sentence. The nature of the wife's misconduct is always considered. When she is solely to blame for the divorce and did not have property at the time of the marriage, and has not accrued any property by her "industry and thrift," she is not usually entitled to alimony. However, when the property has been jointly acquired, she is entitled to something, and may be paid in a lump-sum settlement. If a husband agrees to pay alimony to a "guilty" wife, the court will award it.

Behavior of the spouses after divorce does not usually affect the amount of alimony set at the time of divorce. In one jurisdiction, it was decided that "The failure of the wife to lead a chaste life [after divorce] affords no more ground for depriving her of alimony previously fixed than does the misconduct of the husband call for an increase of the award." (From *American Jurisprudence.*)

The amount and duration of alimony is not absolute and is subject to modification by the court at the request of either party at any time following the divorce, for good reason, such as change in husband's income, the illness of one of the parties, the increase or decrease of the wife's needs. Payments are usually made in installments at stated intervals. If alimony is paid in a lump sum, it is based on the husband's total net worth. The awarded sum is either paid all at once, or in installments over a certain period of time, usually several years. Sometimes where alimony is justified only for a short period of time, a lump-sum award may be made.

Alimony stops with the death of either party (unless there was a prior agreement between the parties that the wife is to receive alimony from her former husband's estate after his death). The husband is not relieved of paying alimony when he remarries—the claim of the divorced wife to his earnings takes precedence to that of the second wife and her offspring. However, alimony ends when the woman remarries.

The wife is entitled to support at the level of her station in life *at the time of the divorce,* so if the husband's income rises substantially and there are no children, she is not entitled to an increase in alimony. A substantial increase in her property or estate may justify a reduction in alimony.

If an ex-husband refuses to pay alimony or child support, his former wife can start contempt proceedings against him. Willful nonsupport is a serious state crime and carries a penitentiary penalty, although imprisonment is a last resort. If your former husband leaves the state and stops sending support, ask your attorney about the "Run-Away Pappy Act" (the Uniform Reciprocal Interstate Support Act). This law is not easy to enforce, but it does offer protection to women and children who are stranded by the family provider, whether there has been a divorce or not.

Alimony is in no way a property settlement, is not discharged by bankruptcy, and is taxable to the woman because it is considered income to her.

Child support. Payments are made to the mother or whoever else has custody, such as a grandmother. The amount of child support is determined by the needs of the child; the father's earning capacity and financial condition; the standard of living when the family lived together; the age of the father and the ages of the children; and the mother's ability to support or contribute to the support of the children. In some jurisdictions, both parents are required to support their minor children. If the child can contribute to his own support, this is also considered (if, for instance, the child is an actor or a professional entertainer and earns more than the father). A divorce court cannot award any part of the father's property to his children.

Child support can be increased when there is a nation-wide increase in the cost of living. A mother can apply for larger support payments when the father's income has increased substantially and the child's needs have also increased (a 10 per cent salary increase might not be considered substantial).

How does the remarriage of either party affect child support? One judge said: "A father's first duty is the support of his children. They are to be given preference over new automobiles and new wives." The father's remarriage is not a ground for his reducing child support; however, if he has children by his second wife and the first wife seeks an increase in child support, the court considers the needs of the second wife and children. If the mother remarries a man of substantial means, her second husband's financial position may be taken into consideration if the father tries to have support payments reduced for a good reason of his own.

Child support is intended to cover the necessities of life for the child, as close as possible to the standard he would have had if he were still living with both parents. If the father has the means, he is required to pay for private-school tuition and summer camp fees. When the child reaches college age, if the father can afford it and if the child desires to go and is a good student and deserves higher education, the father would be expected to support him through four years of college. However, there is usually no provision in divorce settlements made for this if the children are, for instance, eight and ten years old at the time of the divorce, because there is no way of knowing what the situation will be in eight or ten years when they reach college age. This is something both parents should prepare for at the time of the divorce; they should be willing to set aside a certain amount each month for the education of their children.

What about child support during vacation time? Suppose a child spends a month or the entire summer with his father. Some jurisdictions require the father to pay the full amount of child support all year long, others may allow him to pay a percentage while he has the children with him, and still other jurisdictions say he does not have to pay any support to the mother for the period of time his children are with him. (It would be fair to determine how much is spent on groceries, recreation, and baby-sitters per week per child and make some adjustment for that if the father has the children for a month or so in the summer; however, it is unreasonable to permit a man to pay no child support at all for that time, because the mother still must maintain the home, the children still require clothing, shoes, medical and dental attention, and so on.)

Mothers should know that child support can be terminated or reduced in some jurisdictions if a mother interferes with a father's visitation rights. If a mother wrongfully removes a child from the state, the court can order the support canceled or suspended, where the father is denied visitation as a result of the move. Also, if a child refuses to visit his father and the mother does not try to correct the situation, child support can be terminated.

A father is not entitled to credit for clothing and gifts presented directly to his children where the mother has not agreed to accept such goods in substitution for money, nor can he take credit for insurance premiums he has paid, since they are not support. A father who wrongfully and without reasonable justification takes possession of his children is not entitled to credit for arrears accruing while he supports his children, and a father who makes overpayments for several months, because of his erroneous interpretation or recollection of the terms of a contract for child support approved by the court, is not entitled to credit in most jurisdictions.

If a father becomes lax about sending child support, the mother must assert her children's rights promptly. The ways to enforce a child support order are with a civil contempt proceeding or an attachment or garnishment of the father's wages, or the court can appoint a receiver for the father's property. A father's inability to pay child support is a defense to a charge of contempt for nonpayment and arrearage; however, if the inability has been caused by his own neglect or misconduct, the inability is no defense, nor are his remarriage and assumptions of additional burdens a defense. The earnings of a minor have no bearing on a father's guilt or innocence in contempt proceedings; a father is not guilty of contempt if the child was removed from the state by the mother who did not let the father know where they were and the father was up to date in his payments until they left the state.

Child support ends when the child reaches legal age, when the child marries even if under age, when the father dies, or when the child goes into the armed forces with the permission of the mother.

If the father had not paid all the child support sums due prior to his death, the amount of arrears is a proper claim against his estate. The court may award a lump sum from the estate in lieu of future payments. Each state has different statutes regarding these matters.

It makes sense to provide life insurance on the father's life for the purpose of child support in the event of his death. Perhaps the mother and the father could share the cost of the policy. Ask your attorney and insurance agent to advise you regarding this. While you're at it, check on the kinds of policies available that could be used for college expenses.

A child born after divorce has the same rights as any other legitimate child of the father's marriage. Child-support payments are not a tax deduction to the father but he may claim the children as his dependents if he pays more than half of their support. Be certain there is no confusion about this—if you are both claiming the children as dependents, there could be a problem later. You must pay income tax on the alimony payments you receive unless it is paid to you in a lump sum but no income tax is due on child support. Have a tax expert check your settlement so that you know exactly what is taxable and what is not.

In settling on alimony and child support, be certain you do not accept less than you need or less than your husband can reasonably afford because of your eagerness to end the marriage. It may be worth it to wait until you are calm enough to ask for, and if necessary fight for, what is fair. I know several women who were so anxious to end their marriages that they settled for much less child support and alimony than was wise in their particular situations. Be sure to find out exactly how much your husband earns and owns before you make any final agreements.

It may be necessary to have your husband's income verified by his employer, if he has been secretive about what he earns. This can be done with a subpoena if your husband refuses to cooperate—it is one sure way of getting an accurate statement of his annual salary and commissions, bonuses, and other income. An injunction or restraining order may be issued to restrain your husband from disposing of property until after the divorce decree. It is entirely up to you to find out what your legal rights are—this is why you need the best divorce lawyer you can find—to assert your rights, and to fight for them when necessary.

The woman who refuses to do anything about an ex-husband who has fallen behind in child support, and knows he can well afford it, because she does not want to face the unpleasantness of a legal battle, does her children and her former husband a great disservice. The children feel much better about their father when they know he is regularly sending money for their support, and the man feels better about himself when he is facing his legal parental responsibility, even though he may not like to send that weekly or monthly check. He'll get used to it.

At all times be ready to assert your legal rights, but do remember that your husband is a human being you once loved and chose to live with—don't threaten to jail him for nonsupport if he has good reason for being late with a check.

One divorcee I talked to believed that she was not "morally entitled" to either alimony or child support and felt guilty about receiving money from a man she was no longer married to. If you feel the same, rid yourself of such a notion right now. There is a definite need and purpose for child support and alimony because (1) women have traditionally been dependents in marriage and generally still are in spite of the fact that many work after marriage and (2) women—married or single—who work generally do not earn as much as men do for the same type of work and even when qualified, they are not usually allowed to compete with men for the better, higher-paying jobs.

When asked "What do you do?" many women say "I'm just a housewife." There is often a real embarrassment at not being able to name some specific *paying* job or career. Unfortunately, no one pays a wife and mother what she is worth in dollars. If you are soon to be a divorced mother and have never held a paying job, make realistic, purposeful plans about work that could lead to a good career.

In addition to the weekly or monthly child support, the father is usually required to pay for any major medical and dental expenses and to maintain health and accident insurance for his children. The mother is expected to pay for "colds and cavities" (as one attorney put it) from the child-support allowance she receives. It is best to have these issues specifically spelled out in the settlement, because it may be difficult to determine who is to pay for things such as braces for a child's teeth or a stay in the hospital. It is advisable to have the amounts for child support stated separately in the settlement, as well as the amount for alimony, if any. If these payments are lumped together, there may be confusion later if either parent attempts to have either child support or alimony payments modified.

Property settlements. How should couples getting divorced divide their property? The laws on this vary from state to state, but usually an individual is allowed to keep what he or she owned prior to the marriage. Anything that has been accumulated during the marriage (such as real estate, stocks, bonds, valuable items such as antiques, paintings, and so forth) has to be divided. This division of property and the manner of dividing it causes much pain and heartache for many divorcing couples, and often delays the divorce proceedings. Competent attorneys can do much to assist a couple to reach a satisfactory property settlement.

The average couple getting divorced probably does not have much property to divide—usually there is a home with a mortgage, one or two cars, some furnishings, books, records, a diamond ring or two, some silver and china. Where there is much money and property involved, the terms may be most complicated. What can delay the process is the bitter attitude many husbands and wives develop before either one ever sees an attorney. To get even the wife may hold out for "all I can get" and the husband may feel "I'm not giving her anything I don't have to." If they cannot reach an agreeable property settlement with the help of their attorneys, the court will divide their property.

Items which have emotional meaning may be the hardest to divide. I know a couple who fought about a silver candlestick which was a wedding gift from a dear friend of both. You will have to compromise when it comes to records, books, snapshot albums, cameras, and such things.

A property settlement settles property rights but says nothing about custody or support of children, alimony, or the right to live apart. In the northeastern part of the United States a property settlement is called a "separation agreement." A property settlement does the following:

1. Determines the rights of the parties in jointly owned property and states the disposition to be made of it.

2. Settles all claims of each spouse in the property of the other and claims of each spouse to title to property held in the name of the other.

3. Mutually releases all past and present claims except as established by the agreement.

4. Waives and releases all future rights as spouse in each other's property.

5. Surrenders the rights of each on the death of the other, including rights of inheritance, homestead, dower, and the right to administer the estate of the other and to have exemptions and allowances from the estate.

6. Agrees that each will execute all documents necessary or desirable to carry out the purposes of the agreement.

Courts do not always have the final say about division of property. Community-property states * may penalize the "guilty" party in a divorce.

In division of property, the following points have bearing: did the husband buy the personal property with his own money, or did the husband and wife purchase it out of mutual funds? Did he own the property before the marriage took place? Did the wife buy the property with her own funds? In general, the wife keeps furs and jewelry purchased for her by the husband; the husband may keep the television set and hi-fi equipment if he purchased them with his own funds; money in checking and bank accounts is usually divided equally; wedding presents are usually divided equally; household furnishings belong to both, but usually the person getting the house and custody of the children gets most of the furniture and appliances (perhaps in exchange for a cash allowance). If the family home is sold, the wife is entitled to half of the net proceeds from the sale of the home and property, after paying off mortgage balance, liens, real estate commissions, and similar expenses. The husband usually gets the newer of two cars—unless, of course, the wife purchased the newer car

* Arizona, California, Idaho, Louisiana, Nevada, New Mexico, Texas, and Washington.

with her own funds and it is in her name. This all varies with each case, and where a couple cannot agree, much will depend upon the judge hearing the case.

The divorce court has the inherent jurisdiction to attach a husband's property or income—this means he is not able to sell, dispose of, or remove his assets before a divorce. An injunction or a restraining order may be issued by the court to prevent a party from disposing of property until after the divorce is heard.

There is no fixed rule or mathematical formula to set property awards; the general level is one-third to be given to the wife, except in those states in which property acquired by a husband and wife after a marriage is community property in which each has a half interest. Where there is a large amount of debt and the husband is insolvent, the court can order the homestead sold to pay the bills; the difference is split between husband and wife. The court may restore to the wife any property she brought to the marriage.

The "guilty" party may be penalized in a property settlement, depending upon the state. The court may award the homestead to the innocent party.

The wife's remarriage terminates installment alimony but has no effect on payments in settlement of property rights. Installment payments in the settlement of property rights are not taxable to the wife or deductible by the husband. The wife loses insurance benefits, but sometimes a man keeps policies for the benefit of his minor children in the event of his death, and his ex-wife would then collect on them as the legal guardian of their children.

A receiver may be appointed to manage the property after a divorce. If an action regarding a property settlement is based on fraud or duress, the agreement may be annulled as a whole, on proof.

Child custody. The law says that the primary consideration in determining child custody is the best interests of the child. It is unfortunate that our courts do not have the facilities to make a thorough and proper investigation of each parent to determine which is really better suited to have custody. Mothers are awarded custody most of the time because traditionally their place has been in the home with the children. Some women should be denied custody of their children. Mother does *not* always know best, and the custody of a child should not be arbitrarily awarded to his mother primarily because of tradition. The qualities of the mother and father as *human beings* should determine which parent is better suited to care for and guide the children.

There are many children from broken homes who would undoubtedly rather be with their fathers, and would be better cared for and more loved by them. Children are too often treated like any other piece of property and their rights as human beings are forgotten. Lawyers and psychiatrists sometimes are aware of the "Santa Claus complex"—a situation in which a divorced father tries to induce his teenage sons to live with him by promising a car, motorcycle, boats, etc., and greater freedom than he would have with the mother.

The laws regarding child custody have not kept pace with the needs of a modern and fast-changing society. The social stigma of divorce is great, no matter what anyone says. The stigma for a woman losing custody of her children is even greater—often a woman will bargain with her husband regarding alimony and property so she will get custody of her children. Neither party in some cases cares that much about the kids—one is interested in saving face, the other in saving money.

More care should be exercised in determining which parent is better suited morally, emotionally, and intellectually to have custody of the children. If the father is, then he should have them. Children are not a prize to be awarded to the winner of a contest, but that is what happens too often in many divorce suits. A woman can be a good person of superior intellectual capacity, she can be a marvelous homemaker; perhaps she was not legally at fault in the breaking up of the home and marriage—but suppose she is more interested after divorce in a career or in social pursuits? Suppose she would gladly be relieved of the full-time responsibility of parenthood (which is one of the problems in most broken marriages—neither party actually wants the full-time responsibility of marriage and parenthood). She can hardly say to her husband: "I think you should have custody of the children because you have more to offer them. I'll visit them on weekends and in the summer." Such a woman would be regarded as a freak in our society. However, such women do exist and they are neither to be condemned nor given custody of their children!

I know of two such cases where mothers have custody of their children, but the fathers are better suited to care for them. One woman does not want the responsibility of rearing her children, but she is so hostile to their father that she would rather die than have them live with him. He suffers when he sees how his children are being neglected. When he makes a suggestion to their mother about anything regarding their care, she goes into a rage. She turns her children over to incompetent baby-sitters, has no interest in training them or spending time with them in the home, and in general permits them to run wild. They are nervous, undisciplined, and unhappy. Yet when this man asked his attorney what he could do, he was advised that he would *never* be able to get custody because their mother is not "grossly unfit, an alcoholic, a narcotics addict, a prostitute, a criminal, or insane"—but she *is* selfish, mean, unconcerned, too busy, irresponsible, and lacking in patience and self-discipline. Most persons who know this couple agree that the father should have the children. However, tradition and our legal system have conditioned him to have a defeatist attitude about fighting for custody.

The essence of custody is the companionship of the child and the right to make decisions regarding his care, control, education, health, and religion. There are three kinds of custody:

Joint custody, in which the child lives most of the year with one parent, and the other parent has regular visitation. Supposedly, both parents have an equal voice in decisions pertaining to health, religious training, schools, trips, vacations, and summer camp. But in general the parent the child lives with decides most of the things regarding the child's welfare and upbringing.

Divided custody, in which custody of the child is divided between the parents or other persons, usually for a period of six months each; this type of custody is not considered in the best interests of the child. Each parent has reciprocal visiting privileges.

Split custody, which divides the children between the two parents. The court may award the older children to the father and the children of "tender years" to the mother, or the boys to the father and the girls to the mother. However, the court ordinarily strives to keep brothers and sisters together unless for special, valid reasons it is necessary to separate them.

A decision regarding custody can be changed if a father can prove that the mother is emotionally unstable, morally unfit, and grossly neglects the child. If the court finds both parents unfit, a child may be awarded to a third party. A mother who cannot provide a home for her child will not be given custody. A woman who has committed adultery does not necessarily lose custody of her child unless she is extremely immoral or promiscuous; but she *can* lose custody if she alienates the child from the father, if she seriously interferes with the father's visitation rights, if she is unable to keep the child in school, or if she unlawfully removes the child from the state.

The child remains under the jurisdiction of the court until he reaches legal age; the parent with custody is not allowed to remove the child from the state without permission of the court. A woman who does so may be found guilty of kidnaping or fined for contempt of court. A court may grant permission to remove the child from the state for reasons of health or business, or if the woman marries a man from another state.

A mother without custody who remarries may apply for custody. Among things considered are the character and disposition of the stepparent, the acquaintance of the child with the stepparent, their attitude and feelings toward each other, responsibility of the stepparent for the divorce, moral atmosphere of the home, and racial or religious differences. The primary consideration is always the best interests of the child.

A great improvement in the father's financial condition does not warrant a change in custody. In case of the death of the parent with custody, the surviving parent is entitled to custody if he or she is fit. However, the child may be awarded to a third person if a child's best interests are served by doing so. A third person may file a plea of intervention seeking custody of a child.

The court can appoint an investigator to make a report on conditions before it makes a decision regarding custody; in a contested case it is not usual for a judge to interview a child privately before making a decision on custody, but it has been done.

If a divorced mother denies visitation rights, a father can start contempt proceedings to enforce these rights; the court is reluctant to deny visitation rights to a man who is behind in alimony and child support. A parent can lose visitation if he has been cruel to his children or is habitually drunk when he sees them. A father who has served a prison term does not lose visitation rights if he behaves himself after serving his sentence. Sometimes visitation is denied if a father has abandoned his wife and children; a man who does not keep current with child support payments does not necessarily lose visitation rights, if he has good reason for falling behind. Visitation is not at the discretion of the person having custody of the child. It is advisable to have both parents agree upon visitation at the time the property settlement and other agreements regarding the divorce are made, and to spell out as specifically as possible in the agreement when and where the parent without custody is to see the children, and also to settle such issues as holidays and vacations.

A child may express a rational opinion regarding which parent he prefers to live with, but this is not conclusive upon the court. (A recent study made by psychiatrists indicates that it is better for the child to live with the parent he did *not* choose because he will receive better guidance and discipline from the tougher parent.) The courts retain a continuing power to modify a custody order (after divorce, you do not have the final say about your children)! The courts try to avoid making orders of temporary custody, feeling it is better to settle this so that a child is not shifted around from one household to another.

A parent is not disqualified from having custody of a child because of his religious beliefs, or because he or she is an agnostic. However, if the parent is a member of a religious sect which takes up so much of his time that there is little time to devote to the child, the custody may be awarded to the other parent. Agreements between parents concerning the religious training of their children will not be enforced by the court because the parent getting custody is not bound by such an agreement.

A father is obligated by law to support the child until that child is of legal age, no matter how often the mother remarries. However, if the mother and her new husband file to adopt the child and the father decides to sign off and let the adoption order be granted, he is thereby relieved of his financial obligation toward his child, and he loses visitation rights, or the chance to gain custody.

Rights of children of divorce. For more than five years, children in the state of Wisconsin have had court-appointed lawyers to protect their interests when necessary where the parents are seeking divorce. According to one judge in Milwaukee, children are often used as a "bargaining lever" in matters pertaining to money and property settlements.

In Milwaukee, divorcing couples are screened by a Family Court Commissioner and a court aide trained in social work to check the possibility of a reconciliation. If it looks favorable, the court's professional staff, with a psychiatrist for consultation, gives marriage counseling. In the United States about 30 per cent of all divorce actions are dropped before decree; in Milwaukee today the figure is 48 per cent, and most of these cases are in families with children.

The Wisconsin courts try to see that the children of divorce get educational trust funds and administer more than 500 such trusts. After the divorce, social workers watch for signs of disturbance in the children: are the children being poisoned by one parent against the other? To teach a child to hate one half of his ancestry is to teach him to hate one half of himself, and the courts there are doing all they can to see that children of divorce suffer as little as possible.

Lawyers are not appointed in every case—only when it is evident a child's rights need to be protected. These guardian-attorneys receive an average fee of $100, paid by one or both parents. They can issue subpoenas, make investigations, cross-examine parents and other witnesses in court, visit the home to see the children, and recommend to the court what they think is best for the child regarding custody, visitation, support, and so on.

Each parent who files for divorce receives a copy of a "Bill of Rights for Children in Divorce Actions," based on opinions handed down by the Wisconsin Supreme Court, and the Family Court of Milwaukee insists that all divorcing parents recognize that their children have these rights in and out of court:

1. The right to be treated as an interested and affected person and not as a pawn or chattel of either or both parents.

2. The right to that home environment which will best guarantee an opportunity to grow to mature and responsible citizenship.

3. The right to the day-by-day love, care, discipline, and protection of the parent having custody.

4. The right to know the noncustodial parent and to have the benefit of that parent's love and guidance through adequate visitation.

5. The right to a positive and constructive relationship with both parents, with neither to be permitted to degrade the other in the mind of the child.

6. The right to the most adequate level of economic support that can be provided by the best efforts of both parents.

7. The right to the same opportunities for education that the child would have if the family unit were not broken.

8. The right to periodic review of custodial arrangements and child-support orders as the circumstances may require.

9. The right to recognition that children in a divorce are disadvantaged parties and that the law must take affirmative steps to protect their welfare, including, where indicated, a social investigation to determine their interests and the appointment of a lawyer-guardian to protect their interests.

Efforts are also being made in the state of Michigan to have children of divorce represented by counsel. Perhaps more states will follow the good example of the state of Wisconsin.

Marriage counseling and reconciliation. To locate a marriage counselor, write to the American Association of Marriage Counselors, 27 Woodcliff Drive, Madison, New Jersey. Members must have a master's degree, be doctors or psychiatrists, or have a doctorate in psychology, sociology or a related field of study, or a three-year graduate degree from a theological seminary.

A serious difficulty for those analyzing marriage problems and trying to arrive at solutions is the lack of complete statistics and data, state by state; there are no statistics on the outcome of therapy or counseling for those who have considered divorce.

Mexican divorce. After 1915, Americans were able to get Mexican divorces (sometimes called "mail-order divorces") without either party needing to set foot in Mexico. A divorce took six months from the date the petition was filed. After 1926, a decree was possible within twenty-four hours from time of filing petition. The biggest problem with Mexican divorce is the validity—the only state that recognized Mexican divorce had been New York. No state is required to recognize a Mexican divorce. Ordinarily our courts will not recognize a divorce obtained in a foreign country if neither spouse had a domicile in that country; the divorce may be recognized if the plaintiff appears and the defendant appears in person or by attorney.

Some additional information: United States divorces are recognized in each of the fifty states and are valid even if the ground for which they are obtained is not a ground in the state in which recognition is sought.

In absolute divorce "the marriage relation is as absolutely destroyed as if by death" and one's status is changed to that of a single person. However, absolute divorce does not affect the legitimacy of children born or begotten during the marriage.

A limited divorce or legal separation is provisional and conditional, and terminable at the will of the parties; terminates defendant's right of cohabitation. The wife can establish her own domicile, but it does not put an end to the marriage—it merely suspends certain mutual rights and obligations.

In Wisconsin, under Judicare, 84 per cent of the cases have involved divorce or divorce actions. Judicare was originally designed to give legal protection to the poor against unfair housing, welfare, credit, and consumer practices. In Britain, where a Judicare-type system was begun in 1950, 80 per cent of the government-subsidized cases in the first year were suits for divorce.

Your day in court. Unless your divorce is contested, your day in court is likely to be quite uneventful. You will be required to have one corroborating witness, but it is not often that divorce witnesses have to testify in uncontested cases. My own day in court was typical of most uncontested divorces:

I approached the appointed day with great trepidation and anxiety. I was awake about two hours earlier than usual and had slept poorly. I dressed simply that day, and wore little makeup. I called my witness before having my breakfast to make sure she was up. I played the piano for about fifteen minutes until the sitter came, and left at 7:30 A.M. to be in court by eight-thirty.

My witness and I and my attorney and my husband's attorney went to the jury room. The two attorneys checked over some papers and had a final consultation. My husband's attorney signed papers withdrawing his defenses to my complaint, thus making my case an uncontested one. I was nervous and had a hard time composing myself. I see now that as a defense mechanism, to fight my anxiety, I felt flippant that day and had a terrible compulsion to be silly. My attorney briefly reviewed my file with me. As I read over the copy of the Bill of Complaint, filed nine months earlier, some of the statements in it seemed insignificant and even irrelevant. I had to remind myself that I had been miserable while I was married—because most of the time since my husband had moved out of our home had been busy, tension-free, and even happy for me.

For a panicked moment I had the apprehension I would not be granted a divorce. What if the judge thought that my grounds were not substantial? Not enough to end a marriage? My husband did not show up (defendants rarely come to court in uncontested cases, I have since learned). My witness and I laughed as we watched the two attorneys trying to straighten piles of legal documents. When we entered the courtroom, it took all my control to sit still and realize how serious it all was. My attorney began talking, addressing the judge, and I took the witness stand. My attorney began to ask me about my marriage—routine questions at first, then we got to the ground for divorce. As I began getting into my testimony, it all came back to me. I was getting divorced for a good reason and this was the right thing to do. The judge hardly looked up but seemed to listen intently. I wondered how many times he had heard similar questions and answers. He never looked at me and did not ask a single question. It was not at all what I had expected.

When I was through giving my testimony, the judge asked both attorneys if there had been an attempt at reconciliation. Both said "yes." In less than ten minutes after entering the courtroom I was free.

The two attorneys, my witness, and I went back to the jury room. I looked at my copy of the divorce decree (seven pages long) and saw the judge's name stamped on the first and last pages. I was still giddy and felt the need to laugh. "What the hell is this? Can't he at least sign in ink or put his thumbprint on it? I didn't go through all this just for a rubber stamp!" Everyone laughed. Then my former husband's attorney said I had been a very good witness and that he liked witnesses who gave complete answers to questions. At that point I hardly remembered exactly what I had said. He also said, "Oh yes, your husband told me last night to be sure to say good morning to his wife." I replied, "Now it's too late."

My witness and I stopped at a mutual friend's home for a cup of tea, then we went out to lunch. At the restaurant, I was asked for my identification. I thought that was quite funny because I was twenty-nine at the time. The waitress still did not believe my age after seeing my driver's license and I recall thinking to myself that perhaps I looked better than I realized. I went home and took my sons for a swim, and felt relieved about the way the day went. I was even having kind thoughts about my ex-husband. That evening I went out to dinner and was told later by the baby-sitter that he had called. I never did find out what he wanted that night. Earlier in the day I had considered sending him a telegram, but did not because I could not think of an appropriate message.

Focus clearly on exactly what it is you want; an attorney is not a miracle man and there is a limit to what he can do for you as a client. If you and your husband are able to work out an agreeable settlement, that is better for you both than turning over every personal detail to two lawyers. Don't let your attorney talk you into anything that does not seem right or fair—remember that if there are children, you and your husband will have to stay in communication for many years. If there is a minimum of bitterness at the time you work out a divorce agreement, you will have an easier time with one another later. You are not trying to turn your husband into an enemy for life—you are simply trying to get out of a contract that is probably not very satisfying to either of you. If your divorce is handled wisely, your husband will be just as relieved as you are when it is over. The worst thing you can do is end a marriage that you think has a possibility of working. No one can convince you to stay married—that decision is yours alone. A lawyer may let you talk yourself into a divorce before you are actually ready for one, but most attorneys do their best to convince their clients to stay married.

Know what you want, then proceed to get it in a logical, calm way. Make a list of questions to ask your attorney at your first conference. I had a notebook with me and wrote things down. I also had a list of questions that I wanted answered. One divorcee I know took a tape recorder with her when she went to see her attorney!

Consider these points:

If you are to receive alimony, avoid making an agreement to share your husband's income. This can lead to court battles about his net income.

Be sure to have a flexible alimony or support arrangement— have an arbitration provision in your divorce agreement to modify it if necessary—do not agree to waive alimony. You never know when or how your circumstances may change.

Your lawyer will tell you if a lump-sum alimony settlement makes sense in your case.

Arrange for provisions for medical and dental expenses, psychiatric treatment for the children and yourself if necessary during and after the divorce.

Be sure to have arbitration clauses on as many issues as possible, including visitation rights.

Own life insurance on your former husband's life, because alimony usually ceases in the event of his death. Ask for irrevocable insurance coverage to protect alimony payments, also to cover support requirements. A court order might require husband to pay premiums and produce evidence of payment, notice, and the like. Have a disability provision in the life insurance policy or noncancelable disability income coverage on him.

Try to agree in advance on higher education for the children and make provisions for it; perhaps your alimony can include this (but make sure you save the money or invest it in a special insurance policy for this purpose).

Never agree to any property settlement unless you have a statement executed by your husband signed and sworn to and declaring his assets—the list to be a complete, detailed, and accurate accounting of all his possessions.

Enter into no agreement with your about-to-be ex-husband unless your attorney approves it. If you and your husband do discuss settlement and other matters, listen politely and thoroughly, and offer to advise of your decision after you discuss the arrangement or offer with your counsel.

In case of your own death, make provision for guardianship, support payments, and other important matters. Consider insurance on your own life for your children's education. Make a will.

Speak to your attorney about equality of inheritance for your children.

Know your rights if your husband leaves the state or country.

Be sure there are no mortgages or liens you do not know about on your home or other property. Take precautions that your husband does not strip his assets or keep them secret.

Be certain you have not co-signed or endorsed any note or installment obligation; be sure the liability has been paid off before the divorce agreement is finalized.

Be sure the household bills are up to date (including school and college fees).

Be aware of the dangers of a joint tax return before the divorce is final—you could get stuck with an income tax liability later. Keep in mind any refund that may be due you on joint returns filed for the previous year. Have a tax expert look over your divorce agreement.

Good luck.

Chapter 6

The Children of Divorce

A CHILD need not be traumatized by the legal ending of his parents' marriage. Each year, approximately half a million children under eighteen become children of divorce. As of 1961, there were seven million stepchildren out of a total of 62 million children under eighteen—the majority of these youngsters became stepchildren because of their parents' divorce and subsequent remarriages.* What are some of the special problems these children of divorce and their parents face? The mother with custody must handle an endless array of unprecedented problems, many of which are practical and can be solved quite easily. But many more of them are psychological problems, which are too often the undoing of young people whose families have been split by divorce, whether legal or emotional.

Sometimes the existence of her children is the one factor that forces a divorcee to mature quickly. After divorce, if the father vanishes or defaults in any way, the children may have no one to turn to but the mother. Perhaps the mother will not receive child support—she may be forced to use all her ability and talent to survive so that she can provide for herself and her youngsters. Some mothers and their children become a strong, courageous unit, working and cooperating to make a happy life for themselves. Perhaps she realizes now, for the first time, just what her responsibility is to

* See Anne W. Simon, *Stepchild in the Family* (New York: Odyssey Press, 1964).

these children of hers. Her job will be far more difficult and exhausting than she expected. She may be dismayed at receiving little or no emotional support from family, friends, or community. She'll have to make it on her own, sometimes with the help of a sympathetic friend or two or a new romantic attachment. The problems she faces are much like those of the widowed mother, but the response she evokes from those around her is different. The widow usually gets help, sympathy, and emotional support for herself and her family in their bereavement because most persons feel she has been dealt an unfair blow. The divorcee is bereaved also, but too often onlookers feel "she got what she deserved" and in many ways she is made to feel she has done something wrong or scandalous. It is in this emotional climate that she must learn to solve her family's problems.

Sometimes the divorced mother will feel her children are a burden —they now demand so much more from her because their own world has been toppled. If they are very young, they will still require much physical care, comforting, and loving attention, and they may not be able to give much in return. If she finds herself thinking her children are more a burden than a blessing, it is time to examine her attitudes toward herself, her divorce, her children, her goals.

Is she trying to get emotional support from her children by turning to them before they are old enough to be a comfort? Is she trying to get from them the kind of love and approval she never received from her husband? Is she a burden to her children? Is she too involved in their lives and activities—is she unable to maintain a healthy objectivity about them? She must realize that they can never replace an adult male in her life. Although she may choose to wait before she tries to love a man again, she must prepare herself and her children for the time she falls in love again and remarries. At the same time, she must help her children to continue to love and respect their father. This may be difficult at first. If she was put aside for another woman, she may feel bitter resentment toward him. If she wanted the divorce, she may be entirely correct in her belief that her former husband was inadequate, neurotic, weak, cruel, or whatever. But she must allow, even encourage, her children to love their father.

It is the responsibility of the parent with custody to instill values in the child. Before this can be done, the parent must have a clear idea of what his values are, or it will be impossible to state them clearly, concisely, and simply. Because custody is ordinarily awarded to the mother, these comments are addressed in the main to women. Much of what is said here applies equally to fathers with custody.

THE CHOICE: EMOTIONAL DIVORCE OR LEGAL DIVORCE

Unhappily married people who are also the parents of children often make the mistake of staying together "for the sake of the children." Though they are legally married and live in the same house, they remain *emotionally* divorced. One of the inherent responsibilities of parenthood is to guide one's child and provide for that child an environment that will enable and encourage him to reach healthy adulthood. Part of being a sane adult is possessing the ability to have rational romantic love relationships with members of the opposite sex. I ask anyone who claims she is staying married to a mate she despises or merely tolerates "for the sake of the children" how she expects to communicate to her child that *marriage is a value, that love is possible, that sex when combined with love is a human being's way of celebrating the joy of being alive.*

After you have answered that question for yourself, it is up to you to choose: emotional divorce or legal divorce.

Children who live in a home filled with tension, discord, and conflict are constantly torn and disturbed. They are hurt when they see their father being hostile and indifferent to their mother; they are confused when they see their mother consistently reject their father's gestures of affection; they are even more destroyed when there is no evidence at all of respect, love, or affection in the home. The child may not intellectually understand the disharmony in his home life, but he will feel it and manifest it by being confused, anxious, insecure, and disturbed himself. The parent who is focused on preserving the *form* of the marriage relationship but does nothing to improve the *content* harms herself and her children.

If you say "I am staying married for the sake of my children," think about what that statement actually means. You are in effect saying "I have no right to happiness, therefore I must sacrifice myself for my children." A sacrifice is trading a higher value for a lesser value. It is not a sacrifice to fulfill one's responsibility to one's children, but it *is* a sacrifice to forgo the opportunity to pursue one's own happiness for the dubious benefits of staying married to a mate one does not value, love, or respect. You will gain nothing and your children will gain nothing. You are bound to feel resentment toward your children if you make such a sacrifice; your resentment may not be regularly expressed in words, although you may cringe the first time you hear yourself say to your child when you think he is being ungrateful or unappreciative: "How can you treat me this way after all I've done for you?" Your unspoken attitude will surely convey your martyrdom, and one day your children (and you too) will wonder why you have given up your personal happiness for a life no one enjoyed. I have heard many people say "My parents should have gotten divorced a long time ago—but they stayed together because of me [or us children]." Such a sacrifice on the part of either parent will burden a child; if you make him the reason for staying unhappily married, you give him a debt he does not deserve and can never repay.

TELLING YOUR CHILDREN ABOUT THE DIVORCE

How can you prepare your child for your divorce? Much depends on his age. An infant will not be able to say "Where's Daddy?" but he will miss the presence of his father after a separation and will need to see him regularly to be secure. A child who can talk well enough to ask questions will surely ask where his father is if he mysteriously disappears one day and is gone for what seems forever. It is a mistake for the couple to separate without preparing their children for it first. It is almost a certainty that your child suspects something has been wrong if he hears quarrels when he is supposed to be asleep and if he sees tense, unhappy faces around him. Some children do not dare ask what is wrong because the answer might be more than they could bear. Your child has a right to be told that something is wrong, and you must let him know that you are both trying to solve the problems you have. This is essential to his security. If something so terrible is going on that no one dares mention it, a child becomes extremely anxious. Tell your child that conflicts in marriage, though unpleasant, are not the end of the world, and that no matter what happens he will have two parents to love him and take care of him.

If yours is a well-planned, sensible divorce, you may both be able to sit down with your children and tell them you are not going to live together. Most couples probably would be better off telling their children separately because of the danger of an emotional flareup and bitter accusations if they tell their children together. Make it simple, tell the truth—and do not include sordid details or things your child cannot understand—assure your child that he is not the cause of the divorce, and stress that you will both always love him and continue to take care of his needs. Let your child talk about it and ask as many questions as he needs to. You can say quite simply: "Daddy and I [or Mother and I] have not been getting along together. We fight so much that we decided we would both be happier if we did not live together, and you would be happier too. You will stay here with me, and Daddy will see you every Saturday" (or whatever the visiting arrangements are going to be).

If you are having a trial separation first, tell your child that you are going to live in separate places for a while. Do not give your child false hope, and do not be evasive. You can say, honestly, "We are not happy together and we want to live apart for a while to think about everything. We will do our best to settle our differences." Let your child know that adults do have serious differences, although he is probably quite well aware of it by now, and that divorce is sometimes used as a solution when nothing else works.

At all times remember that your son or daughter has the right to be the child of both parents. A child can survive almost any painful experience if he is secure in his parents' love. Be certain you do not make your child feel hostile toward the parent who has left. If you say "Daddy doesn't want to live with us any more," your child will feel abandoned by his father.

Your children must learn to think of divorce as a welcome solution to a serious problem, not as something evil that will harm them or bring them only misery. If your child blames you by saying "You made Daddy leave," try to be patient with him. Do not vent your anger toward your husband on your child or take out your unhappiness on him.

Divorce is a major crisis for young children, just as it is for adults. There will be behavioral changes in your child. If you have handled things chaotically, your child will feel abandoned, shocked, depressed, or angry. If you can calmly prepare yourselves and your children, you may be surprised to see a change for the better in their behavior after the conflict is resolved and the home atmosphere improves.

I know of two children who were prepared well in advance for what was coming. When the parents went for marriage counseling, they told their children they had problems they were trying to solve with the assistance of a professional counselor. The children felt free to ask either parent from time to time "How are you doing with the counseling?" After about eight or nine months, the father sat down with his children (they were teenagers and quite bright) and said, "Your mother and I have decided to live apart and get a divorce. I'll still see you regularly after I get my own apartment, and we will spend weekends together and take vacations whenever possible. You needn't worry because I will continue to support you. You will still live in the same house, go to the same school, have the same friends. Even though your mother and I will not be living together, we will both always love you and take care of you. I expect you both to obey your mother. When you are having a problem that she cannot help you with, you can come to me with it, just as you did when we all lived together. The major difference in your lives will be this: I will not be in the same house with you every day. But I will still be available to you at any time you need me—you can call me at the office to talk, we can see one another in the evening, we will do many things together on weekends just as we have done in the past. We will have difficulty at first, because I will miss you and you will miss me. But you will see in time that this is the best solution to the problem. Because your mother will return to her job, you both may have some new chores around the house. But the extra responsibility will be good for you."

Several months after this father left, one of his children said: "You know, Dad, I did think the end of the world would come after you moved out, but things aren't so bad. It's just like you said— things are better because there's no more fighting, and Mom is a lot happier. We like seeing you by ourselves because you're a lot happier too."

One thing many fathers lose sight of is that their children need them. Divorce does not have to cut a man off from his offspring. Getting together and staying in close touch will be more difficult, but it can be done and it is certainly worth it. I know a number of divorced fathers who have better communication with their children after divorce than they ever did during the unhappy marriage.

In preparing your child for your divorce, remember that your child is likely to worry about the following: he may believe he was responsible for the divorce; he may worry that no one will look after him; he may think "If Dad left, how do I know Mom won't leave me too?"; he may feel different—left out—because most of his friends have two parents at home.

WHAT ARE CHILDREN OF DIVORCE LIKE?

According to a study by Dr. Judson T. Landis, professor of family sociology at the University of California, the emotional shock of divorce is greatest where the child believed his parents were happy before the divorce. Some children felt the need to "save face" and may therefore have associated mainly with children from divorced or separated homes. However, children who were not surprised by the divorce, because of open conflict at home, were relieved when divorce finally came and had greater security and happiness afterward because of the lessening of tension in their lives. Children who were used as pawns or exploited by either parent suffered, especially where the parents were vindictive and tried to get information about one another's activities.

In general, divorce increased the emotional distance between children and their fathers; girls usually grew closer to their mothers. Children of divorce were rarely close to their fathers before, during, or after the divorce. The unhappy father-dominated marriage is more likely to end in divorce than the unhappy mother-dominated marriage. Children from divorced homes are less likely to have strong religious ties, and are more willing to make interfaith marriages. Though they often doubt their ability to be happy in marriage, they are not generally bitter about it, but are more cautious, realistic, and afraid.

Children of divorce date later than children from happy families, and they date fewer persons and less frequently than those from a happy background. They go steady more often and don't "play the field" the way most children from happy families do. They seek security in their relationships because they have so little security at home. Boys make friends with girls more slowly, and in general the youngsters from divorced and unhappy homes are more likely to be promiscuous. Children from divorced families got less detailed sex education from their parents. These teenagers are often lacking in self-confidence and feel different from other children: inferior, ashamed of their parents' divorce, less attractive. They usually have less confidence in their own ability to have normal relationships with the opposite sex. They also had higher grades in school than children from untorn families—perhaps they worked for grades to compensate for their feelings of inadequacy.

According to Dr. Landis, divorce tends to run in families and children of divorce tend to go steady with, become engaged to, and marry others from divorced families because they have much in common. One of the conclusions of his study was that continued home conflict harms a child more than a divorce and that it is not the divorce but rather the unhappy home situation that determines how a child faces life.

TEACHING YOUR CHILDREN TO FACE REALITY OF DIVORCE

One of the most serious mistakes a divorcee can make is preventing her children from accepting and understanding the reality of their new situation. Because many of us are confused and upset during the period of divorce, we are unable to face the reality ourselves and consequently mishandle the situation with our children.

Children *must* be told the truth by their parents. It is far more intelligent to say "We made a mistake when we married and we are now going to live apart. We will do our best to love and care for you in spite of our problems with one another" than to invent a monstrous lie. Mystery will make children anxious; lies will make them distrustful.

Do not encourage your children to believe you will get together again if you know it is not so. Children spend much time in a fantasy land where everyone lives happily ever after; it is cruel to lead your children on when you know there is no hope for a reconciliation. If there is a possibility you will settle your problems, of course tell your children "We're working on it" or "Your father and I are doing our best," but do not lie, do not give false hope, and do not evade.

I recall one time my former husband came to pick up our sons for the day. We were in good spirits and he accepted the offer of a cup of coffee. We sat and talked and laughed in the kitchen for about ten minutes. Our boys came in and saw us together, obviously enjoying ourselves. A look of hope passed between our sons, and one said, heading for the door, "We want to play some more." At the time we didn't understand their ploy. They came back about forty-five minutes later. The next day my older son said to me: "I saw you and Dad having fun together yesterday—maybe you can get married again." I shook my head, said "Don't count on it," and briefly explained that just because his father and I could laugh together was no indication that we wanted to be together again.

Children, beautiful optimists, will pin their hopes on the slightest incident. You must not continually shatter their dreams, but you *must* level with them. Of course you can also say nothing, or be vague and evasive. This will only lead to anxiety. I could have said to my son, with a misty look, "Yes, maybe Daddy and I will fall in love again," but it would have accomplished nothing. There was no chance of it then and there never has been since because we have conflicting values. I had to let my son know that I respected his father's right to think and act differently than I did, but that we had entirely different ideas about almost everything of importance and consequence.

Another mistake some divorced mothers make is to sacrifice too much for their children. The financial picture changes considerably after most divorces. Perhaps Mother must get a job that does not pay enough to maintain the former standard of living. Perhaps Father cannot send much child support. This is not shameful, it is simply an unpleasant fact of divorce. Do not continue to give your child expensive dancing lessons—unless you have another Nureyev, of course!—and elegant clothes if you cannot afford them. You will be doing your child no favor if you go without necessities to give him luxuries. If you are receiving child support from your former husband, tell your children that Daddy is sending money to pay for part of the rent, their groceries, their clothing, and the like, but let them know that all of you must do without some of the things you were accustomed to in the past.

Very few divorcees are satisfied with the child support or alimony they receive and find it hard to adjust their needs and desires to their reduced income. There is the danger of divorced parents trying to expiate their guilt with elaborate gifts for their children; some divorced mothers and fathers may get a kind of competition going to see who can buy and do the most and material objects become a payoff for guilt. A child who does not get enough love and attention from his parents will learn to blackmail them by demanding even more toys and expensive equipment.

After my divorce, I decided to sell our membership in an expensive swimming club. My children nagged about it for a while, but I explained to them that our membership had become a financial burden, we did not have the opportunity to use the pool enough, they were not allowed to swim there unless I accompanied them (and I worked several days a week that summer), and the water was loaded with bacteria, giving many children infections. I also pointed out to them that their father had access to a pool where he lived then, we lived near many pleasant lakes, and we also had a number of friends who had swimming pools or lived on lakes in which we could swim. The nagging stopped once they had the facts.

When my sons need or want something special that I cannot afford, I consult their father. If he thinks they should have the item and he can afford it, he may buy it. Sometimes we share the cost of something, and we have consulted one another regarding special birthday and Christmas gifts. Our method demonstrates to our sons that we are both concerned about their needs and welfare, and it discourages them from trying to play one parent against the other.

Some divorcees make the mistake of permitting their children to believe their father stranded them all to run off with another woman. Most men do not voluntarily leave good marriages—they are often maneuvered into seeking another woman by a wife who is neurotic and an unsatisfactory mate.

Your child will be able to accept the situation only as well as you do. He did not ask to be born, nor did he ask to be handicapped for life by your problems. You have a responsibility to him. The way you handle your marriage problems and divorce is important to his development. You would not want your child to reach adulthood believing that life is hopeless and frustrating, that human beings were meant to suffer, that happiness is impossible to achieve, or that either parent is evil. You must teach your child (and your former spouse must assist, if able and available) that difficulties can be overcome, that goals can be reached, that time and money can be managed, that it is possible to fail in a love relationship and marriage and learn from that mistake (and hopefully, try again with another and succeed), and that he can have a good, happy life even though he is a child of divorce.

FATHERS, MOTHERS, AND CHILDREN OF DIVORCE

The father, as the absent parent, still has many responsibilities and rights that should not be interfered with. If a man is reluctant to assert his rights, such as taking disciplinary action when necessary, the mother must encourage him to act as a father. If he neglects his responsibilities, such as sending support, she must remind him of his children's needs and, if necessary, give him proof of her expenses.

Concentrate on his positive qualities when you discuss your former husband with your children. Children need to identify with both parents, particularly with the parent of their sex. When you are angry with your child, do not say "You're just like your father," because your child may conclude that you hate him the same way you must hate his father. Make positive comparisons, such as "John is an excellent swimmer, like his dad," and your child will be proud of himself and of his father. It is simple enough to say to your son "That's the best haircut you've ever had—no one can cut your hair as well as your dad." It hurts a child to think that his parents dislike one another so completely that they can see only the negative qualities in one another. And don't discuss your former husband or the reasons for your divorce with friends when your children are around! You may think they are busily engaged doing something else, but children have a way of tuning in on adult conversation when we least expect it. Also watch your phone conversations when they are around. They can be quite upset by remarks they do not fully understand. I heard a sad story recently about a ten-year-old girl whose separated parents quarreled on the phone regarding a property settlement. She heard her mother say she would call the police if her husband tried to take anything out of the house (the girl knew her mother was talking to her father because she answered the phone and spoke to him first) and she lay awake all night thinking her mother was going to have her father put in jail.

Your child's father will be granted visitation rights by the court. This can be one of the saddest aspects of divorce—children, fathers, and visitation. Too often it is mishandled by both parents—the woman who tries to keep her ex-husband away because of her own bitterness loses sight of his rights as a father. In court his rights may not amount to much: he may be granted the right to visit his children one day a week, or one weekend every other week, or perhaps just once a month. Most of the time a man is granted "reasonable visitation rights" and this can be interpreted in many ways. It is imperative that both parents stay in communication with each other; if they have set up a schedule with the help of their attorneys, they should both try to stick to it as much as possible so both children and parents can have some regularity in their lives. The man who finds it too difficult to pick his children up every Saturday or Sunday and claims he must work, golf, or clean his apartment forgets that his children need him *now*. They need to know they are important to him—important enough for him to make a special effort to spend time with them.

Mother, do not spoil these visits for your children or their father. If your ex-husband is half an hour late, don't say "He probably forgot he was supposed to pick you up today." Make it your business to know what is happening, know when he is supposed to come, and where he is taking your children. If you are in doubt, it is simple enough to call and say "I understand you are taking the children to a picnic Saturday. Shall I pack their bathing suits or any special toys?" If he picks your children up regularly at a certain time, have them ready and properly dressed, with suitcases packed if they are staying overnight. If there are chores to be done, allow plenty of time for your child to take care of them—don't make your last five or ten minutes together unpleasant because you have to nag! Don't use unnecessary phone calls about the visits as an excuse to argue about some other problem. You should have settled those matters with your divorce—your only concern with one another now is your children's happiness and welfare.

If your children are participating in a special program at their school, let their father know so he can plan to attend. When your children get their report cards, show them to their father, as well as any special work they do in school, or any papers and projects which are outstanding and interesting, or even ordinary. You will have to make an effort to keep their father posted on their progress and activities—he may forget to ask about these things, and your children may also forget to tell him.

My sons spend every other weekend with their father. I try to find out what they will be doing so that I can pack the right clothing. If he plans to take them to dinner right after he picks them up, I devote an extra half-hour to helping them select their clothes, and assist them with hair-washing and grooming. This makes my sons know that it is important to me that they have a good visit, and it also shows that I want to be proud of them. I want them to be happy with me when they leave, happy with themselves, and ready to relax and enjoy their dad. Some women may be afraid that their children will like Father better than Mother. If you have this fear, examine it carefully. If you are a loving and concerned mother, you will want your children to love their father. Any love they give to him or to any other human being will certainly not detract from the love they feel for you.

When your children return from a visit, try to be home to greet them. If they want to talk about where they went and what they did, listen with interest. They want to share their experiences with you, and their time with their father is very important. Refrain from making snide comments about their activities with him. If you learn they are unhappy during their visits, try to find out why, and do what you can to improve the situation. Do not prevent them from seeing their father for a flimsy reason and *never* deny them a visit because of some misbehavior on their part. These visits are not a reward.

Your former husband can actually be your greatest ally where your children are concerned. Does that sound impossible? If you feel resentful and negative now, try to work out your hostile attitude and try to understand your own motivations. You will need his backing on many decisions regarding your children. You were doubtless not able to communicate well during your marriage and it seems to be asking more than is humanly possible to expect you to do any better now. However, the real problems for children of divorce are caused by the constant tug-of-war between their parents, or by the father's indifference to his children or the mother's over possessiveness. Your children need their father or a reliable father substitute, and they will benefit from his psychological as well as his financial support.

There will still be many problems facing you as parents, and you will have to work harder than parents living together to solve these problems. This is one of the prices of divorce—but be sure you are the one who pays, not your children, because you can afford it better than they can.

You may have bad days with your children—days when you feel tired, ineffectual, discouraged. You may wonder what you have done wrong, what you can change. You may turn to your children's father for help and assistance, only to have him remind you "The divorce was your idea. The kids are your problem now." Or "I'm busy with my work. I don't have time for these matters." Or "I'm busy with my new family now. I'm sorry."

Realistically, it *is* difficult for a man who lives somewhere else to play an active role in his children's lives. If he has not remarried, he may live in a bachelor apartment with facilities inadequate for his children. His schedule may be full with work, new social contacts, and recreation. Perhaps he lives far away and driving to and from the children's home is a two-hour proposition. If he has remarried, his new wife may have children of her own and he now has to think about the problems of his second family. His first family may be forgotten at times. If the new wife has no children, she may want to be alone with her husband as much as possible: it is a rare second wife who can assist with her husband's children, remind him of his responsibility to them, and even urge him to live up to it when he is slacking off. Many second wives unfortunately think of the first wife as a natural enemy and a constant threat to their own security.

You will have to work out a fair and satisfactory arrangement about birthdays, holidays, and vacations. Much will depend upon the individual circumstances of both mother and father (how much space you have, whether or not you have both remarried, the other demands of your lives) and where the father lives. If he lives several hundred miles away, your child's visits will of course be less frequent, but no less important. Try to be as agreeable as possible when making arrangements for your children to go out of town to see their father. Perhaps they will take the bus or train or plane and stay for an extended visit. Perhaps they will have to spend alternate holidays with each parent. If their father lives in another town, encourage your children to write to him, and allow them to make long distance calls regularly. Remind your children to buy presents for their father's birthday and other special occasions; fathers need to be remembered too.

AN OPEN LETTER TO DIVORCED FATHERS

After a divorced father asked if I had tried to give men any help or suggestions in this book, I decided to write a letter to divorced fathers.

First suggestion: *Do not divorce your children.* Your divorce has upset you—you probably feel bitter and rejected if your wife asked for and was granted the divorce. You probably feel you have been unfairly treated by her, by the attorneys and the court, and now you think the easiest thing to do is fade away quietly and see very little of your children and their mother. Many divorced fathers have tried that. It seems to be the easiest course to follow at first, but it's the coward's way out, and it is also immature. You cannot run from your children—they are living realities and proof of a relationship you would prefer to forget. Forget the relationship but don't forget your children. Do not think of your children as mere extensions of a woman you no longer love or who no longer loves you. Your children need you, their natural father. Sometimes a woman seeking a divorce may say—perhaps to justify her action—"The kids would be better off without you!" You cannot listen to that kind of talk and you must not believe it, unless she is right—then what you must do is straighten yourself out so that you no longer harm your family.

The most painful aspect for a divorced father without custody is likely to be his inability to see his children every day and not being able to play a vitally active part in their lives at all times. You will have a difficult time staying in contact. It will be hard to know your children well when you see them just once a week or once every two weeks.

The present system does much to separate fathers permanently from their children. The law appears to favor women, although it really doesn't. The divorced mother has to continue to be mother, try to be father (and learns this is impossible), and be a wage-earner. She is eager to remarry, which means she must spend time away from home husband-hunting. Whatever she does, she feels she is not giving her children enough of herself. The divorced father has the frustration of not being able to give his children his time and love every day. He may be so embittered by his divorce that he leaves town, with serious effects on his relationship with his children.

A divorced father without custody must first determine just how much he should blame himself for the failure of his marriage. Did his wife give him a warning; did she give him several chances? Did he take her seriously, or continue to treat her and perhaps their children poorly? Did he make her life so unbearable that divorce was her only choice? If he finds he was at fault, he should try to change his attitude.

In the United States, the divorced father is almost stripped clean of his parental rights. He must pay child support for children he sees once a week, and he usually has little to say about how that money is spent. If I had an ex-wife who was a reasonable woman, I would try to meet with her from time to time to discuss our children—how they are progressing, how they are being disciplined, educated, and so on. I would use the phone regularly to talk to my children and my ex-wife. I would try my best to maintain an active role in making important decisions, but I would realize that according to law the children's mother had the upper hand. I would try to make her see that this is not always *morally* correct and that, to do the best job for our children, she and I should communicate, consult, and cooperate.

I would certainly not use child support or alimony to *control* her, as many men try to do, thereby alienating their ex-wives and children even further. I would talk calmly with my children's mother about their future; I would expect her to honor and respect my rights and position as the father. I would patiently point out to her that our children's welfare, health, and happiness depend exclusively on how well we communicate and act in their behalf. I would not engage in a stupid contest to see who can give the children more privileges and goodies. I would not try to be just a pal or a playmate to my children when I saw them, but a real father. I would always remember that my child has the right to be the child of both parents.

If my ex-wife opposed me on this, I would have someone she

respected and admired talk to her about the situation—perhaps a clergyman, or the family doctor, or a good lawyer who knows the sad outcome of many divorces. Or a marriage counselor or psychotherapist. After I got my ex-wife to listen to reason about our children, I would continue to be reasonable myself. I would try to show her that I am not trying to win our children away from her, that I am not bribing them with gifts or privileges they should not have, but that I am genuinely interested in sharing the responsibility for their upbringing, even if I live quite a distance away. I would say, "When you are having a problem you can't handle alone, call me. I will talk to our son or daughter, and I will back you up if I think you are right."

I would try to arrange a reasonable and satisfactory visiting schedule, and would do my damnedest to stick to it. I would not make promises I could not keep, and I would not talk against my children's mother to them. Neither would I overpraise her, because then my children would wonder why I could not live with such a paragon. If I had to say something negative about their mother, I would try to keep malice out of it.

If I thought my kids were trying to get me to agree to something their mother was against, my response would be "I will discuss that with your mother—we will both make the decision."

I would realize that the main reason we divorced is that we have conflicting values; I would nevertheless try to get along.

A youngster who sees his dad once or twice a year treasures letters, postcards, or little gifts. A long-distance phone call can be a big event in a ten-year-old's life if it comes twice a month from his father.

Don't antagonize your ex-wife now, because she may retaliate by pulling things like telling you the kids have colds and cannot visit you this week. Some women are inclined to do some pretty awful and stupid things to their ex-husbands to get even for years of misery. Of course this is wrong; it is equally wrong if you play the same game. The children are hurt most. Don't give your ex-wife an excuse to be difficult—and don't let any unreasonable behavior on her part determine how you shall handle your parental responsibilities. Remember that she may be quite emotionally upset immediately following the divorce. You must do what is objectively right whether she does or not. In time she will settle down.

Don't pump your children for information about their mother's activities. Her private life is private—as yours is now. If she is failing to be a good mother, you will have to speak to her about it. You can probably expect an argument, and it may take time for your criticism to sink in. It is almost impossible to accept criticism from one's ex-husband gracefully, but a man has a right—in fact, a duty—to speak up when his children are not being treated properly. Don't back off, thinking "I don't want to start any more trouble." And do be sure you are making a legitimate complaint about a legitimate problem. If you nitpick and nag at her for any insignificant matter, she'll simply tell you to go to hell. She may reject your important advice, but give it anyway; in time she will learn you are primarily interested in your children's happiness and health.

Now to the matter of alimony and child support. Most divorced men think they are financially raped in divorce suits. I will repeat the obvious: women have been discriminated against for centuries; that is why most of them are still dependent on men. The law recognizes this and makes provisions for women who divorce or are divorced by their husbands.

If you have minor children, you must provide for them after divorce. Forget what the law says about child support, because it is often unrealistic. It is usually not enough (see page 69). If you can afford it, you should be willing to provide for your children to the best of your ability. If you can send enough money so that they have their *own mother* at home with them while they are very young (at least until the age of six or seven) instead of a housekeeper, do so without quibbling or being forced by law. I am not suggesting you support your ex-wife and children in a grand manner, but do figure out something reasonable and keep in mind that part of the child support should pay for your ex-wife's time. Most baby-sitters earn from 50¢ to $1.50 per hour; your children's mother deserves some consideration for all the time she spends at home if she is not gainfully employed.

If you want a divorce because you have fallen in love with another woman, you should do all you can to help your wife become independent. Pay for her tuition to night school or make arrangements to send temporary alimony while she studies. Be realistic about your ex-wife's ability to earn a living.

You know what it costs to run a household. You know how tough it is to work full-time. You know how demanding children are, how much time and love they require from their parents. Do not expect your ex-wife miraculously to rear happy, well-adjusted children alone. She needs the child support (send it on time!), she needs a chance to relax (this she can do when the children visit you), and she needs a chance to develop any skill or talent she has so she can eventually get a decent job.

I have heard men remark: "If she thinks I'm going to send child support after a divorce, she's nuts." Let's hope you are not one of these. Money is love. The money you send for your children demonstrates your love and concern for them—it's that simple. My children know they have been able to live in the same house since their birth and the divorce because their father loves *them* enough to send the child support regularly.

At the time you work out a divorce and property settlement, you will no doubt work out a visitation schedule, which can be revised if it is not satisfactory. You will probably see your children every Sunday while you are unmarried; if you remarry and have larger living quarters you may decide to see them every other weekend, Friday to Sunday.

After about six months you may tire of being a recreation director. Most children of divorce spend Sundays with father going to the zoo, to movies, to sporting events, to museums, to the circus. You do not have to spend the rest of your life "dating" your children. What they need most from you is your love and guidance. Think of something simple to do when you see them, like staying in on Sunday reading the paper, playing checkers, or just watching the ball game on television. You don't have to spend a fortune every time; you don't have to buy them a lot of toys and gadgets they would not get if you lived with them; and you don't have to entertain them constantly. Learn to relax with them; let them be children, introduce them to other children in your new neighborhood, and be their father. If they're bored occasionally, it won't kill them.

Your children need to talk to you about whatever is bothering them, so keep your ears open. One of our greatest problems in America is a result of the fact that boys and girls do not have enough healthy contact with their fathers. Children are with their mothers constantly until they go to school, then they have women teachers. If mother works, there is a female housekeeper or a female relative. Daddy is too often someone who is a grouch in the morning before he leaves for work, and a grouch when he comes home from a hard day at the office or factory and perhaps a hard hour on the expressway. On weekends he golfs or participates in some other sport; he may spend part of one day recovering from a hangover; perhaps he must spend part of the weekend maintaining his home and property. Or, if he's a go-getter, he spends Saturday at the office or he brings additional work home. How much time does that leave him with his children?

It has been reported that the average American child spends a total of two hours a week with his father. As a divorced father you may have the opportunity to spend many more hours weekly with your child—but in one stretch at a time. You can make this time constructive and rewarding. We have a nation of children growing up without the necessary healthy influence of mature men. Our crime rate reflects these weaknesses: the problems of our young people—young men especially—cannot and should not all be blamed on mothers. As a divorced father, you will have to make an extra effort.

Maintain an interest in your child's activities. Whenever possible, go to his school when there is an open house or a special concert or play, meet his teachers, go to see him play baseball if he is on a team, go to his recitals if he plays an instrument. Give your child emotional support. You can make yourself more a reality in your child's life by occasionally inviting his friends along when you do something special. Your child wants to be proud of you—he wants his friends to know you too. He doesn't want them to think he is different because his dad lives somewhere else, or that his dad doesn't care about him.

If you have several children of widely different ages, planning your time with them will be more difficult than if they were all in the same age group. Your teenagers might think the zoo a bore, and a hockey game is not likely to be appealing to a six-year-old girl. One of your problems will be how you spend your visits with your children. The situation is often easier when a man remarries and has a home again instead of a bachelor apartment. There will also be a lack of opportunity for casual contacts with your children, for those precious minutes alone with this or that child. Perhaps at times you can arrange to see each child separately or to have occasional short visits during the week.

Perhaps you can take an apartment not far from the family home. If you and your ex-wife are agreeable about this, it could be a boon to your children to be able to see you in the morning before you all start your day, or stop in at dinner time. One remarkable couple was able to work this out. The father is an attorney and the mother attends law school. They have three children (and a live-in maid). Father lives about two blocks away, and his children have seen him as much after the divorce as they did while they all lived together. Their parents have handled visiting intelligently.

Some people feel that children are better off if they see father infrequently after the divorce. This may be valid if the father's presence is quite disturbing to the children. Nevertheless, a man should see his children regularly, whether or not their mother re-marries. As for giving one's children up through adoption, I would think very carefully about that if I were a man and would get the best professional advice before reaching such a decision. I would also consult my heart.

I have talked to a number of adults who were children of divorce. Those whose fathers faded away felt cheated and wished they could have been able to maintain some contact and relationship with them. One young man told me he had always missed his father and won-dered about him, even though his parents divorced when he was three years old and a year later his mother remarried a wonderful man, who adopted him. One of the saddest facts of this twenty-two-year-old man's life was that he had seen his natural father just three times in eighteen years and he felt abandoned by him. He learned when he was eighteen that his domineering mother had prevented the father from seeing his son and forced her former husband to give the boy up. If you need legal advice to enforce your visitation rights, get it. Don't give up in despair.

An attorney read me part of a letter from the teenaged daughter of one of his clients. The girl had written to her father, wondering why he had stopped visiting her and her little brothers. She was lonesome for him, and the letter was pleading and heartbreaking. The child had no understanding of the sick and evil game her mother had been playing. The mother had told her children that their father did not care and did not wish to see them. She then told her ex-husband that his children hated him and were afraid of him. The truth came out when the girl wrote to her father, and he was smart enough to take the letter to his attorney. Soon after, father and children had their visits again even though it took a court order to enforce his rights. If that girl had not been old enough to write, this heartsick man might have stayed away from his children indefinitely.

It is sometimes said that many divorced fathers would prefer to spend their free time dating. No man should give up the opportunity to form a new romantic alliance, but don't lose your perspective about your children while you are trying to find a new love.

Certain activities will be more enjoyable for you and your children if there is a woman along, but try to limit this in the beginning. Your children may come to resent a woman who is always with you immediately after your divorce. They will undoubtedly report to their mother, and she may turn them against your new friend if she herself is not romantically involved. She may convince your children that you are cheating them of your exclusive time and attention. Give your children time to accept the idea that another woman is replacing their mother in your affections. Don't make comparisons between her and their mother. Your children want to be loyal to both parents. Until they have accepted the divorce, they may regard the romantic interest of either parent as an interloper. They will learn to like your new choice, but in their own time.

If you have sons, be aware that they need you. Make sure their mother does not overprotect and overcontrol them. It is well known in psychoanalytic circles that most homosexuals have had all-powerful and domineering mothers and weak, passive, disinterested fathers. You must provide them a strong male image because if they do not identify with males, they are likely to identify with females. If you see signs of trouble in your sons, talk to their mother about it and get professional help if necessary.

Your daughters need you too—there are things you can tell and teach them that they cannot learn from their mother. A girl gets her first, lasting impressions about men from her father. A child who has the love and attention of both parents gets a balanced view of both sexes. Above all, you want your children of both sexes to grow up with healthy ideas about themselves, marriage, love, and sex. Your divorce need not cripple their emotions and outlook.

Your children will need to talk to you about many things—their personal problems, their school activities, their questions about morals, ethics, current events, politics. Keep the channels of communication open; you may have to ask them more questions than you would if you were still living together to find out what they are thinking because such subjects do not always come up naturally or spontaneously. Be sure you do not spend all your time playing with your children—this happens to many divorced fathers, and they actually forget how to talk with them.

You have the moral responsibility of providing for their educational needs. Make provisions early so you are not suddenly hit with a financial burden when your first child reaches eighteen. You may be remarried by then and you may also have more children. Don't forget your responsibility to your first family; you have no business having more children with a second wife if you cannot provide for the children you had with your first. Also, the children of your second wife by a previous marriage should never come before your own natural children. Discuss educational requirements with your ex-wife. If she is employed, perhaps she can share the expenses with you, just as she might do if you were still married.

Be patient with your ex-wife. Her adjustment is probably going to be far more difficult than yours. She is faced with more responsibility now than ever before in her life. No matter which of you wanted the divorce, it is likely her new role is more demanding, at least until she remarries. She may act strangely immediately after the divorce in her attempts to become independent. Sometimes she may be demanding, threatening, or just plain mean. Then, perhaps the next time you see or talk to her, she may be pleasant, almost kind and sweet. If there is any way you can help her adjust, do so. Any assistance you give will benefit your children. A woman who has the practical problems of maintaining a household under control will have more time to concentrate on the needs of her family. You are primarily interested in your children's happiness. It follows that if their mother is happy, she will be a better mother.

This is part of a letter from a divorced father about what happens to a man's fatherhood after divorce:

A man may become almost a father to his lover's or his new wife's children. Yet he would always act to some degree as a guest. The woman would always have a primary responsibility and a kind of final veto concerning the kids. After all, they are hers. This is inescapable and calls for very clear definition, constant clarification, careful understanding. Also the man has a peculiar responsibility for his own children's behavior. They are his, and yet he has little daily say in how their personalities are formed. He has no legal rights with regard to their upbringing at all, except in extreme cases. If things go well with them, he can feel only partially proud; if they do poorly, he can feel only partially responsible. For the women, there is too much irrefutable, undeniable, inescapable responsibility. For the men, everything becomes slippery, nothing is real, final. All relationships with kids have an aspect of having been borrowed. A divorced man's parental motives and his parental energies cannot be made to coincide, at least not fully. These are the prices of poor judgment and poor choice.

WHEN FATHER REMARRIES

Eventually most divorced mothers must face this: your former husband is considering marriage again, but not to you. Your attitude about his remarriage will depend in part upon which of you wanted the divorce. If he left you for another woman, and he is now going to marry her, you may feel publicly humiliated. But consider this: perhaps she now has or is going to have what you did not value or cherish while *you* had it.

The woman who has been put aside for another will have many emotions, most of them destructive, but you cannot really increase your self-esteem by bad-mouthing another. It may sting when your children say "Dad's getting married again." You may wonder if *she* will try to woo your children away from you, as you may believe she wooed your husband away. You will have cause to worry only if your own relationship with your children is poor. If you're letting them down, they will naturally seek love, guidance, and friendship somewhere else. That somewhere else can be from a favorite teacher, their grandmother, a motherly neighbor, a female relative, or your ex-husband's new wife.

Children do not automatically love and respect us—we must earn and deserve that love and respect. If you find yourself actively competing with your child's stepmother, something is drastically wrong. Suppose she is smarter, younger, more successful, or better-looking than you? Your children may come home praising her, or they may speak affectionately of her. They may tell you about some special dish she prepared just for them. They may use a nickname when referring to her. If you respond negatively to all this, perhaps you feel threatened. Can you accept her as just another human being with hopes, fears, and desires much like yours (you both would be surprised to learn how much you have in common—at least you found the same man attractive)? She cooks, cleans, laughs, makes love, cries, perhaps holds a job outside the home.

Of course, she is not *just another human being:* she is the woman who married your ex-husband. She *will* be an influence in the lives of your children, though to a limited degree. With luck, she will be kind and friendly to them and will try to make their visits happy and rewarding. She undoubtedly is not the wicked woman you might prefer to believe she is. If your children can like and respect her, they'll be better off.

Would you actually want them to hate or dislike her? This would mean they'd be upset and anxious around her. Your children have the right to make up their own minds about this new and important person. If she is given the chance to know and like your children without their having been poisoned against her by you, it is possible a healthy relationship will develop. Try not to question your children about her. Of course you are curious—who would not be curious about the woman one's ex-husband chose for a second wife? The degree of your curiosity will depend on how rich and full your own life is. If you and your children have good communication and rapport, in time they will talk about their visits to Dad's house and they will mention their stepmother. Don't make cutting remarks about her—your children may surprise you by defending *her!* If you're catty, they'll think you're a bad sport.

It is reasonable to be concerned about what effect she will have on your children; you may worry that they will develop habits or tastes or ideas that you find objectionable as a result of their association with her. It is necessary for a child to have a wide exposure to many different activities and styles of life. In the end he will make his own choice, just as you did. Your child's stepmother is just one of many other adults who will come into his world. If you know your child is being harmed by something his stepmother does, then by all means put a stop to it. You have this right and responsibility. However, if you have no evidence that she has done harm intentionally, do not derogate her. Don't make your child feel guilty about liking her, and don't say *"She's* the one who caused the divorce." I am not suggesting that you must pretend to like the woman. Your children will not be fooled by any phony friendship on either side, but they will respect you more if you do not lose your dignity. If your husband openly left you for this woman, you will experience feelings of intense jealousy, rivalry, and competition. Your first impulse may be to blame someone else for your marriage failure, but that will not bring you one bit closer to understanding yourself and the reasons for your wrong choice and subsequent failure.

It is hard to be noble when one has been deeply disappointed in a marriage. Perhaps when your children are adults you can safely and frankly discuss the reasons for your divorce. However, while they are children there is much you should not share with them. First, because children have big mouths. Holding your tongue is mainly for your own protection. Second, children cannot understand adult emotions and will misconstrue much you say. The end result could be that they learn to despise their father, to mistrust him, and to feel that he has abandoned them, when in truth the only thing he did was try to find his own happiness.

I heard a not very funny story from a divorced friend. Her eight-year-old daughter asked her mother what she thought of "Daddy's new wife" and my friend said unthinkingly, "She's a conniving bitch." Guess who repeated the remark to her stepmother the following Sunday? As a result, the stepmother let her own emotions get out of control and retaliated by saying something equally nasty. The girl repeated the remark to her mother and the battle was on. The hallmark of maturity is self-control. We cannot teach self-control to our children unless we have it ourselves.

Suppose *you* instigated the divorce and were glad to be out of your marriage; yet when you learn your former husband is getting married again, you experience emotions you neither like nor understand. Perhaps you were wishing he would undergo a stupendous change for the better, come back to you chastened and humbled, and you would fall in love all over again. It doesn't usually work that way. Now someone else has what you didn't want, and you may even wonder what she sees in him. Don't waste your time wondering; get on with your own life. I have heard some divorcees say they felt sorry for the second wives of their ex-husbands. Whatever the situation, whatever your reaction, don't talk against your children's stepmother. If you are in love again you're probably not too much interested in your ex-husband's love life. Make no mistake about this: it will take time for the scars of an unhappy marriage to heal. If you have children, it is not fair to them to make them feel your pain. They have their own pain. The best justification for divorce is that all individuals involved come out winners, not losers. If your ex-husband can love again and be happy, he will be that much better a father.

Some divorced families can have compatible, cordial relationships within the new groups formed by the new marriages. It helps to be courteous and civil. Some will stop right there—just enough courtesy to enable each adult to speak on the telephone when something must be discussed. You do want to be able to tell your child's stepmother whatever is necessary to insure his health and welfare while he is in her home. Mother and stepmother will have to work this out. Remember there will be much passing back and forth of children and their assorted clothing and equipment from your house to their father's house. There will be times you may have to speak to the stepmother about holiday plans, birthday parties, one child or another needing to take medicine or get extra rest.

Encourage your child to treat his stepmother with courtesy and respect. Remind your children that even though they are at their father's house, it is also the home of another woman and perhaps other children who are entitled to respect and consideration.

An excellent book that can add to your insight about all step-relationships is *Stepchild in the Family* by Anne W. Simon.

Your child's stepmother will be relieved if you are at least cordial to her, and unhostile. She is no doubt a little nervous about you too. She may have heard favorable comments about you from your former husband, and perhaps she considers you a threat to the stability of her marriage. Perhaps she too has children and her weekends are confused and busy now with all those children coming and going. Perhaps she is doing her utmost to be friendly and pleasant to your children but is having a hard time because they are rejecting her. She has probably heard your children say how wonderful, talented, kind, loving, and smart you are.

If your child's stepmother has a religious belief different from your own and your child comes home with some new ideas, it's the signal for open discussion. No one has a priority on morality or truth: don't be so close-minded that you arbitrarily forbid your child to benefit from his association with his new stepfamily.

At first your children may not talk about what happens during their visits, perhaps mainly because they are not sure of your response. Perhaps they're not having a good time at all—there may be difficulty adjusting to stepbrothers and stepsisters as well as the new stepmother. Perhaps their father is having a tough time too, and he may be harder on them than usual. Be ready to listen when they're ready to talk. They may start with something which seems insignificant, such as a discussion of their father's new dog or pool table. If you cut the discussion off with an "I'm busy now" you may miss the opportunity to help them with some incipient problem.

In your circle of friends it may be difficult to discuss divorce; it is not as common an experience as having a baby, for example. You may never find yourself in a group of women discussing step-relationships and how to handle them. You, as an overtired, overworked, often overemotional divorcee, may not have the necessary patience, experience, and wisdom to handle each problem as it arises. There will be many times you will have to be magnanimous for the sake of your children. You wield a power that can be devastating to them. Use that power wisely. Remember to have patience with your child—he does not yet have good judgment about handling these delicate new relationships. If your child is having inner conflict about his father's new wife, he may cause dissension in his father's home. If he is so hostile that the visits become miserable for everyone, soon the visits will stop altogether. This would be a loss to your child.

RELATIONSHIPS WITH OTHER FAMILY MEMBERS

After divorce, children need reassurance, love, comfort, and company more than ever. There is evidence that children from broken homes, foster children who have been moved around a number of times in early childhood, orphans—children who have not had secure, permanent places in a loving family—are more often emotionally disturbed, and show more signs of neurosis and serious personality disorders in adult life than those who had secure childhoods in stable, loving families.

Some mothers are not able to keep their children together immediately after divorce, and there is extreme family disorganization. If there are brothers and sisters and their relationships with one another have been close and happy throughout their lives, they will need to turn to one another now for companionship, understanding, and solace. It is bad enough that your children have been separated from their father; if it is necessary to separate them from one another and also from you, do be aware of the serious problems this could cause. It is best if you can keep your children together, with you, and change their daily routines as little as possible. Your new arrangements will depend upon the ages of your children and your financial situation. If you have older, college-age children and you have waited many years to end your marriage, remember that your children will still need a home base for weekends, vacations, and holidays.

Sometimes, of necessity, a mother is forced to send one child to this relative and another child to that relative immediately after a divorce. If you have to separate your children because you have sold your home or are looking for new living quarters and are trying to get settled in a permanent job, be sure the separation is temporary and that you *reassure* your children. Some children live the lives of refugees for many years while their mothers or fathers ineffectually try to make more permanent living arrangements. The small child who is shifted around from one relative's house to another while his mother lives somewhere else trying to get settled will feel lonely, unwanted, and afraid. It will take many years to get rid of the insecurities brought about by these impermanent, irregular modes of living, and some children grow into adulthood never feeling they belonged anywhere or that anyone really loved them. If, for instance, your child must live with your mother or a sister right after your divorce, be certain *you* think of it as an emergency visit.

If you find it necessary to live with your parents after divorce, ask yourself some questions about what your life might be: can you be a part of their household without being treated like a child? Can they accept and honor your right to have the final say about your child's discipline, privileges, behavior? Is there enough room for you in their household? Will you be using them as baby-sitters, day and night, so you can ignore your own responsibilities to your children?

Or will the situation be temporary and happy and healthy, with your parents willing and able to help you get organized enough to control your own life and look after your own children?

If you are planning to take a flat or an apartment near your parents' home, be sure you have carefully thought out the advantages and disadvantages of such a move.

If your children have been close to members of your former husband's family, make it possible for them to continue having warm, close relationships. Children who have had the benefit of a big, loving family should not be cut off from grandparents, aunts, uncles, and cousins. Encourage your children to write to relatives of your ex-husband on birthdays and holidays, to exchange small gifts with their cousins, and so on, even if you may prefer to stay out of touch with them yourself. Usually the father makes the arrangements for his children to visit with his relatives after a divorce, but there is no reason a divorcee cannot maintain cordial relations with a former sister-in-law if their children have always gotten along well and have spent time playing and visiting overnight at one another's homes. You may have to make the first move about things like this after your divorce. Other family members will be friendly in return if they see that you are not going to be bitter and uncommunicative.

If your former in-laws are hostile toward you it may seem natural to you to want to keep your children away from them. It may be necessary for you to go to your former in-laws and talk to them calmly about any derogatory or inflammatory remarks they make about you to your children. Perhaps they are overemotional, out of control, and have become too personally involved. Make it clear to them that you do not wish to permanently separate your children from them, but that you will not tolerate their talking against you. Most young children would not be able to handle unkind, unfair remarks made about their mother by a close relative, and if you discover this is happening, you have the right to protect your child from such threats. If you cannot visit your former in-laws in person, it may help to write to them about any problem.

One wise grandmother I know pays for her divorced son's children's day-camp fees every summer because their mother must work full-time, and this is one way she can show love and concern for her grandsons. She has also instigated the tradition of birthday parties at her apartment for each of her five grandchildren. This way her two grandsons whose parents are divorced get to see their father's relatives in a happy family setting.

Children of our so-called nuclear families (just mother, father, and children) of today miss out on a lot of solid, old-fashioned family life when that nuclear family has been exploded by divorce. Do not deny them part of their heritage by cutting them off from their father's relatives.

A NORMAL HOME LIFE IN A ONE-PARENT HOME

The divorced mother will ask "Can I still give my children a normal home life?" By Webster's definition, *normal* means: "According to, constituting, or not deviating from, an established norm, rule, or principle; standard, regular, natural."

A knowledge of our country's history brings to mind the pioneer women who managed homes and reared children while their men were away, of women who did the job alone during wars. Mothers today often have to do the job alone: their husbands are in the service, or away at business most of the time. Actually it is quite *normal* in our country for a mother to do the job without a father around all the time. Remember, however, that normal does not necessarily mean *best*.

We consider it the birthright of our children to have the best that is available in schooling, medical and dental attention, clothing, shelter, and food. Giving one's children "the best" requires a certain amount of money and a certain standard of living. There are some things involved in parenthood that have little to do with the amount of money one has. It does not cost *money* to give one's child love and good values. It is your responsibility to guide and protect your child.

See to it that your child is protected from constant danger to his physical and psychological well-being. Your child is entitled to an environment that is free of ugly tensions, hatred, anxieties; of disease-producing germs and filth, of constant physical threats. Give him a place of his own to work, play, and sleep—even if it must be just a corner of a room he shares with others. He needs privacy at times, he needs to be able to entertain his friends in his home, he needs a place he can mess up at times without being severely chastised.

No matter how poor you are, it is still possible for your child to have an occasional overnight guest, or a friend in to lunch or dinner. Remember what your own childhood was like—think of what made it happy or unhappy, then look at your own child. A child needs to be loved, wanted, accepted, and enjoyed.

Listen to yourself as you talk to your children—do you nag, whine, demand, shout, and complain, or are you courteous to them? Think about what you say and do regarding your child—teach him to think about what *he* says and does.

If your child feels embarrassed, guilty, or somehow responsible for your divorce, get him to talk about his feelings. Explain to him that *he is not alone,* that other children have lost one or both parents for one reason or another.

Do not say "no" arbitrarily to everything your child requests. If there is a reason why he cannot have or do something, give him the reason. Don't permit your child to learn the habit of emotionally blackmailing you every time he wants something! *You* are the adult, you are in charge, you are the one who must be aware, informed, alert, and responsible. If you are not any of these things, you will not be able to teach your child anything worth knowing.

You will have to determine to what extent your child has the right and ability to help you make a decision. You would not permit a six-year-old to decide where your family should live, but when you make the decision whether to stay in your old home or move you certainly must consider the needs of that six-year-old.

Your child needs to learn that actions have consequences, he needs to learn that he does not have the right to run the household, to tyrannize his mother or brothers and sisters, to shirk chores. In a good household there is an atmosphere of love, respect, trust, patience—and humor. You will set the pace. You need not live in disorganized chaos. Meals can be eaten at fairly regular hours; each member of the household can be held responsible for jobs that are right for his age and ability.

If it is necessary for you to work outside your home, you will have to organize your life and your household around your job and increased responsibilities. Your child will have to adjust to the changes in his way of life. An eight-year-old can wash a floor, boil an egg, bring up a basket of laundry and fold it. A ten-year-old can clean the bathroom, run errands, polish furniture, set the table, and so on. Give each child work to do. Don't try to do it all yourself.

Don't expect your child to work without some rewards, but do try to pay him for more involved chores. I pay my sons for certain kinds of work; a penny a minute. They like this because they can work ten or fifteen minutes without getting too tired or bored and still have something to show for it. I learned that my sons were efficient, competent helpers when I returned from the hospital after major surgery several years ago. It was impossible for me to get around and the plans I had made for help fell through. My sons pitched in and did everything a cleaning woman can do. I sat on a chair and supervised, and they worked with vigor and dispatch!

Involve your children in your social life when possible. Invite your friends and relatives who have children for lunch or dinner and let your children help with the cooking and entertaining. You need not limit yourself or your family to a meager social life because of your divorce. Children need to have happy times with friends and relatives; they need to learn how to be gracious hosts, and good guests.

Don't forget about outings with your children. You can plan these according to your likes, where you live, and what you can afford. Do not cut yourself or your children off from the benefits of work, play, and love. Your job is teaching your child to be a worthwhile adult—that's what parenthood is all about. Admittedly, it's harder to achieve in a one-parent home, but others have achieved it and so can you.

THE DIVORCED WORKING MOTHER

The way you will approach the problem of working will depend on many factors: the ages of your children, your training and former work experience, your present and future financial needs, where you live, your state of mind and health at the time of your divorce, and even your plans for remarriage.

The divorced working mother may find herself trying to lead three full lives at once: that of a career woman, or "working girl," depending upon her age and her self-image; that of mother and homemaker; and that of the single woman in search of a new social life (and new husband—no matter what she says to herself or her friends, she *is* looking for HIM). A year or two of attempting to lead three lives will surely put her in a state of extreme physical, mental, and emotional exhaustion.

How can you maintain your sanity and your balance now that you have the often-overwhelming responsibility of rearing your children alone, in addition to earning a living for yourself?

You are not a superwoman. If you try to take on too much all at once before you are sufficiently prepared, you will collapse—physically, spiritually, and financially. Your children will suffer and perhaps the damage done to them will be irreparable. Every move you make now is crucial. Ask yourself honestly: can you handle a full-time job outside your home, remain in good health, take care of everything, and still give your children what they require? If you have been a stay-at-home mother for years, the change in your schedule may be difficult for your family to handle.

If you can possibly afford it, ease into the working world on a part-time basis. This will give you an opportunity to learn to manage your time and energy while you gradually increase your responsibilities. Your children will also have a chance to adjust to your having another demanding life away from home. If they are preschoolers who must be left with a relative or a housekeeper or put in a nursery while you are at work, their adjustment to this new change will be easier if you are with them at least half their waking hours.

Approximately seven million women have part-time jobs in this country—this seems to be the answer for the woman who wants the stimulation of productive work. For the divorced mother who must work, a part-time job solves a number of immediate problems. She is left with enough time and energy to be a mother and homemaker, but she can use any talent or skill she has on the job. She can develop other interests that have nothing to do with earning a living or being a mother.

Do not think that relaxation, recreation, and rest are a waste of time. Remember always to save time for yourself. Forget when you can that you are somebody's ex-wife and somebody's mother: first you are a human being. Because of your nature as a woman you need time for certain pursuits to be at your best. One of the reasons you wanted to be divorced was so that you could enjoy your life more.

There is a growing need for women workers in all fields—employers everywhere are willing to hire women on a part-time basis. Nurses, teachers, lab technicians, and women with other special training and skills can find excellent jobs that require just two or three days a week. Women who can do office work can work through agencies such as Kelly Girl or Manpower or others that locate temporary and part-time jobs for women. Good part-time jobs may be harder to find than full-time jobs, but they do exist. If you prefer night work, consider being a waitress, cashier, hostess, hat-check girl, desk clerk in a hotel. However, your part-time work should lead you into a good full-time position when you and your children are ready to manage a forty-hour week.

If you are a professional woman, it may be possible for you to arrange your schedule to dovetail with your children's schedules. Most mothers want to be with their children as much as possible immediately after a divorce—although if you personally think the challenge and stimulation of a full-time career will be good for you, ask yourself if it will be good also for them. They must have enough time to adjust to father being gone. If you are also gone much of the time, they may feel lonely and abandoned. This all depends upon their ages and development, of course. If you have a family of three teenagers who are not home much either, the problems will be different from those of the woman with one preschooler and a child in third grade and one in junior high. If you are exhausted after being away from home forty-five or fifty hours a week (thirty-five or forty hours for work, three to ten hours for getting to and from your job, another five hours for lunch—say you leave at 8:15 A.M. and return at 6:15 P.M.) you will all have difficulty when you are together. Your children will clamor for your attention when you come in tired; your temper will be short; and there may be much crying and yelling and chaos. You will need an angel of a housekeeper, but such women, I am told, exist only in heaven.

At this critical point in your life there are two very important words to think about: *re-evaluation* and *organization*. Because of the enormous practical problems facing you and the horrendous demands that will be made on your time and energy from now on, you must re-evaluate everything. How much money do you need? Where can you cut expenses so a part-time job will do instead of a full-time job? If you are keeping your home after your divorce, do remember that whatever work your husband did will now have to be done by you or your children, or you will have to hire others to do it. (It is estimated that the average man does approximately $51 worth of work around his home a week.)

Your property will decrease in value if you let too many things slide—lawns must be fertilized, trees and shrubs must be trimmed, walls and outside house trim needs painting regularly, equipment must be maintained, repaired, and replaced. You will be in charge of all this "man's work" in addition to your "woman's work" (worth about $159 per week at today's prices). If you do not have the funds to have this necessary work done by others, you will surely wear yourself out doing it all alone, or you will constantly nag your children to help. Children have their breaking point—there is a limit to how much work they can handle. Perhaps you will decide to sell your home. The section called "Where and How Shall You Live" in the next chapter may have some tips for you.

Whatever you decide to do, major changes in your way of life will be necessary. There won't always be time to clean up after your children. (If you have always waited on them, they are in for a shock.) Some things will necessarily have to be eliminated from your daily schedule. If your responsibility as a parent is clear to you, and if your goal as a human being is also clear, you will not have much trouble communicating your ideas to your children. They will respond to the need for simplifying and streamlining your lives; they may even cooperate eagerly! Your attitude is important. You need not be grim or threatening about the changes—just calmly point out that if they can give you an extra fifteen or thirty minutes a day or whatever is required, life will run more smoothly for the whole family.

Occasionally a not-so-calm attitude works, too. One Saturday morning I asked my sons to do a few chores and they began bickering about who was to do what. I said they could finish by the time I took a shower and dressed. The work was ignored. I came out of the shower wrapped in a towel and saw one boy on the couch and the other sitting on his bed. The broom was on the floor. I lost my temper. I raged for a few minutes, chased one son with the broom (being sure to hang onto that towel), and ended my tirade by showing my eleven-year-old son a long list of repairs that had to be made in the house. All three of us ended up crying (I had worked in a slap or two), and I went into my room to calm down and put on some clothing. When I came out my younger boy was sweeping the recreation-room floor and the older boy had the list and a screw-driver. That morning he fixed the locks on both storm doors, he painted the address plaque and numbers (and washed the paint-brushes), he changed the burned-out light bulb at the side door, he replaced the globe for the outside light at the front door, and he fixed a sliding door that always stuck. They finished off by taking their new dog for a walk and when they returned we all had a big breakfast together. We talked about cooperating to get the work done in the house. I apologized for blowing my cool, and my older son said: "I understand, Mom. You had every right to get angry. We had it coming—we'll try to help more and fight less." They carried their dishes to the sink after breakfast and put away all the equipment they had used that morning without being asked. My tantrum brought things more sharply into focus for us all. (Of course, I felt afterward that I had aged about three years, turned at least seventy-two hairs gray, and given myself an enormous splitting headache.) My sons learned that I too have my breaking point. They also relearned that they are competent when they want to be, and that gave them a good feeling.

Don't expect your children always to respond to your requests promptly, and don't be afraid to lose your temper occasionally if the occasion demands it. Just be careful *how* you lose your temper—don't lose complete control.

There are several books written by working mothers * that offer suggestions about how to handle things while you work away from home. As you read these books, remember they were written by mothers who are also *wives*—they have husbands at home at night and on weekends to give them a hand with chores and the children. You will not have this help. Don't forget that our society is largely organized for and by married persons. Our culture is still based on the idea that woman's place is in the home. Our attitudes about women working are strangely old-fashioned compared to those in many other countries. The general attitude in America is that family ties are weakened when mothers are encouraged to pursue activities

* Including *The Case for the Working Mother, A Complete Guide for the Working Mother* by Margaret Albrecht (Garden City, N.Y.: Doubleday, 1967).

that do not relate directly to family life. The truth is that a number of American mothers are *forced* to work full-time outside the home because they are divorced, separated, deserted, widowed, or their husbands do not earn enough to support their families, not to mention the many women who work because they *want* to because they have some special interest or talent. Even though more and more mothers are employed (there are thirteen million children under fourteen whose mothers work, according to the 1960 census report), there is a shocking shortage of day-care centers and nursery schools. We might do well in the United States to copy the Scandinavian countries, which have a nation-wide network of low-cost nurseries.

One of your biggest problems will be to find the right person to look after your children while you work. You cannot escape this: our complex, increasingly urbanized way of life is so designed that a divorced mother with a full-time job is too often desperately driven to a hasty remarriage because of trying to juggle two lives—the life of a single person and that of a mother.

The first year after my own separation and divorce I worked an average of two or three days a week as a model, and part of my time at home was spent keeping my wardrobe and myself ready for the camera. When I worked out of town occasionally, I hired an older woman to come in and take over. After more than a year of that hectic pace, I re-evaluated. My children needed more quality and quantity of my love, time, and attention. I decided to change my life. I applied for entrance at the local university. I cut our expenses, worked less, took no out-of-town jobs, and used my savings for household needs. I went to school three days a week, from about 9:30 A.M. to 1:30 P.M. and was free to take modeling assignments in the afternoon, on my days off, and during the weekend. I saw my sons at breakfast, and I usually was home when they returned from school (sometimes they came home for lunch if I was there). Some of the time they went to modeling jobs with me if one or both of them worked too. I earned enough to squeak by, and sometimes we performed miracles with money.

Our schedule may have seemed insane to others—it seems I lived much of my life during those six years in fragments, but that appears to be the story for most modern American women. I had an hour or so in the morning with my sons, then I cleaned up after breakfast, dressed and went to school or to work, then I got home by three-thirty or so to greet my sons, did some homework, housework, cooked dinner, cleaned up again, spent some time with the boys before their bedtime. Some nights I would go out after dinner. Other nights I went to bed at 8 P.M., when the children did. But I'd get up at 3 A.M. to study or write when the house was quiet.

Two years ago I agreed to work in my agent's office for two months while one of the girls went to Europe. I had the opportunity then to learn what it was like to be a divorced mother working full-time. My sons were quite cooperative during that period. They helped with morning chores, they sometimes made breakfast (some mornings I had to eat two breakfasts if one son fixed pancakes and the other prepared scrambled eggs). They liked seeing me made up and dressed every morning rather than stumbling around in my robe in a half-awake daze. They left at eight-thirty and I left shortly afterward. The drive to the office twenty-three miles away took forty-five minutes to an hour, depending on traffic and weather. My hours were 9:30 A.M. to 5:30 P.M. except the two days a week I attended a morning class. I hired a sixteen-year-old neighbor to stay three hours after school until I came home. (The mother who must work regularly would do better to hire a woman to come in daily; I do not recommend teenagers as baby-sitters five days a week—too many problems can arise from such a permanent arrangement. However, an extremely mature and competent seventeen- or eighteen-year-old girl, preferably from a large family so she knows about children and household chores, might solve your problem temporarily.)

At 6:30 P.M. when I returned, my sons and I worked together in the kitchen, preparing dinner. They didn't mind setting the table, fixing a salad or mashing potatoes. Working together gave us more time to discuss our day's events. I was sometimes quite exhausted and jangled after the long drive in heavy traffic on the jammed expressway, and after the first week I sometimes had a small glass of wine while we prepared dinner. I had a *different* kind of patience with my sons because I had been quite stimulated by my day's activities. We spent more time than usual talking at the table. About once a week we had dinner guests, often friends of theirs. Usually by 8 P.M. dinner and cleaning up were over. Perhaps we relaxed together in the living room, perhaps one boy played the piano. Sometimes they watched television in their room. Occasionally there was homework to be done. Then came bath time. By 9 P.M. they were in bed. By 9:15 P.M. I was ready to die. The last of my energy had vanished completely at this point.

But there were still chores. Maybe a few loads of laundry, or folding and putting away what had been put into the dryer that morning, perhaps some ironing to do. Once a week I cleaned the refrigerator. Once in a while I went back into the kitchen to prepare the next day's dinner. If the phone rang, I utilized the time I talked by mending. If my hair needed washing and setting and my own clothing needed attention, that took about another hour. By eleven-thirty or midnight I was ready for bed. There had been little or no time for reading, writing, studying, or thinking. Somehow I managed to read the required books for my one English class, but I realized I would never be able to work full-time and attend classes regularly.

By the end of the fourth week the glamor and novelty of working every day was wearing off. I wondered how other divorced working mothers managed. It seemed that even if one had excellent full-time help, there would be little time or energy left for other activities. I had to steal time to go out in the evening during the work week—if I wanted to see a play or hear a lecture it would mean staying downtown and miss seeing my sons at dinner.

How did other divorced mothers who worked daily manage a social life? My weekends had become a frenzy of serious activity, with tending to the other chores left over from the previous week, housework, errands. The only time I could go to the bank was on Friday evening. It seems I spent a good part of every Saturday racing around from the post office to the dime store to the cleaners to the drug store. One Saturday afternoon I went to the electric company to pick up my iron, which was being repaired, only to learn that they always closed at noon on Saturday. They closed at 5 P.M. other days, so there was no chance of getting the iron until the following week. I sadly learned that the hours of most places of business are geared to the two-parent family in which the wife is around during the necessary hours to shop for food, clothing, paint, wallpaper, and so on. When did working mothers go to the dentist, the doctor, the hairdresser? These errands had never presented a problem before.

I did not have my car washed for those two months because the place I patronized near home closed at five-thirty daily and was impossibly busy on Saturday. The girl I was filling in for returned several days before Christmas. As I scurried around trying to get ready for the holidays, I was relieved that I did not always have to work full-time. A forty-hour-a-week job just left too little time for living.

The hours spent in the office took my mind off the problems of running a house without a male partner, and it was fun to be with adults I knew and liked. However, the drive to and from the office was killing—seven to ten hours a week lost in a useless activity.

During those two months I learned to organize more and re-evaluate. My take-home pay was less than $100 per week and my expenses were as follows: sitter, fifteen hours a week at 60¢ per hour (cheap—a woman would have cost much more) came to $9; no cost for lunch because I brown-bagged it or was taken to lunch by clients; gas to and from work about $5 per week—no parking expense; a cleaning woman once every three weeks averaged $3.33 per week; add to that about $1.50 for items which were broken or wasted weekly when I was not home to supervise; add another $6 or $8 to the grocery bill because there was not time to plan economical meals, and the kids and their friends snacked more (teenage baby-sitters consume snacks too). There was not much take-home pay after the average $28 per week it cost me just to walk out the front door! I did not have to buy special clothing because my work as a model necessitated having an up-to-date wardrobe, and I did not have to pay for a full-time housekeeper. The divorced mother who has not worked in years will certainly have to add to her wardrobe (don't forget items such as cosmetics, extra nylons, and cleaning bills); she will need good, dependable help that will cost on an average more than 60¢ an hour. Her expenses will be higher than mine were for that trial run as a full-time working mother.

A nonprofessional woman does not make much money—the woman with little or no training cannot command a good salary. Her expenses just to leave the house properly prepared every day are quite high. If she receives little or no child support or if it comes in irregularly, a good part of her income will go for living expenses.

No matter what we are told about "equal rights" and "emancipation," most women who work are still economically discriminated against. In America, females are not always taken very seriously in the business world. (For a number of valid reasons, I might add: in general, we take more days off than men—not for alcoholism but for all the reasons connected with being female, such as caring for our sick children, having illnesses and health problems that men never have, pregnancies, etc.; also we are not always as well prepared or trained as most men, and we may not have as many years of work experience behind us.) Men, in general, still prefer to have us stay home and keep house and I think this attitude creeps into offices and factories. (It is amazing and amusing how rapidly an ex-husband can do an about-face on this. While I was married, my husband did not want me to work and he was dead against my continuing my education—in those days I was an "obedient" wife, so I stayed home and baked pies and minded the children, and also became boring and bored. After divorce, my former husband suggested regularly that I get a regular job! But who will mind the children and scrub the floors and bake the pies?)

Women's salaries in almost every field are considerably lower than men's and there are still a few fields not open to women at all. We are too often treated as second-class citizens when it comes to productive work outside our homes. This will not always be so, but it is no comfort to the woman who requires the salary of a head of the household to know that ten to fifteen or twenty years from now she will be more "equal." The job-hunting divorcee is distressed to learn that her earning potential is generally not even half her former husband's, except of course for the minority of women in the professions or in certain other fields.

While you are struggling to make it, your former husband has a much easier time. He's free to work longer hours, he can take a second job if he wants to, and he's been working for years and years and therefore has a regular income and a delightful thing called seniority. They will put up with him while he adjusts to the marital breakup if he has always been a good employee in the past. But just you wait until you get a new job and take time off because your children are sick, or you are too fatigued and desperate to get to work punctually every day, or you make a few mistakes on the job. They have every right to fire you too, because they do not know from previous evidence what kind of employee you are when there is less stress in your life.

Back to your former husband—he knows from past experience

how much he can earn, what he's worth, and he can shop around for a better job. It's also easier for him to cut expenses than it is for you. Even if he is earning much more than he did when you divorced, and even if your children's needs increase, it is very difficult to get a substantial increase in child support or alimony. Furthermore, you will have to pay your lawyer for this service and you may not receive enough weekly to make up for the lawyer's fee!

Often divorce is the impetus to spur many a man on to earning more money—it happened with my own ex-husband and with other ex-husbands I know. A friend of mine who is divorcing his wife said to me "I've never thought about how much money I was earning before, but now I need more money and I'm planning to double my income if necessary." Usually one of the problems the unhappy couple had was not enough money for their needs, or else poor management of what they had. Soon after the marriage ends, some men double or triple their incomes. Sometimes it seems that the man could have earned the money all along, but he stayed at a low-paying job or performed poorly to spite his wife. One divorced father confessed that he never cared about earning enough for his wife and two children because "my money was always eaten up by their necessities—I didn't feel like exerting myself so *they* could benefit." This same man has now doubled his income, a year after his divorce. A question for male readers: examine your motives for staying in a poorly paid job—is it to spite your wife and kids? And one for women: are you making your husband so upset that he is incompetent and inefficient at his work as a result of the conflict between you? Lack of money can make a miserable marriage even more miserable. Enough cash for vacations and a luxury or two might ease the pain while you work out your problems.

You may *never* find another man you want to marry—you can not count on being the second wife who gets to live in the bigger house, unless of course you are getting a divorce because you have tagged your future second husband.

If you divorce with the hope of finding true love the second time around, remember that *men* write the songs that tell us "love is lovelier the second time around." The average divorcee discovers that by the time her carpeting and old winter coat are threadbare, she has given up on the true-love dream. She is willing to marry a decent, steady man she likes, if she has been fortunate enough to meet one, and she hopes for a different, mature kind of devotion to come later. Many of the divorcees I know who have remarried could not hold out for "true" love, and they settled for less than their original dream man. Don't be so naïve that you expect a world full of wonderful, exciting, idealistic, successful men waiting to know and love you! A wise divorcee commented: "Any man you get is a mixed bag." Naturally, this applies to women too, but we are talking about future husbands here. The men you'll meet will probably be in the thirty-to-sixty age group. Perhaps some have never married— you'll wonder what their problems were; perhaps some have been divorced once or twice, and you'll wonder about *their* problems; and perhaps one or two will be widowers—you may find yourself wondering one day as you get to know him better "Did he drive his wife to an early grave?" You'll be trading one set of problems for another. Make sure you do not settle for the first man who comes along because of your financial desperation. Your best insurance against that disaster is to have a good job with good potential and to manage your time and money wisely.

To make your life as a divorced working mother easier, here are some suggestions:

Consider a job within walking distance of your home. You may be paid a few dollars less per week than you would earn "downtown" but consider what transportation (your car or bus fare), parking, and lunches would cost; think of the peace of mind you'd have if you could get home immediately in case of an emergency. Also, think of the precious time saved daily because you don't have to travel a great distance to work. You can go home for lunch when you like, put a roast in the oven, take something out of the freezer, put a load of clothes in the dryer, etc. The walk in the fresh air is good exercise (you may think you're getting enough exercise, but it's probably the wrong kind!).

Baby-sitting arrangements: If you do not have or cannot afford that angel of a housekeeper, perhaps you can share your home with a retired woman or a widow in exchange for her baby-sitting services and some light housekeeping. Be sure you do not get a person *you* have to take care of; if the woman is very old she may not be good with extremely young children. However, if your children are school-age and rather independent, it might be nice for them to have a grandmotherly type around while you are at work. You can locate such a person through ads in the paper, or perhaps through local churches. Be sure to interview her carefully (have your children appear at the end of the interview and watch the reactions) and ask her questions that will indicate to you whether you want her to live with you. One divorced mother shared her home with a widow who was a religious fanatic—my friend was quite openly an agnostic, but religion did not come up during the interview. Several months later she learned the woman had been reading Bible stories to her three children every day and filling their heads with many fearsome ideas.

I would want to know the following if I hired a person to live in my home and look after my children and our possessions:

1. Does she like children?

2. Has she had good work experience and have her jobs been steady (I'd ask for references)?

3. *Why* does she wish to work as a housekeeper?

4. How long could I expect her to stay with us if we were all compatible?

5. What are her religious beliefs?

6. How good is her mental and physical health?

7. What does she expect from the person who hires her (not just in terms of money and hours, but what are her particular needs as a human being, living and working with others)?

You may say "I don't have time to be so analytical," but you had better be. It is a serious mistake to turn your children over to just anyone who happens to answer an ad. I know about one divorced working mother who has had seven or eight housekeepers in the past seven years—the last one was quite mentally ill, was on welfare, and had her two illegitimate children with her. She did not keep house or cook and was otherwise incompetent. You cannot afford to turn your children over to such a person.

An ideal situation would be to own or rent a duplex with another divorced (or widowed) mother, and you could both afford to hire and share a really first-class housekeeper. It could work well if you planned it carefully.

Other possibilities for child care are neighbors, relatives, day-care centers, nurseries, and so on. If you cannot afford a competent adult, try to find a teenage helper.

We all have 168 hours a week. I made a schedule of how the full-time working mother may spend her time. See how your own busy schedule compares with this one.

Rest and sleep	8 hours a day	56 hours a week
Full-time job	10 hours a day	50 hours a week
Meals: preparation, eating, cleaning up	30 min. breakfast, 1¼ hrs. for dinner	12¼ hours a week
Housework, shopping, errands, "man's work"		20 hours a week
Children: homework, baths, talking, outings, trips and visits		12 hours a week
Yourself: personal care, bathing, dressing, beauty routine, etc.	30 minutes a day	3½ hours a week
TOTAL		153¾ hours a week

Clearly the biggest chunks of your time are for rest and work. If your job takes you away from home fifty hours a week (counting transportation and lunches), and you spend twenty hours a week working at both "woman's work" and "man's work" in and around your home, and another twelve and a quarter hours preparing and eating meals, you can see that an extremely small portion of your time is left for you and your children—less than 10 per cent. Simone de Beauvoir says in *The Second Sex* that the average French housewife spends approximately thirty hours at her chores.

Subtract 153¾ hours from 168 hours and you have fourteen hours and fifteen minutes a week, or two hours and two minutes a day average for hobbies, crafts, reading, furthering your education, husband-hunting, social life aside from dates, attending church, clubs, letter-writing, exercising and sports, and so on.

What about time with your children? An hour a day for help with homework and baths and just talking, and four or five hours a week for an outing, such as dinner out, bowling, a concert in the evening, or a visit somewhere, is probably average for school-age children. Infants and preschoolers have different schedules and different needs.

Don't count time you and your children sit staring at the television set—you're there together but hardly communicating. Unless of course you turn off the set after a program and discuss it.

Where can you cut, where can you save time so there will be more hours available for fun and living? If you feel good with just seven hours of sleep a night and a fifteen-minute nap or rest during the day, you can add five and a quarter hours a week to your time (but be careful about taking time from your rest). You can gain time by working closer to home, saving perhaps five hours a week. If your children help prepare breakfast and clean up afterward, that's another hour and forty-five minutes a week; if you cook in large quantities and use a freezer to store whole dinners, and if you simplify your meals during the work week (but splurge on weekends!) you can save perhaps about fifteen minutes a day, or an hour and a quarter a week.

You can eliminate all unnecessary jobs (such as drying dishes). Sweep the floor every other day instead of every day. If you buy clothing and linens made of perma-pressed fabrics, you may cut your ironing time in half. If you use every labor-saving device and trick you can afford or think of, you may possibly cut several hours a week from your work (but don't go in hock to buy labor-saving devices or spend many hours working overtime—that defeats your whole purpose). If your children become accustomed to saving steps for you (such as putting milk bottles in the chute, bringing clothes up from the dryer, helping you carry in grocery bags) and doing small jobs in the house, such as vacuuming, polishing mirrors, windows, and furniture, and you can count on them for at least fifteen minutes a day and another hour each day of the weekend, you can get three hours and a quarter per week per child.

Add this together and you can have an extra eighteen and a half hours a week—added to fourteen hours and fifteen minutes, that's thirty-two and three-quarter hours a week for recreation, sports, education, hobbies, and the like. It's worth planning and organizing to get this much extra time.

Learn to do two things at once. If you like to watch television, you can iron, mend, or exercise while you do so. I sometimes keep our portable set in the kitchen and work when a special program I want to see is on. Phone addicts can get very long cords and be free to move around. Here are a few quiet jobs you can do: clean the bathroom, wash woodwork, mend and hem clothing, iron, polish shoes, wash floors, prepare food, polish mirrors and furniture, clean kitchen appliances, polish silver. You can even exercise as you talk, but don't do headstands—they make your voice sound funny!

It is essential that you learn to *group* things—keep cleaning supplies in a box or basket in one spot—when you must work, simply take out the basket in which you keep the necessary polishes, soaps, brushes, and cloths. Keep your personal supplies grouped, too—cosmetics, preparations for the hair, your own little cleaning supply kit in your closet (I keep a shoe box with polishes and dyes to keep my shoes in shape when I have a rather long phone call).

Teach your children to group things too. Your example will teach the children to be organized. They will like keeping their toys and possessions in order after they learn how much easier their lives can be this way. People must *learn* to create order—it is not an instinctive or innate drive. My sons have a box in the bathroom for their personal items: comb, hairbrush, nail file, clippers, Q-tips, "greasy kid stuff" for their hair, Band-aids, shoe-polishing things. They know exactly where their things are. If you have daughters, help them organize their own things. Be sure they have what they need so they are not taking nylons, hand lotion, or cosmetics from you. Teach them to respect others' property.

You will need to keep tools in a handy place because you are going to be using them more than usual. I keep a supply of assorted nails and screws in my bedroom, along with a few basic tools like screwdrivers, pliers, hammer, all-purpose scissors for cutting wire and string, black friction tape, Scotch tape, spackle paste for plaster repair, wood putty, and so on.

More tips: always iron and fold clothes as soon as they come out of the dryer, and keep a supply of hangers and a small mending kit near your laundry area. You might need mending tape for jeans, a selection of buttons, snaps, and so on.

When you shop for groceries, take your children along (if they are the right ages) and give them a grocery list. I do not have the problem so many mothers have of children who whine for a bag of potato chips or a package of popsicles. My sons are told in advance how much I can afford for their treats, and they select what they want. If I think one of their choices is poor, I have the final say about whether we buy it.

Make lists—keep papers and pencils at handy spots and learn to write things down. Your mind will be overcrowded now with many details and it is much easier to let a slip of paper remember for you. Use a bulletin board or a blackboard. Write notes and let your children know what you expect them to do when you are away from home.

Don't become fanatic about organization—there is no need to become so super-orderly that you spend two hours a day making labels and stacking and folding things.

This letter was sent by a child to a newspaper:

It's my mother's birthday, but I can't get her the present I want. She's divorced and has to work hard, so when things break down, they don't always get fixed right away. The dishwasher's been busted for a month. Mom has the broken blade in her car. She was going to take it to a dealer so he'd know what she needs, but she never got there. I'd like to do it for her so I can fix the dishwasher myself. For three nights I got up after she fell asleep, and tried to find the blade. But there's no light in the garage (that's broken too) and I can't find it. Please help me.—Miss C. (age 12)

The above letter was sent to Action Line and this was their reply:

It was under the front seat. Action Line tracked down the lot where Mom parks during the day, paid the attendant to look the other way, and swiped the blade, then enlisted a neighbor to take it and you to the dealer. We also took care of the washer, dryer, and the garage light that gave you a 110-volt jolt for three nights. Happy birthday, Mom.

Not every divorced mother is fortunate enough to have such a thoughtful daughter—or a fairy godmother like the Detroit *Free Press*—come to the rescue.

A good attitude between mother and child is important. The mother needs to be able to say, either in words or in actions, "Look, we're in this situation together and I need your help and cooperation to get us all through this. Give me a hand and don't make life more complicated than it need be. I'll give you as much of my love and energy as I possibly can." Children respond if they are treated lovingly and firmly. You must have sufficient self-esteem to earn their respect, and if you have their respect, getting their cooperation is easy.

YOUR CHILD'S SCHOOL AND TEACHERS

Many parents who are either contemplating divorce or are separated hesitate to tell others about their problems perhaps because they are hoping the marriage will be repaired. Let your child's teachers know what is happening.

If there has been the kind of conflict and tension in your home that usually precedes divorce, you can almost bet that your children have been showing signs of the trouble in school. Most kids who have behavior problems are ripped up inside because something is wrong at home. Your child's teacher will have a greater understanding of how to deal with him in the classroom if the facts are known.

When my former husband and I separated, I had one boy entering kindergarten and one in the first grade. I was so involved in my own emotional problems that it never occurred to me to tell my sons' teachers about the impending divorce. As it turned out, my older boy had little difficulty handling the new adjustment—he had many friends at school, and he could function fairly well away from home. In fact, school became his refuge. But my younger son had problems.

About a month after school started, I was called in for a conference, as all the parents were. My son's kindergarten teacher told me she thought David might do better to wait until the next year to enter kindergarten, because his behavior was erratic. One day he was passive and withdrawn, another day he was happy and working well, still another day he was mean and aggressive. She thought he was simply too young to be in school because he had just turned five. I told her that his father and I had been separated for about two months. Her face crumpled and her eyes filled with tears. I still remember her exact words: "Oh, the poor little honey—and I thought he was just too young and naughty." We then had a frank talk and agreed that she would give him another month in the classroom. We both thought he was bright enough to be there, and she thought it would be too heartbreaking for him to stop school and have to face another disappointment in his life. After she knew our situation, she was able to help him get along, and she reported to me a month later that things were much better and that he should finish the year. I thank that teacher for her kindness to my son. She was able to help because she knew what was upsetting him. I only wish I had been wise enough to tell the principal as soon as school started that there was a marital breakup coming.

Since that day I have felt free to discuss any problems my boys were having. By working and communicating with the principal and teachers, I have been able to help my sons avert any serious emotional problems in school.

Although you need not become a participating member of the P.T.A., it is a good idea to attend as many school functions as possible and get to know your child's teachers and principal. Education is not a matter of forcing facts into a child's head—the emotions are involved too. If a child knows his teacher is on his side, or is at least sympathetic, he will behave and do reasonably well in school.

If your child's teachers make suggestions about how you can help, consider the advice seriously before you reject it or decide you are being picked on because you're divorced. Most schools have specially trained persons to help the emotionally disturbed and their parents, such as a visiting teacher with an advanced degree in social work or a psychologist who can test your child to see if his problem is emotional or intellectual. Don't be embarrassed or hesitant about taking advantage of this help.

A child's suffering does not happen suddenly—it builds up gradually and may come to a head about the time the parents separate. Be sure to communicate with the child's father during this period regarding school, grades, and problems.

Another teacher told me that teenagers seem to have more trouble adjusting to divorce than younger children. They are embarrassed and ashamed of what has happened; they are more aware of the social stigma than the elementary school child, and may be more defensive and apologetic about the situation. Some kids actually enjoy the drama, according to this teacher. They may tell their friends about the terrible fights their parents have, may repeat things about either parent that should be kept quiet. In general, the younger child adjusts quite well in a short time if he has at least one stable parent.

There is now a trend to offer guidance and counseling at the elementary-school level, to help troubled children. It has been found that children from broken homes benefit greatly from having male teachers. A good, firm, understanding male teacher can make a child's adjustment during the first year or so after divorce much easier. Speak to the principal of your child's school about this to see what can be arranged. I am told that if the school is aware the child comes from a broken home, there is an effort to put the child in a man's classroom rather than a woman's.

The child of a working mother may get lost in the shuffle. If mother is on a tight schedule, she may not have time to meet all her child's needs. Be sure you check your child's progress in school. If there is a new crisis at home, such as a death in the family, or mother going into the hospital, the school should be notified.

FRIENDS—SOCIAL LIFE—NEIGHBORHOOD

When a family that is breaking up moves away from the "old neighborhood" the child experiences a double loss—a parent is gone, and now his friends are too. Where he is removed from school, friends, and familiar surroundings, he has nothing left but his family. Often mother is emotionally upset, preoccupied; other brothers and sisters are suffering also and may not be able to offer the necessary warmth and security.

The parent with custody must make the final decision about whether to continue living in the old neighborhood. If it is possible to stay in the same house, part of the child's world is still intact. If the home must be sold or if the family must move, consider living in the same neighborhood. There is often a tendency to want to move to completely new surroundings—even to leave the city or state.

Consider all the implications of staying, all the implications of leaving. If a move is inevitable, do try to give your children enough time to adjust. Perhaps they can help you choose the new place.

If you do stay in the old neighborhood, at first there may be some difficulty for your child regarding the divorce. He may feel embarrassed about it, and perhaps some of his friends will tease or taunt him. In time his friends will accept the new situation—in fact, about the time your child accepts it, they will too.

You must see to it that your children are especially well-behaved in the neighborhood. Your whole family will be watched closely for a while. Perhaps for a year or so you will get complaints from neighbors that your children have been guilty of one minor offense or another. Do whatever you can to redress each situation.

The neighborhood children will not be as hard on your children and you as their parents will be. You must realize that a divorced adult is a threat to other married adults, but children know nothing about this. They accept other adults and children for different reasons than most adults do, and though children are often honest to the point of cruelty, they are also less prejudiced. If you are fair and friendly with your children's friends, they will see you are not an ogre or monster in spite of what they may hear at home. If you have a daughter who is a good student and fun to be with, her friends will accept her on that basis; if you have a son who is an excellent athlete, his buddies will admire and accept him for that—what the parents have done will not matter to other children.

Your child will develop a new strength as he adjusts to the divorce. He will, of course, be hurt by thoughtless remarks made by others, but in time he will learn to speak up for himself when necessary, and you must teach him to do so if he doesn't.

Kids like to be able to play at a house where there is a combination of sensible rules, fairness, and freedom. You do not have to turn your home into Grand Central station, but do remember that it is wonderful to hear children's laughter in your home.

Your job as a mother will be more demanding and difficult because you will often be called upon to handle roles father always handled. You are now the protector and the one who makes rules about fair play. You will have to defend your son or daughter, and it may bother you to know that your children will never have their own father around to defend them. Perhaps the first time a father in the neighborhood comes to your door to speak to you about something one of your children did will be a turning point for you. Perhaps customarily your husband handled such incidents. Don't get a chip-on-your-shoulder attitude when these things happen. Listen patiently, try to get the facts, then do what you can. Eventually your neighbors will stop complaining.

DOES YOUR CHILD NEED THERAPY?

How can you tell if your child needs psychotherapy? There are three main areas in which a child's behavior can be judged: home, school, and the social area. The average well-adjusted child gets along well most of the time in two of these three areas; some children of divorce may show their disturbance in all three areas, or two of three. Be certain you are not unduly alarmed about behavior that is considered normal for a particular age.

According to Dr. Benjamin Spock, the following could indicate your child needs help: bed-wetting, stealing, lying, fire-setting, rebelliousness, excessive interest in sex and sex play, poor social adjustment, sudden low grades and lack of interest in school, withdrawal, stuttering, uncontrollable anger, excessively poor appetite, inability to sleep or relax. Things like nail-biting may indicate a child is under a strain, but would not necessarily require counseling.

The child whose emotional development is not up to par with that of other children his age, who is hostile and aggressive to everyone, cannot focus on his work, or seems to have no conscience may need a change in environment as well as psychological counseling in order to become happy.

It is a good idea to discuss any problem your child may be having with your pediatrician and, at the same time, arrange for your child to have a thorough physical examination. If the need for counseling is established, your child's pediatrician or your family doctor may be able to recommend a psychotherapist. (See "Selecting a Psychotherapist" for more suggestions.)

If you are in emotional control, you will be better equipped to help your child with his problems. Contrary to popular folklore, children do *not* outgrow many of their problems—situations that develop in early childhood because of a poor home environment lead many individuals into crime, homosexuality, drug addiction, and other serious personality disorders. If your child sees you attempting to solve your emotional problems with alcohol, drugs, and other forms of escape, he may develop the tendency to solve his in similar ways. If he is unhappy and always in trouble, get the help he deserves. Make whatever changes in yourself and your home environment are necessary to insure improvement.

TEACHING YOUR CHILD ABOUT SEX AND LOVE

The mother who is bitter about men, who believes she was "done in," may give her children the idea that marriage is evil, that men cannot be trusted, and that love is either a sham, nonexistent, or destined to disappoint. The divorced parent must be on guard how she speaks to her children about sex and love. Children in happy families learn about male-female relationships by observing their parents, and by asking questions of both. Yours won't always have that opportunity.

Regarding the sex education of your children, if you do not feel qualified to give them adequate instruction, you can call their school and ask about books, films, tape recordings about sex education. Most schools have one or two P.T.A. meetings a year devoted to the subject of sex education that parents and children can attend together. If there is a problem with your children regarding sex, make an appointment to talk to the counselor or social worker at their school; there is no need to feel hesitant or embarrassed about such matters. The services exist for those who want to use them. If any of your children is having confusion about the biological aspects of sex and you cannot inform them properly, ask your pediatrician or family doctor to give you books or pamphlets regarding this, and then read them with your children and discuss any questions they have.

The mother must be certain she is not subconsciously conveying negative attitudes to her child. You can say "Yes, I made a mistake, and now I have tried to correct it. I hope to find another person soon whom I can love and respect and eventually marry." If you believe that love and marriage are values and act accordingly, your children will learn to have a positive attitude about love and marriage in spite of your divorce.

Boys whose mothers condition them to believe that "father was a rat, therefore men are rats" will either identify too strongly with their mothers and females instead of their fathers and males, or go to the other extreme and defend their fathers so vigorously that they end up rejecting their mothers and become woman-haters. A boy who cannot make the proper identification with his own sex will have a hard time in his own romantic love relationships as an adult. The same applies to girls who are conditioned to distrust men, or told to use them to obtain material objects and comforts.

Mothers and daughters. Some mothers make the mistake of overprotecting their daughters, of trying to delay their growing-up process by forcing them to dress a certain babyish way or by preventing them from having normal friendships and dating relationships. What makes a divorcee severely strict with her daughters?

One divorcee I know will not permit her sixteen-year-old daughter to date at all or to have boys to their apartment. "I was wild and began dating at fifteen," she says. "I ended up married at seventeen and divorced at twenty-five. I don't want this to happen to Cathy." But her pretty young daughter is sullen, rebellious, and resents her mother. She daydreams about boys constantly and is doing poorly in school. Her mother does not trust boys, but Cathy thinks her mother doesn't trust *her*. This girl needs to test herself with members of the opposite sex—she needs the chance to know boys, to date, and to have many friends of both sexes. Her mother could help by permitting Cathy to have friends in for dinner or to study, or for the casual parties and get-togethers teenagers like and need. Cathy will either be forced to date on the sly and tell lies about where she is going, or she will abandon the idea altogether and become stiff and awkward around boys.

Mothers and sons. When a boy has no symbol for maleness, according to a leading pediatrician he will attempt to find it in rough talk, using four-letter words, and in sex and aggressiveness. Boys need men to teach them to be at ease—men can present the outside world to them with realism and humor. In the traditional family situation mothers provide love, security, and comfort. If there is no father available to teach your sons about sex, see to it that your sons develop a close, trusting relationship with a man they can talk to and admire. Perhaps your own father or another male relative can fill this need for your son. Boys need to be with men, whether they are from united or from broken homes.

Your children of both sexes need to know what healthy maleness is. Girls need to have kind, sane men around in order to learn which qualities to respect and admire. When they wish to choose husbands they must be able to identify those characteristics that make men good husbands and fathers. Perhaps father is away, unavailable, not interested, or too disturbed to be of much help to your child. If there is a choice between two good music instructors, for example, one male and one female, choose the man. Remember that your child is in school all day with mostly women teachers, then he returns home either to you, a female relative, or a female housekeeper.

Consider what activities in your community will provide your child with male relationships; if you can afford summer camp for your child, choose one that has college men as counselors. Encourage your children to be active in sports, scouting activities, church clubs, and so on, giving them the opportunity to come into regular contact with stable men.

Sometimes during this period the husbands of friends can be a help to your children. Stay in touch with individuals you know who are happily married—entertain such people in your home, and visit them with your children.

If you don't particularly care to date for a while, and you are wondering how you can bring stable, interesting men into your family life, the solution one divorcee used may work for you. She was in her late thirties and wounded by a bitter divorce. She did not care to date and had very few male friends and no nearby male relatives. Her children were starved for male companionship. A professor she knew suggested she invite some foreign exchange students to her home. She contacted the local university and was soon able to develop friendships with students, both male and female.

SOME SERIOUS PROBLEMS OF CHILDREN OF BROKEN HOMES

Homosexuality generally speaking is learned behavior; the divorced mother who poisons her sons against their father or who succeeds in forcing an interested father to stay out of his son's life may be unknowingly setting the stage for her son's eventual homosexuality. Mothers are blamed for almost everything that goes wrong with children—if you are the one who is responsible for your child's character and personality development, you must acquaint and instruct yourself regarding the dangers to your child. If the father is not on the scene, he can't be blamed for something he did not do, although many American fathers have defaulted and let their children down. If your son's father lives out of state or does not spend regular time with him, problems with your boy may increase.

It has been estimated that one in twenty-five men is homosexual; some experts say one in six. The male homosexual seeks masculinity through his male partner. According to what is known at the present time, homosexuality is not innate—it is a psychological *disturbance,* not a physiological disturbance. According to psychoanalytic theory, adult homosexuality is rooted in childhood situations—it is considered an outcome of exposure to highly pathologic parent-child relationships and early life situations. Homosexuality may represent a fear of the opposite sex as well as a desire for persons of the same sex; male homosexuality has also been considered a flight from masculinity and an actual or feared inability to live up to male-role expectations.*

Drug addiction. An unstable and inharmonious family environment can lead to drug addiction. The troubled and disadvantaged child is more likely to use drugs, but there is growing evidence that unhappy middle-class adolescents use drugs also. The addict has a weak ego, a defective superego, an inadequate masculine identification (girls use drugs too, though less frequently), a lack of realistic levels of aspiration with respect to long-range goals, and a distrust of major social institutions. The personality type typically involves strong dependency needs and pronounced feelings of inadequacy. There is usually a history of poor parent-child relations, as well as poor interparent relations, personality problems of the user, and a disorganized family life. The fathers of addicts are usually absent most of the time, or are themselves highly disturbed and deviant. Young persons are often led into crime in order to support their habit. In New York City, about 25 per cent of all crime—particularly prostitution and petty larceny—results from the necessity to maintain the habit; these crimes are usually nonviolent crimes against property.

How can you tell if your son or daughter is using drugs? The question bothers the parent from the suburb as well as the one in the slum. The drugs increasingly used by the young are barbiturates, stimulants, hallucinogens (LSD), and marijuana. Watch for sudden and dramatic behavior changes, neglect of health and grooming in your teenager. The barbiturate user seems drunk, has a staggered walk, erratic emotions, and slurred speech. He may fall asleep suddenly and frequently.

The pep-pill (stimulants) user is extremely nervous, irritable, and argumentative. He may have dilated pupils and may constantly

* See Edwin M. Schur, *Crimes Without Victims* (Englewood Cliffs, N.J.: Prentice-Hall, Inc., 1965).

scratch his nose and lick his lips. He also eats infrequently, cannot sleep, perspires profusely, talks constantly, or chain smokes; perhaps his hands tremble.

Beginners with narcotics may have the medicinal odors of paregoric or cough syrup (for codeine) on their breath. LSD users have symptoms ranging from terror to a trancelike state.

Marijuana produces animation at first, drowsiness later. The user's pupils are dilated, his breath and clothing smell like burnt rope.

The only positive proof of drug abuse is through a blood or urine test. If you suspect your child is using any kind of drug, take him to your family physician immediately.

Suicidal tendencies. Child suicides are on the increase in the United States. More attempts are made by children who are bereaved because of the death of a parent or the divorce or separation of their parents than by children in happy homes. Children who have been abused are more likely to attempt or commit suicide than those who have been treated well. The suicidal child has a background of misery, is accident-prone, self-punitive, and always harming himself. Some children become so miserable they may attempt to starve themselves. Be aware of any of the above signs of danger, and see to it that your child's home life is not unbearable because of quarrels and tension surrounding your marital situation.

Other problems you must be aware of are juvenile delinquency, your child dropping out of school, your daughters becoming sexually promiscuous, your boys running away from home. If you have lost control of your children because of your own problems, there are a number of social agencies that can give you advice and assistance while you try to get your own life back to normal. The problems you may be having with your children, no matter what ages they are, cannot wait.

DISCIPLINE AND CHILDREN OF DIVORCE

A child needs a balanced amount of discipline, and he needs it consistently, whether he lives with one or both parents. The child of divorce, like any other child, needs to know where he stands, what his limitations are. The mother who feels guilty about her divorce may try to compensate by giving in to her child's every whim or pampering him when he needs to be dealt with firmly. She may feel tired, ineffectual, discouraged, and go from one extreme to another, from permissiveness to severe punishments. Allowing a child too much freedom and independence before he has self-discipline is a serious mistake. A household without rules and standards is often chaotic and unhappy, and the children in such a household need firm guidance. You won't have time to repeat yourself or threaten your children with penalties you do not enforce. There will be no father coming home every night to help settle minor and major problems. If you are going to be employed and have someone else look after your children, you must tell that person how you want your children to be disciplined.

The essence of discipline is misunderstood by many parents. Discipline is a method of controlling, altering, and *changing* human behavior; it is a consistent way of teaching, developing, instructing by exercise, training and educating a child.

Consider what your child is like, how he learns. You must realize that discipline is intended to teach a child how to live, and how to achieve ends or goals. You must show your child how to reach his chosen objective by using logical steps. Successful, productive human beings know how to achieve order in their lives; your child must learn control through practice, and you must be both educator and disciplinarian.

Discipline is *not* punishment. If in dealing with your child you impose a penalty each time he breaks the "rules," you may believe that children are naturally inclined toward evil. Neither is discipline blind obedience. If you demand compliance at all times, if you impose a penalty when your authority is questioned, if you make arbitrary rules that have no reasonable foundation, and if you expect your child to conform without questions or choices of his own, he may merely learn "manners" and hide behind a façade of etiquette, but he will *not* achieve self-discipline.

The other extreme is permissiveness, or noninterference. The mother who allows her child to run the household and thinks that all children are innately "good" and that she will destroy his creative impulses if she disciplines or imposes adult standards on him does not understand human nature. All human behavior is learned. At birth we are neither *innately* good nor bad—all each human being has then is a potential for good or evil. We must be taught how to behave, and the mother must teach her child through reasonable methods how to be good and how to make right choices for himself.

A child learns primarily by imitation and example. The mother must know and understand the needs of growing children. She must also be sure that her own behavior does not contradict her words. The needs of other family members must be considered when a mother is training her children, and how much each individual child can handle must be considered. There is always the possibility of conflict in achieving any goal, so a child must be taught to plan ahead. An allowance, for instance, will teach a child how to handle money and plan for things he wants to do or own. You must be ready to answer his questions and introduce him to others who will broaden his thinking. He needs the opportunity to explore, discover, and develop many interests. You must lend support when he needs it and insure his safety, but you must not overprotect him. You cannot teach your child the value of effort, of seeking truth, of finding answers to everyday problems and also big problems if these things are not of value to you. Your life with your child should set the stage for him to acquire skills and knowledge with a minimum of conflict, and he must be free to question, refuse, and test his own powers.

This does not mean that he can make choices about everything. Some things are mandatory. It is necessary that he have medicine when he is sick, that he go to the dentist, that he eat and rest properly, and so on. The rules you enforce must be essential and objectively valid. You would not let a child decide whether he will have an inoculation to protect him from disease, but you would let him decide if he wants to play the piano or the trombone or have pineapples or ice cream for dessert.

Your child must learn that actions have consequences—if he stays up until midnight reading with a flashlight in bed and wants to go on a hike early in the morning, he will learn that you were right when you told him to turn out the light. When he can see the causal result of his behavior and makes the connection between action and consequence, he learns and increases his control and sense of personal worth. When a goal is highly desirable to him, he will be willing to work and gain skills. Your consistency in dealing with him teaches him he must comply with certain things to achieve a desired way of life.

When you require something of your child, you must understand the logic of your requirement, and the consequence of your requirement must also be logical. Your child needs simple explanations. Arbitrary consequences have a negative effect on a child—do not use anger, love, rewards, bribes, or the like as *reasons* for your child to do something. Do your goals for him make sense? If you set unrealistic goals for your child, there is bound to be friction. His misbehavior can be a result of his—and your—unresolved conflict. When there are several children in a family and there are frequent outbursts of meanness and fighting, there may be too many demands and not enough reasonable rules.

What about spanking and force? Force is often necessary in time of danger; sometimes you may have to force your child to face reality if he is avoiding it. How does physical pain show cause and effect—ask yourself *where is the logic of deliberately inflicting pain on your child?* Perhaps you frequently resort to spanking or other severe punitive measures. If you see you are using physical force and severe punishments regularly to deal with your child, reconsider your method of discipline. Spanking may teach your child to obey, but it will not teach him to understand *why*. In short, your function as a disciplinarian is to teach him self-discipline.

Suppose your child's father has different ideas about discipline and you clash. If it is not possible to discuss the matter with him reasonably and he permits your child to do things during visits you believe are wrong or ultimately harmful, you will have to undo any damage. If your child's father uses gifts and special treats as a way to bribe the child, if he permits him to stay up too late, to eat improperly, to engage in harmful activities, you will have to take a firm stand with your former husband and explain that your child's welfare is being endangered. Be certain you are not nitpicking— sometimes fathers maintain a "holiday atmosphere" during their visits with their children and prefer to leave all discipline to the mother. You will have to determine if your former husband's discipline or lack of discipline is harmful. If he chooses to relinquish his responsibility toward his child in this way, you will have to reinforce things at home consistently.

If you find it necessary to say to your child that you believe some of the things his father allows are wrong, explain why you think so. If you learn that your child has been permitted to stay up late every night for a week watching horror movies while he has been on a visit with his father and he is upset and nervous when he returns home, you could say "You are tired and unhappy this week because you did not get enough rest last week. The next time you are with your father, tell him that you would like to keep your regular bedtime." This can be done without turning your ex-husband into a monster. You can say "Your father made a mistake. I am sure he does not want you to feel tired or upset, and perhaps he has forgotten that you need more sleep." Your child will eventually learn what makes him feel good and what makes him unhappy or upset, and he will be able to speak out.

Chapter 7

Adjusting to Divorce

Loneliness can be conquered only by those who can bear
solitude. . . . We want to feel what we are—namely,
alone—not in pain and horror, but with joy and courage.
—*Paul Tillich,* The Eternal Now

As A wife you were part of a social unit. You have become accustomed to thinking of yourself as part of a *we* and now you must return to thinking of yourself as *I*. After divorce you are alone; without the status, comfort, or security that social unit provided. For some, the biggest complaint about marriage is too much togetherness; for some, the biggest problem after divorce is too much aloneness. Each person's adjustment is unique and personal and involves myriad factors, including one's hierarchy of values, age, length of marriage, reasons for divorce, number and ages of children, educational and cultural level, temperament, and emotional and physical health.

If *you* wanted the divorce, you'll be vastly relieved at first to be out of the marriage. If you were divorced by a man you still love, your problems of adjusting to living without him will be many. No relationship other than marriage offers the opportunity for such intense rewards—yet no other relationship can be as unbearable as a dying or dead marriage.

There are few women for whom divorce is not a crisis. We have been conditioned to believe that marriage is our highest goal, that motherhood is our most important and treasured role. Because the meaning and effects of marriage are usually broader and deeper for women than for men, it follows that the meaning and effects of divorce are also broader and deeper. There is no way to get around this reality. Hopefully, our sons and daughters will not have the same problem—but that is in the future. In our present society marriage has a positive value and divorce a negative value. As a divorced woman you must learn to think of yourself in positive terms as you adjust to a negative situation.

Not easy. A real problem for many divorced women is handling the sense of alienation after everything is over. Because you need to have a satisfying love relationship, you believe you will no longer feel alienated if you can be in love again.

But before you attempt to live with another man, you must first learn to live with yourself. Your new aloneness will provide you a chance to learn who you really are and who you can become. There is no one to stop you now but yourself. Do you have the courage to find out, to take the risk? Your children cannot fill every void and gap—it would be unfair to expect of them what only another adult can give. But they will keep you busy and may even provide you a purpose for living, until you discover that *you* are the purpose.

The woman who wants to live joyfully and intensely can do so any number of ways. Some divorcees see the need for counseling or therapy to help define their personal problems; they realize that half of solving any problem is *knowing* what it is. Others heal themselves by filling the needs of their children and others, by throwing themselves into their own productive work, by furthering their education, by doing volunteer work or finding a new cause. Some seek spiritual fulfillment through a reawakened interest in religion. Whatever your "thing" is, do it, but don't become so completely engrossed in it that you leave no time for solitude and introspection. You have much to think about: why did you marry the man you did? What do you want for yourself and your children now that he is gone? Do you want to marry again? Do you have a good idea of what your failings are?

Some of us must spend years becoming that right woman before we're ready for the right man. While you are involved in this new demanding life, you will keep searching for love. You'll have to know yourself well to know if you have found it again—no one but you can be the judge of that. *Don't fool yourself.*

You'll probably grow and learn much more in the next few years than if you had stayed in your unhappy marriage. At times you'll be pushed far beyond yourself. (My mother called divorce "instant maturity" because I was forced to grow up fast.) It has been said that human beings operate at about one-quarter of their ability and potential; as a divorcee, you may have the opportunity to reach more of your potential.

Reflect on how alone you felt while you were unhappily married: you were actually more alone then than now because you had little or no communication with your mate. So long as you were tied to one another, there was little chance of finding another man to love, to relate to intimately. Now you do have the chance to enjoy your solitude. The feeling of aloneness is universal:

> Each of us is alone: sometimes we escape from solitariness through love or affection or perhaps creative moments, but those triumphs of life are pools of light we make for ourselves while the edge of the road is black: each of us dies alone.*

It is not dying alone that concerns you—it is living alone. If you wanted the divorce, you could hardly wait until he was gone. But now there is no one physically present to protect you and your children at night. On weekends, when your children may be gone and your work is done, you may wonder what to do with yourself. There may be a proclivity to drown yourself in self-pity. Each of us who has gone through a divorce must also go through a period of grieving. We cannot escape the inevitable identity crisis. Your loneliness will be unique—it will sometimes be tinged with frustration, bitterness, or despair. There is a nostalgia for something you could have had but didn't utilize to the fullest: you *did* have the chance to make a rich, happy life with another.

The longer you put off your self-confrontation, the more layers you'll need to peel off. There is no course at your local high school or college that will teach you to like being exclusively in your own company: it will come about only by working through the problems that brought you to your present state.

For a time you may feel vulnerable and weak because you are alone. The weakness can be emotional, physical, mental, or spiritual. Until you have your *self* under control, you may even feel that your life is in a constant state of emergency. You may panic and think "Oh dear, what shall I do now . . . what will happen to me,

---

* C. P. Snow, *The Two Cultures: and a Second Look* (New York: The New American Library, 1963), p. 13.

to my children?" But now you are entirely responsible for your own life, your own future. This is a tremendous adjustment to make for most women who have been protected all their lives.

Others will think differently about you now, too. Though you might have been desperately miserable as a wife, you possessed a certain enviable status—at least to those who did not know the truth about your marriage. Don't let the stigma of divorce distort your self-image. This statement, from a sociology textbook, fosters the idea that "marriage is a woman's highest goal," an idea sometimes destructive for both men and women:

The primacy of marriage as a sexual relationship is evidenced by the greater economic and legal security and the *higher respectability* accorded the status of being a wife as against any other role for a woman.*

Your adjustment can be as quick or as slow as you choose to make it, and it depends upon a number of factors. A thirty-year-old professional woman with one school-age child, an outgoing personality, many interests besides home and work, who is in good health will no doubt have an easier time after divorce than a poorly educated fifty-year-old going through menopause who has never held a job outside her home and whose three children are grown and married. But the fifty-year-old woman may have something the thirty-year-old does not: more experience and more wisdom.

I asked one thirty-year-old, a nurse in charge of a ward, about her adjustment. "Adjustment? What adjustment? I work all day, come home at five to cook dinner, help my children with their homework and get them ready for bed. Two evenings a week I go to school [she is working on an advanced degree so she can teach] and one evening to group therapy. On weekends I clean, shop, and cook. It's no different now than it was before, except *he's* not around to bug me and the kids. There's no more conflict at home and I'm certainly not having any trouble adjusting to that! Occasionally I go out on a date, but I'm just as tired and busy as I was while married. I don't mind being alone, though. I know *why* I'm divorced and I hope to find a man I can marry soon."

* Edited by Robert K. Merton and Robert A. Nisbet, *Contemporary Social Problems* (New York: Harcourt, Brace and World, 1966), p. 329.

She was working through her problems and had done much adjusting to the idea of divorce before seeking one. Though you may think you've adjusted well to the *idea* of divorce, you may be surprised at your reactions when you have one.

A feeling of emergency, of constant crisis, can make enduring one's new solitude most difficult. Your entire family is adjusting—your children may need to be completely rehabilitated if the marriage was disturbing enough. There is for you the added problem of learning to relate again to others as an individual. Some women feel little or nothing is required of them if they can hide behind a man's name. Their lives were structured around the needs and demands of their husbands; this gave them their identity. Divorce can leave such women bereft.

What about you? What do you want to do with the rest of your time, your life? I recall a toast: "Here's to tomorrow—the first day of the rest of your life."

Some divorcees fall into a destructive pattern of escaping reality through too much drinking, reliance on drugs, spending too much time and energy socializing and partying (although some social life is good), having one casual affair after another—which can lead to promiscuity. Escape usually leaves you feeling more alone, empty and exhausted.

"We are healed of a suffering only by experiencing it to the full," wrote Proust. Must you throw yourself completely into despair now that you are divorced? Must you "put on the agony"? Paul Tillich said in *The Eternal Now:* "He who can endure the loneliness of disappointed love without bitterness experiences the depth of man's predicament radically and creatively."

You will learn to be glad you're alone. You can do as you like every day without irritating another adult, and there will be no other adult to irritate you. I confess as a divorcee I enjoyed being able to listen to whatever music I preferred in the evening, to stay up as late as I liked, to cook whatever I liked, to invite in what guests I liked, whenever I liked. (This may make me sound like an indulgent brat to women who have shared everything for years and years.) It's the old value problem again—when one is married to a man with different values, there are usually violent clashes about music, hours, food, guests, and other things. It's great not to have to *share*. I am now sharing with a man whose values are not too different from mine. But as a divorcee it was delightful to do things because of my choice, not a husband's demand.

You may be so delighted to be alone at night and on those days your children are with their father that you'll say "I'm never going to marry again—who needs it? This is the only way to live." Then one evening you'll be at the home of happily married friends. You'll go into the bathroom to wash your hands before dinner. On the back of the door you'll notice a woman's nightgown with a man's pajamas hanging over it. You'll remember the pleasures and intimacies of marriage and, with a stab of anguish that surprises you, you'll wonder "Will I ever live in a house again with a man, will I ever share a medicine cabinet and a bed and a *life* with a man I can care for?" You'll stand a while in front of the mirror, looking into your own eyes, perhaps questioning the real meaning of the remark you might have made earlier after your host asked "Well, tell me the truth now, do you ever miss Henry?" Your quick reply—"Would you miss a nail in your shoe?"—made everyone laugh. But inside, you didn't laugh.

There will be times your married friends seem to overdo their joy at being together. You'll think "Come off it. I know your life together isn't all that good." You'll wonder if they're putting on a show for your benefit. Sometimes you'll believe they're only trying to convince themselves of their own happiness. Every divorcee I've talked to has experienced this. Eventually it goes away, after you are no longer so sensitive about persons being couples instead of individuals who happen to live together.

After filing for divorce, I wanted to be alone. The tension of being within the same walls after making the decision to divorce was excruciating. Right after I was alone, I felt happy, relieved, and glad to be busy with other things. The next six months were euphoric. I was working hard, enjoying my sons more than ever, meeting new friends, painting and sewing and changing things around. Suddenly it hit. The overwhelming realization of what I had done, of what my life had become and how unprepared I was for it, frightened me. I felt terrified, even panicky. Nothing in my previous experience had really prepared me for the enormous duty and responsibility of this new life. My moods began to change from day to day, swinging from wild gaiety to deep depression. Several times I awoke from a sound sleep, trying to shake myself out of what seemed a very bad dream. I began to worry—that I'd be forced to stop modeling, that I'd run out of money and never find any other kind of work, that I'd end up penniless and alone and even without my children. But at the time I was earning more money than in four years of modeling! And I had what I'd wanted for so long: my precious freedom. I was in a state of anxiety and was restless, insomniac, and plagued by ailments both organic and psychosomatic.*

I hated married couples because they were together and I was alone. Their togetherness implied success; my separateness spelled failure. For a time I was strangely pleased whenever I read about or heard of any marriage breaking up. "See," I thought, "I'm not the only failure." Misery does love company! What a contrast to my present reaction when I learn of someone's divorce—I feel sorry and wish there were something I could say or do to help. Right after my own divorce I think I wanted to believe that conjugal love could not possibly exist.

Fortunately, after a few months of this, I put myself into the hands of a good psychotherapist. I soon learned to stop distorting reality and began to see and understand the variations in the quality and intensity of male-female relationships.

Without a man around, there is at first a tendency to goof off, to let some things slide. Once I had been a good cook and a better-than-average housekeeper. One day it dawned on me that I had always done most things to please my husband. I had to find a new way to run my household that would please me and be good for my sons too. We women who live without men must often force ourselves to be organized, to cook properly, to take care of our personal appearance at home. If you think bachelors live a messy life, you'd be shocked to see how some newly divorced women live! We probably rebel against the standards of a person who is no longer around to approve or disapprove.

If you must work full-time, there won't be many hours to waste, and you'll soon find a schedule that works for you and your family. Some women cannot bear to be alone and must live in the center of much activity. But the woman who wishes to know herself needs

* Morton Hunt describes similar reactions of other divorcees in *The World of the Formerly Married.*

quiet time to work, think, and relax. Some women may feel a temporary lift from a night out, perhaps sitting in a bar. They may try to numb themselves enough to carry on for another day or week. But too many nights in bars and too many hangovers will ruin your looks, health, and disposition.

Try physical exercise—sports, gymnastics, a dancing class or yoga. If you use your body in healthy, constructive ways you'll be able to clear your mind enough to progress to more mental exercise such as learning a new skill, returning to school, or improving a talent.

Don't feel you no longer have a place in your community. At first your friends and neighbors may feel awkward, even threatened, about your divorce and won't know how to react. They'll adjust. You'll undoubtedly be dropped by a few friends, and there may be an organization or two you'll choose to leave. Find new friends and groups geared to your new way of life.

You might consider joining an organization called SOS, which was started in Palo Alto, California, in 1963 and is now expanding throughout the country as part of Parents Without Partners. The purpose of SOS is to help individuals face the loneliness and despair of divorce. Members work in groups of ten with a social worker or other therapists. If there is no SOS chapter, perhaps other organizations that fill a similar need exist in your area. There are a number of new organizations created for the sole purpose of bringing unmarried people together in agreeable social situations.

SUICIDE AND DIVORCE

Divorced persons are more prone to suicide than married persons. The overall suicide rate in the United States is 10.8 per 100,000 persons. Dr. Bruce Danto, founder and director of the Suicide Prevention Center of Detroit, tells me that despite the unreliability of figures, there are approximately twenty to twenty-five thousand persons who die by suicide every year in the United States. Although divorce is one of the top variables in the overall death rate and suicide rate, men predominate three to one in successfully killing themselves, while women predominate in the suicide *attempt* group three to one. One source says the suicide rate for divorced men is *four* times what it is for divorced women, which might indicate that women alone seem to fare better than men do, perhaps because they are busy taking care of children or others. According to Dr. Danto, women use the threat and attempt of suicide as a means of manipulation—a suicide attempt by a divorced or about-to-be-divorced woman may be a bid to establish reunion with her estranged mate.

If you have been feeling suicidal because of your divorce, talk to your family doctor or lawyer right away. Do the best you can to get an interested person to help you. There are approximately 75 suicide prevention centers in the United States; check with Information or your local police department to see if your area has one. If you're planning to do away with yourself, remember that you might not be stopped or found in time. As Dr. Danto told me, some individuals go around "like an accident about to happen." If you are accident-prone lately, you may need help. I recently heard about a young divorced mother who had *eight* single-car accidents in the first year after her divorce—she seemed determined to destroy herself until a relative recommended she seek counseling.

The potential suicide often shows his hand—he talks about how empty he feels, he may tell friends or relatives that he is planning to do away with himself. He thinks "No one cares about me, so why should I care about myself?" He distorts his problems to the extent that he cannot see a solution to them or an end to his misery other than the *ultimate* end.

There is no one universal cause of suicide—the reasons behind suicides vary tremendously from age group to age group and from one culture to another. According to the World Health Organization, there are one thousand suicides a day in the world. In the United States there is a major idea that the suicidal person is the victim of strong aggressive tendencies he fails to express outwardly; as a result, he turns these impulses inward. However, when one takes a look at the reactions of the survivors—the children, relatives, friends and co-workers the suicide left behind—one clearly sees that the arrow has found its target. No other cause of death leaves a family as naked as suicide.

Social disorganization is a big factor in suicide. The suicidal person often is not sufficiently "socially regulated" and consequently has poor social relations; he finds it hard to get along with others and feels unliked and unwanted. The divorced person certainly feels *personally* disorganized at first. His divorce may result in social disorganization or even be a result of social disorganization.

How can you help the divorced or separated person who is showing self-destructive symptoms? First, recognize that his problems are not necessarily caused by his divorce—they are probably what made him unable to choose an appropriate mate or live happily and peacefully with his mate. If you know a seriously disturbed divorcee who is struggling but says repeatedly that everything is hopeless, why not end it all, and similar things, direct him to a doctor, psychotherapist, clinic, mental health organization or an antisuicide organization. He may need just one person to care enough, to show concern that he lives. He's not crying wolf, so don't turn away. Remember that in every instance of successful suicide there frequently is a preceding history of eight suicide attempts. You may be able to help him help himself if you actively involve yourself long enough to put him on a new path. If you should get a phone call from a potential suicide (the hours after 5 P.M. seem hardest to face alone) talk to him until he calms down, offer help, and if necessary and possible, go to him.

I have been called upon several times for help, and sometimes all one can do is offer food, comfort, and perhaps a place to rest until your friend can face reality a little better. If someone has chosen you to be his rescuer, remember that you need not sound like a detached scientist as you try to help. Be legitimately real without completely losing your head—you can communicate you really *do* care by saying simple things like "I care about you and *I* value your life. I would not like the world as much if you were not in it." Don't give up when he or she refuses to listen to "reason"—and don't forget the value of honest emotion and humor. Make suggestions about what he can do to make his situation better. If you don't know how to handle this, ask someone who might have experience to advise you or take over.

Your friend's words and actions are a plea for help. If he jokes about taking his own life, don't take his jokes lightly. He may be laughing to keep from crying. Perhaps you need to put yourself in his place for a few moments to understand.

SOLITUDE AND LONELINESS

Even after you think you have yourself well under control, you will have occasional attacks of loneliness. Perhaps holidays and birthdays will remind you of painful or happy times when you were all together; perhaps a comment exchanged between happily married friends will renew your anguish or nostalgia. Perhaps an old letter or snapshot or a favorite song will do it. Don't take too many trips down "memory lane." A bad trip one day could send you on a long crying binge.

Since your husband left you may have many new insights about how to love. As you learn who you have been and who you would like to become, you'll be plagued with reminders that once you were inconsistent, inconsiderate, frigid, extravagant, a nag, a shrew, a nincompoop, or whatever it it was he called you. You can't help being bitterly aware of your failures at times, and you may even hate your former husband vehemently for his failures. But then you'll feel sorry you couldn't give him what he needed, and you'll feel compassion for him. You may even occasionally wish he was back and that you both had another chance. These conflicting emotions about a former husband are not unusual. However, if thoughts about him are upsetting your whole life, something is amiss. I am continually surprised by the venom with which some women speak of their former husbands, then the respect or admiration they may express in the next breath for some aspect of his character or personality.

SINGLE NOW BUT STILL A MOTHER

There is a widespread notion that a woman is "better off" than a man after divorce because she has custody of the children, she keeps the family home if there is one, and she receives child support and alimony, plus other property. She and her children usually remain totally or partially dependent on the ex-husband until she remarries. If a man does not provide for his family after divorce, someone else must—the divorced mother may be forced to go on welfare or return to her parents' home or marry in haste simply to get a breadwinner. Few women are able to support themselves and their children without any financial help.

After divorce the symbolic emotional, physical, and financial security the husband represented is gone. Perhaps he was weak, ineffectual, unemployed, but he was *there,* and at least some of the time he came through for her and the children. The wife no doubt had hopes he would improve one day and become more responsible, a hope that keeps many women in an apparently "impossible" marriage.

A divorced mother may feel she cannot live without the security and protection a man can provide, so another husband becomes her only hope. A man in the house acts as a good buffer between mother and children when necessary. The divorced mother and her children have no such go-between and are left to their own devices to work out the problems of adjusting, growing up, and finding new and better patterns for daily living.

FRIENDS, NEIGHBORS, AND RELATIVES

If you have chosen your friends carefully and treated them well, they'll be around when you need them. There will be times you need to talk about the breakup, and there's comfort in having someone trustworthy to confide in. You may have to be quite frank with some of your friends now—they're not mind-readers, although a perceptive friend can sense what you need and offer it before you ask. Sometimes it is necessary to cry out for help.

One Sunday about a month after my divorce was final when I was feeling sorry for myself, I called a busy friend. She recognized the despair in my voice and said "I'll be right there."

She walked in and remarked that it certainly was peaceful and quiet (my sons were with their father). "I'd give anything to have a whole Sunday to myself," she said. "Do you know what I left behind this morning? Three teenagers bickering about the telephone, a husband with a hangover, and a cross two-year-old in a high chair." She sighed and looked around the neat kitchen. "Can I borrow your divorce for a weekend?" We laughed a lot that morning, and she made me see that I was unrealistically idealizing the glories of the married state. I began to appreciate my divorce more and more after our talk.

It's unhealthy to repress everything that upsets you. Your friends can be therapeutic now, and your close ones won't mind listening while you let off some steam. If you pretend you neither need nor want them, they may stay away. There's no disgrace in admitting despair, but don't get carried away. Be sure you're ready to return the listening ear and cup of coffee.

If you've had any kind of counseling or are acquainted with such helping organizations as Recovery or Alcoholics Anonymous, you know there need be no shame or embarrassment in permitting others to help you. The point of this help is to give you sustenance when you need it most so you can be self-sufficient again. A sensitive, intelligent friend of mine who is going through an especially upsetting divorce said "I could never get through these weeks without all my friends—everyone has been so kind and thoughtful." Most new divorcees aren't very gay; they need regular bolstering until they adjust to single life.

Without friends, those six years would have been almost unbearable. I've had no relatives at hand to count on; I didn't have the kind of neighbors who come in and pitch in when one is rushed to the hospital or is sick; but I've had the most loyal and best friends I could ever hope for.

Neighbors are important, but in a different way. You may need them in emergencies, but life is more daily than it is emergency. Your day-to-day relationships with those in your immediate community are in a new perspective now. You need baby-sitters, for instance, and the mothers in the neighborhood may stop permitting their daughters to baby-sit for you if your life suddenly becomes wild and blatantly departs from sanity. But don't conduct your life according to your neighbors' standards either. If you are fortunate enough to have neighbors who are also good friends, you are blessed. I'm delighted that my new neighbor across the hall is articulate and friendly, and more than just someone to borrow potatoes from. She also has a fine son who is friends with my sons.

Don't play the *femme fatale* at community functions, or cut the grass in a skimpy bikini if you know your neighbor's husband is hanging over the fence with a beer trying to make small talk every time you pass. You want your children to continue being accepted by their friends in the neighborhood. If you suddenly become squirrelly, your kids may be excluded from many activities. You want to be thought of as a responsible mother and a good neighbor. Keep your problems to yourself; see to it that your children stay out of trouble. Show your neighbors that children from a "broken home" can behave. They'll be watching you closely—some will be waiting to pin all the problems on the block on *your* little darlings. As for your former husband, the less you say about him to neighbors, the better for your whole family. Some neighbors will want to know exactly what happened, who was at fault, how much child support or alimony you're receiving, and so on. Save such confidential information for your closest friend, therapist, or clergyman. It's a matter of self-protection.

Some neighbors will also be quite interested in your new social and romantic life. The less they know about you and your dates, the better. Married persons have a way of sliding into a comfortable rut, and they're often alarmed by the actions of single individuals their own age—they may not realize that even though one is thirty-five or forty years old, dating and becoming emotionally involved after a divorce resembles in some ways high-school and college dating. Your neighbors will start to nag you about settling down again. They'll warn you to watch your health, cut your grass, move your lawn sprinkler. They'll give you odd looks in the supermarket if you're there holding hands with your new love while you're picking out a steak. They'll tell you your children need a father. You know all that. Don't let anyone rush or embarrass you.

Do your best to maintain close family ties with relatives and former in-laws for your children's benefit, even though you may feel like withdrawing from other family members right now.

My former in-laws are part of my children's family and they are important to my boys. I maintain a casual contact with my former mother-in-law and we still remember certain holidays and each other's birthdays. It is foolish and unnecessary to end all good family associations because of divorce. My former mother-in-law summed it up when she said "You divorced my son, you didn't divorce me." She has always been kind to me and a loving grandmother to my sons.

Your parents and in-laws will understandably be upset about your divorce. They are of another generation, and in their thinking divorce is a blemish on a family's history. They married and matured in an age when couples stayed together no matter what—it is hard for them to accept the ease and frequency with which marriages break up today. They may blame you at first to protect the family honor, but in time they'll see the fault was not entirely yours. Be patient, honest, and try to understand them as you expect them to understand you.

My mother-in-law and I differed on how to make gravy, how to discipline children, and which church to attend, as would *any two women* from different generations—but these basic disagreements did not provide a reason to end a close relationship after my divorce. We still don't agree about gravy or church, but we are still friends. This is a safe general rule for the divorced mother: if your in-law is a person you have always liked, by all means continue your association to whatever degree is comfortable and feasible. If you have never particularly cared for the person, then cool it where you are personally involved, but do maintain some contact for the benefit of your children.

FOR THE PARENTS OF A DIVORCEE

If your daughter indicates she's thinking about a divorce, her future is probably of great concern to you. Her response to whatever you say depends upon the level and nature of your relationship. If you have dominated her for years and she has been unable to make mature decisions based on her own judgment, she probably wants and needs to be told what to do now. First question: Do you want the full responsibility for her decision? Second question: How great is your need to dominate her? Re-evaluate your relationship; realize that it's time she assumed full responsibility for her decisions and actions. Are you accustomed to directly controlling—or strongly influencing—her life? Do you want her to leave her husband so she and her children can move in with you? Examine her motives. And while you're at it, examine your own.

If you have a healthy love and concern for your daughter, you'll want her to be independent. It is not wrong to want to help her, but be sure your "help" does not prevent her from facing reality.

If she is self-sufficient and emotionally and physically healthy, she undoubtedly wants to maintain a home for herself and her children. You may want her to come home, but if you think she can make it on her own, it is probably better for her to do so. If she's forced to come home because she married a man who cannot provide for her and her children because he gambles, drinks, does not work steadily, or refuses to accept responsibility, offer her temporary help until she is reorganized, working steadily, and able to look after her own family. If she married against your wishes, don't say "I told you so"— she knows this and has enough regret and pain without such reminders. If she moves back into your home, offer her emotional support when she needs it, but treat her as an adult and expect her to behave as one. Don't pamper her and don't assume the role of parents to her children.

If you've had a close relationship with your daughter and she confides she's planning a divorce, talk to her as you would to a valued friend. Help her examine the problem, ask if they have received help, and share with her any insights you may have about her marriage problems. Tell her about your own early struggles and how you handled them. If you believe she is genuinely making a mistake, tell her as tactfully and honestly as you can. You have the advantage of being at least twenty years older; you've had a chance to experience and observe life for that many more years. As her parent, it is your right to offer any kind of constructive help and advice. As an adult, she has the right to make her own decisions.

Deprecating her husband is largely a waste of time. She knows his faults. Remind her of his virtues, if you think it might help. If they reconcile, it would be awkward for all concerned if you spoke only negatively about him now.

Don't criticize your grandchildren's father in their presence. Do give them extra time, love, and emotional support. Their parents are emotionally shredded and probably not able to pay much attention to their children's needs. If they are old enough to come to you to talk things over, don't break their confidence. You'll need all your wisdom and good judgment here. If divorce seems inevitable, tell your grandchildren you'll be available when they need you, explain to them that divorce need not be the end of the world, and perhaps the family will be better off after the break. You may also have to tell yourself that many times before *you* believe it.

SOCIAL LIFE, HOLIDAYS, ENTERTAINING

If you and your ex-husband had conflicting values, it is probable you did not enjoy the same people and social activities. You now have the chance to make a new and better social and recreational life for yourself, but it will take tremendous effort and imagination. If you're not a "joiner" by nature, you may have to force yourself to become one, or at least to act like one.

Think about things that appeal to you—you'll be free to do them, possibly for the first time since you married. Do you like art museums, skiing, square dances, bowling, lectures on philosophy, foreign films, music? What have you always wanted to do or know about? Do you want to play a guitar, join a theater group, work around racing cars, learn to sculpt or paint? Pick something and make it your "thing" for one year. Whatever pursuit you choose, you're sure to meet new, stimulating men and women. Don't shy away from finding new women friends—remember that other women know men you have not yet met and some new friend may introduce you to your future husband.

After my divorce I branched out. I met several stimulating men and women in group therapy; then I returned to school and met individuals with similar goals and interests; for several years I attended lecture series regularly where I found friends with similar values, and became more involved in my community.

If you have the kind of job that brings you into contact regularly with men and women you want to cultivate as friends, you can widen your circle immediately. After a short time it may become apparent that you have little in common with many of your married friends. Perhaps some of them will introduce you to single men they know, but in time you'll tire of arranged dates. Most large cities have special organizations for single persons, although these groups cater primarily to those who have never married at all. Even if all you can spare is three or four hours a week for a new social life, don't let this go unattended. We are social animals and *need* the stimulation of congenial friends.

Holidays present special problems for the divorcee. It is important to make plans in advance and to know what your children's schedule will be. Who are you dating at the time; does he have children, is he part of a large family group (would you and your three children fit around his mother's groaning board on Thanksgiving day?); do you have enough space in your home to entertain him and his children and other friends or relatives during holidays?

Sometimes holidays become a huge relay race for the divorced mother. One Christmas, when I was regularly seeing a man who had two sons, we tried to work out a schedule to spend part of the holidays together. We had to consult with his mother, my ex-husband, and his ex-wife before we could make our plans! He spent Christmas Eve with his mother and his children; while my children were with their father on Christmas Eve, I visited friends. Christmas morning he took his sons to their own mother's house for the day, and my children came home that morning at ten. My friend came to my house to have brunch with me and my sons. I had invited others for Christmas dinner, and after we all ate and relaxed a while, my friend went to his ex-wife's house to bring his children to my house, where they exchanged Christmas presents with us all. We spent the next day with all four children and took them skating and sledding after they had played together with some of the new toys. The day after Christmas we realized we were exhausted by the complicated logistics involved in having a merry Christmas. We were lucky enough to have the cooperation of our ex-spouses—without it the holiday could have been disastrous. After comparing notes with other divorcees who date divorced fathers, I discovered the procedure was rather common.

The first Christmas after my divorce, my former husband and I decided to spend the day together, with our children. He came on Christmas Eve to help me set up the tree and the toys, and he fell asleep on the couch until the kids came tearing out of their rooms early Christmas morning. We had a big brunch, then he stayed for dinner. The day was strange. We weren't tense being together—there was something almost superhuman about our being able to get along so peacefully that one day. Our sons wondered why we couldn't do it all the time and they asked if Daddy could move in again. We later discovered that we decided to be together that day because we could not face the complications of making plans with other individuals!

Christmas is traumatic for many of us because it cannot possibly satisfy our fantastic expectations or fill our deepest needs. Christmas can be unhappy for the divorced mother and her children if she doesn't plan ahead. This is a time for happy families to be together, and you wonder just where you fit into things. It might help you and your children to forget your own problems and make it a merry Christmas for some less fortunate family.

Your funds are probably going to be limited, and you'll have to explain to your children why they can't have everything on their list.

The first Christmas after your divorce may give you the opportunity to put a new meaning into the season. I have a friend who invites foreign exchange students to dinner for all big holidays; another divorced mother I know invites her friends who have nowhere to go for holiday dinners.

If possible, consult with your former husband about gifts for the children. Don't compete with him to see who can give the biggest, most expensive gifts (a poor substitute for love and attention); if your children need something costly, perhaps you can share the price with their father. Work out an agreeable schedule in advance, and stick to it. Our holidays finally have become happy occasions for us all.

Entertaining can be a problem for the woman who has been accustomed to having a man around. You may feel it's just too much work to have friends in for dinner, bridge, parties, or whatever you usually planned while married. Don't cut yourself off from this part of living. Your children need to have social activities at home, and it is good training for them to help you entertain guests. Who gets the ice, fixes drinks, and runs last-minute errands when you're having a dinner party? *You* do unless you have a cooperative teenager around who loves to be part of things. My sons have turned into excellent hosts—they serve refreshments and snacks, and empty ash trays. When I have guests, they usually are allowed to stay up an extra hour or so. One of my boys sometimes takes over the kitchen detail after my guests arrive (he's good at broiling little sausages and spreading cheese on crackers) and the other is in charge of the living room.

You may want to ask a male friend to be your host until you get accustomed to doing all your entertaining without a man's help. You can enjoy your own parties more if you relax. I invited friends to dinner at least once a month, to stay in practice and to be sure my cooking didn't slide too much. I did not deprive myself or my children of the fun of an enjoyable social life at home just because of my divorce.

WHERE AND HOW SHALL YOU LIVE?

After the split, the divorced mother's needs change, but the needs of her children remain essentially the same. Her reduced income limits her choices of geographical locations and types of living accommodations. Her children's world is in their immediate neighborhood: friends, school, lessons, clubs, parks, while a good part of her world—job, social life, perhaps night school, friends—may be twenty or thirty miles away.

Perhaps the family home will be awarded to the divorcee. She must make a decision: stay or sell. She'll be responsible for all the work now no matter where she and her children live, whether she does it all herself or hires others to do it. Undoubtedly she is working full-time. If the home is in a suburb or the country, the maintenance will probably be too much without a man's help.

There will be a temptation to sell the house and move to smaller living quarters, or perhaps back home with her parents. Several divorced mothers I know who have sold their homes regretted it later. One moved in with her parents; after four years, she and her nine-year-old daughter would like to have their own house, but divorcees have a hard time obtaining mortgages. This woman used the money from the sale of her home for several vacations and lovely new clothing; now she wishes she had not been so impulsive. Another woman gave up a large, lovely suburban home because she couldn't make the house payments. The equity is gone and she is living in a cramped apartment with her two children. She realizes now she could have had someone move in to share her home, at least temporarily—perhaps a widow or a retired couple, or even a young married couple who would not be there much. There were solutions to her problem then, but she didn't think about them.

The ages and needs of your children will help determine where and how you live. If there are preschoolers and you plan to work, you'll need space for a live-in housekeeper, or your home must be convenient to good transportation so the maid or baby-sitter can come daily, or there should be a nursery or day-care center nearby. Teenaged children may get along well on their own if they are responsible and well-disciplined. However, the twin threats of possible delinquency and exposure to unfavorable influences always face the children of the divorced working mother. Though you may be tempted to save money by leaving your older children on their own, this is a mistake—children of all ages must be well cared for and supervised while their mother is away. There are too many temptations facing today's teenagers—you may be lulled into thinking your children can manage without an adult around because you remember your own teenage years. Your child may be stable and dependable, but don't expect a fifteen-year-old to have the judgment of a mature adult.

Evaluate every possible living arrangement before making your decision. Be aware, if you own your own home now and are planning to rent other living quarters, that most landlords do not want either children or pets as tenants. You will soon learn that divorcees in general are discreetly, or often openly, discriminated against. Statistically we have poor credit ratings, we are not as stable as never-married or married individuals, and our children don't get as much supervision as children from united homes (you may be one of the exceptions, but a landlord will not know that).

You must decide in advance if the move is to be temporary—a year or less. Perhaps you think you'll be married again soon and you're not too concerned with the immediate problem of shelter for your family. Though the majority of divorcees with children do remarry, too often the period between a first and a second marriage is longer than a woman may expect or desire.

Don't be hasty or careless when you choose a place to live. Would it be suitable for you and your family for the next three, five, or seven years or longer? Moving is expensive, back-breaking, and time-consuming. You'll spend money on new appliances, rugs, curtains, furniture. You may need additional furniture if your property and furniture were split down the middle. Moving from the old neighborhood may be hard on your children, but this depends mainly on their ages and how well-adjusted they are. I decided to stay in our suburban home until last year because I thought it would be better for my sons than moving immediately. I remembered my own childhood—my parents never divorced, but they separated several times, so we were always on the move. I went to six grammar schools and had little chance to establish firm friendships—it was painful to leave and start again so many times. Because of my emotional disturbance, I was cross-eyed, could not read, and flunked the second grade. (In those days they did not have "visiting teachers" and the counseling services available today for disturbed kids.) My parents eventually called a truce and stopped moving by the time I was in the fifth grade. I was double-promoted in the sixth grade and things improved for me socially and educationally. Therefore I tolerated the problems of owning a home for many reasons—

and I needed the stability of a firm home base as much as my sons did!

Your children's needs must be considered, but it is foolish to overlook your own. The impulse to get away—to another house, city, state, country—must be recognized for what it is: a desire to escape. No matter where you go, you can't get away from yourself or your problems. If you want to move, be certain you know *why*.

Consider the advantages of living not too far from your ex-husband. It would be ideal if you could mutually decide to live a few blocks or a mile apart so that your children would have you both close by. If they could walk to Dad's place or take fast trips there on bikes for help with homework, or breakfast or dinner, this would add greatly to their security. Kids often feel abandoned by father after divorce because he's too far away—telephone conversations are never as satisfying as a person-to-person visit. It is sad when children of divorce lose their fathers altogether—when either parent packs up and leaves the state, the children are cheated. However, if the divorced couple uses the proximity of living in the same area as a means to spy, or hound one another, the purpose will fail. You will have to determine if you and your ex-husband are mature enough to live near one another.

What about the divorcee as a neighbor? She can't socialize much because of the increased demands on her time. If she stays in the same place, she may be considered a threat by her female neighbors, and an innocent conversation with any male on the block about house paint becomes loaded with intrigue in the eyes of her neighbors. I had one reliable helper on our block—he was the father of two of my former baby-sitters and his wife was one of the few neighbors I considered a friend. He sometimes helped me with maintenance problems.

What about city life compared to suburban life? Frankly, I was afraid to move into the city. Detroit, like every other major city in our country, has an alarmingly high crime rate, inadequate police protection, and a poor school system. A family without a father faces too many dangers in the city. Life is quiet and sometimes dull in the suburbs, but the risks are not as great.

I investigated renting apartments downtown, buying a duplex in the city, renting a home in another suburb, buying a cooperative apartment or town house; I have also considered moving even farther out into the country so my sons could keep larger pets and have more outdoor freedom. Once I was desperate enough to consider the dubious delights of trailer living. Six months before my second marriage, I rented a spacious apartment in the country, which appears to meet most of our needs for now. (My sons consented to move only because of the swimming pool.)

I'll discuss the advantages and disadvantages of owning and renting, and also suggest some possible living arrangements for the divorcee to consider. For a more complete discussion of owning and renting, I refer you to *Managing Your Money* by Lasser and Porter (Doubleday & Company, Inc.), available in paperback. It's a valuable book for anyone, and is especially helpful for the woman alone. The following information is from their book:

THE ADVANTAGES OF OWNING YOUR OWN HOME
1. The annual cost of shelter is relatively stable.
2. There is more incentive to save for the improvement of living standards.
3. Owning a home is a fairly safe form of investment.
4. There are income tax advantages in home ownership.
5. Owning a home gives family members a feeling of security.
6. The children can have an uninterrupted school life and the opportunity for stable associations with friends.
7. A homeowner can make any improvements he desires.
8. Can rent out part of the home or conduct business from it if zoning regulations permit.
9. Better living facilities may be available.
10. Greater community and civic activity are available and are part of the pattern of owning a home.

THE ADVANTAGES OF RENTING
1. A definite limit to your financial risks.
2. No high mortgage payments if your income drops.
3. You can leave a rented house or apartment without undue sacrifice of savings or income.
4. There is flexibility to suit changing needs, income, or occupations.
5. The renter is obligated only during the period of the lease.
6. Renting gives you a chance to analyze your community and decide if you want to stay there on a long-term basis.
7. Major repairs and replacements are the landlord's responsibility.
8. You are not tied down financially: water, heat, janitor service, decorating, are usually included in the basic rent.
9. You can move with greater ease than a homeowner if your neighborhood becomes unsatisfactory.

Consider the following:

1. *Staying where you are* (*if you own a home*). Is there too much house and yard for you and your children to maintain? Can you afford the maintenance upkeep of your present home on a reduced income? (Do you know what it costs to maintain your home annually, and do you know what your income will be for the next year?) Will there be too many painful reminders of your husband and your life together? Is your home conveniently located? What about moving your children at this time—would they benefit more from staying in the same school and having the same friends? What will transportation cost to and from your job; what about the cost of a baby-sitter or other child-care arrangements; is your present way of life too costly for your new future income? If you decide to sell your home, can you wait until you find a buyer to meet your price? Can you time the move so your children's transfer to another school will be at the beginning of the semester?

If you decide to sell, show your home to its best advantage to get the best price: take care of exterior painting; grounds—lawn, shrubs, trees, driveway; interior painting; kitchen—is it clean and modern?, bathroom—get new fixtures if necessary; basement—clear it out, paint it, and light it well; keep records of taxes, water, heating and electric bills to show prospective buyers.

2. *Buying a home somewhere else.* Some divorcing couples take care of this before they are actually divorced—they may agree in advance that their present home is too large and expensive, so the husband helps his family move into smaller living quarters. I know one couple who did this, and it worked well. If you have to handle all this alone, are you knowledgeable about real estate and property values, have you enough savings and a reliable income, will the new community suit your family's needs, have you investigated the schools, recreational facilities, shopping, transportation?

When you buy a home, here are some of the costs you should be prepared for: title search and title insurance, which will cost anywhere from $75 to $300, depending upon such things as the price of your home and its location. There is a fee for getting the mortgage and all the necessary papers and legal documents, which ranges from ½ to 1½ per cent of the amount of the mortgage. (Consider too that mortgage costs are constantly rising.) Then transfer charges, including fee to record the deed ($5 to $15), appraisal fee ($15 to $40), credit report ($10 to $20), and property survey ($40 to $50). Also, be prepared for adjustment costs such as a refund on prepaid school and property tax, a prepaid utility bill for which you'll have to reimburse the owner. You may also have to pay part of the cost of a fire-insurance policy or a homeowner's comprehensive policy, and you may also be asked to deposit money into an escrow account with the mortgage-holder to cover future tax bills. You can bargain a bit on costs before you go into a closing. Be sure to consult your attorney if and when you buy a home. Remember that you can increase your income by renting out part of your house.

3. *Buying into a cooperative apartment or town house.* You will be an "owner" but the co-op will hire others to take care of repairs and maintenance. You get some of the advantages of being a home owner and some of the advantages of apartment living. Check the neighborhood and facilities for children. Will there be other youngsters living in or near the co-op? Will there be enough baby-sitters? There is a certain amount of risk involved—you are going into business with other families in the building and you must check the following: is the builder financially responsible, is the price fair, what kind of neighbors will you have, how big a mortgage, will there be a low purchase price and low monthly payments? The maintenance charges may fluctuate—you and the other owners will be responsible. You will have the advantage of an income tax deduction; you may make an eventual profit on your investment if you stay long enough; and you will have pride of ownership and the feeling of being a "landlord" in a sense.

4. *Moving in with your parents.* This may be a necessary temporary solution. Will you be able to maintain your independence? Is your parents' home large enough for two families—will you all have enough privacy? Will such a move be harmful to your children? If they are preschoolers, you may prefer to leave them with your mother while you work. Are your parents neurotic and domineering? If they are stable and happy, the secure and loving atmosphere may be beneficial for a short time, until you get organized. Remember, a move like this may seem a temporary one, but it can turn out to be a long-term mistake.

5. *Sharing a home or apartment with another single woman.* Perhaps you could live with a widow or another divorcee with children (see Thoughts on Roommates, page 178); you can share all living expenses as well as the cost of a good housekeeper. The advantages are many: aside from the reduced financial load, you will have the sympathetic company of an adult in a similar situation. You can take turns cooking and share the housework and baby-sitting. The drawbacks include having someone else's children there all the time, having another adult around when you want to be alone or entertain privately. This can be a good working arrangement or a veritable nightmare. You'll need to formulate rules and regulations carefully, and follow them. You must select your roommate (or housemate) carefully—is she financially responsible, physically and mentally healthy, of good humor and good character? Can you *trust* her?

6. *Renting an apartment.* Can you find a suitable place close to your work? Is the neighborhood pleasant enough for children? Will baby-sitters be available? Perhaps apartment living will afford a better opportunity to meet other single adults. There is currently a trend to offer apartment tenants a country club atmosphere, particularly in California, and some apartment houses are designed specifically for single tenants in the twenty-one-to-thirty-five age bracket. It is not unusual to find tennis courts, swimming pools, game rooms as part of the deal—some apartment house developments are even planning to offer weekly dances, nightly lectures, bridge tournaments, ski and beach outings to tenants. Before you rent an apartment, look around carefully for a place that might possibly offer you an "instant" social life. You might be looking for the anonymity and privacy that is hard to find in the suburban split-level way of life, yet may be surprised to find a wealth of new friends and activities as part of apartment living. In any case, you probably will not be watched closely, because most apartment dwellers are too busy with their own lives. The change may be good for you and your children if your experiences where you now live have been unpleasant.

7. *Renting a house.* Be certain you and the owner have a clear understanding about who is responsible for what. Check other rentals in the area to see if the price is fair.

8. *Other possibilities.* Perhaps you're considering sending your children to a boarding school. Before you make plans for this, dis-

cuss the matter thoroughly with your family doctor or pediatrician, and perhaps your children's teacher and principal. Much depends upon the ages and emotional stability of your children; you need the most complete and best advice possible before you make such a decision.

What about a mobile home? This could be a good temporary solution for the divorcee with one or two children. Some of the attractive features are low-cost, luxurious built-ins, little to clean and maintain for the woman with a full-time job, small lots which require little care because a park operator takes care of most maintenance; there is also safety because the trailer homes are so close together. You can get a fully furnished two-bedroom mobile home for as little as five or six thousand—prices range from $3500 all the way to $15,000 for a mobile home furnished as nicely as a $30,000 home. Some mobile-home parks offer club houses where one can swim, take a sauna, play billiards. There are many different kinds of floor plans and room layouts, and sizes range from a home 10 by 40 feet to 12 by 65 feet. This is perhaps the lowest-cost living available, and something worth looking into. There are disadvantages, of course—perhaps there is not sufficient play space for your children, perhaps you would not meet many suitable dates in such an environment, perhaps a trailer park would be inconveniently located for your way of life.

When planning to move, then, be aware of the following: the neighborhood—is it suited to your cultural and economic level; are there good schools, churches, shopping centers, transportation facilities, parks? Is the neighborhood pleasant and well-kept? Are there many industrial and commercial developments, what kind of building is going on nearby (factories, highways)? Consider the possible expenses involved in your move, your transportation to and from work, availability of baby-sitters.

If you have been awarded the family home as part of the property settlement and you decide to sell, don't sacrifice your home to make a quick sale. Make sure you understand the terms of any leases and agreements you sign—if you are in doubt about anything, consult your attorney.

The divorced mother who can plan satisfactory living arrangements for herself and her children saves time, energy and money.

THOUGHTS ON ROOMMATES

There are distinct advantages to having another woman live with you after you are divorced. Not only is there pleasure and comfort in having another adult around to talk to, but your financial burden can be lessened if there is someone to share expenses.

Consider carefully whom you should invite to live in your home—do you want an elderly woman who could help with your children while you are at work, or would you prefer the company of someone closer to your own age, who is in a similar situation? Be sure she will not be emotionally dependent on you, and also that the arrangement offers you something besides extra work. A college girl might be your answer—perhaps she can baby-sit several hours a week in exchange for modest room and board. If you think clearly about your needs you should be able to come up with a satisfactory arrangement.

If you have a single friend share your home or apartment, don't expect her to baby-sit whenever you ask—perhaps she can trade a few hours a week of her time to stay with your children in exchange for some service you'll do for her such as laundry or cooking.

My experience with roommates has been excellent—the women who lived with us were intelligent, stimulating and a welcome addition to our household. They liked my children and my children liked them. We respected one another's privacy, and my children were expected to treat them with respect and courtesy—and did so. We made a point not to become overly involved in one another's social or personal lives because we knew our living together was temporary and we did not want to tax our friendship. My sons benefited from having other adults to relate to during that period in their lives.

Consider also renting a room in your house to a young couple, if you have enough space. There's the advantage of having a man around to help with repairs, and the added safety and protection of a man in the house at night. I found one of the greatest advantages of having roommates was that I was not always stranded in an emergency. It is difficult to live alone with the total responsibility of children; one can *never* leave without making elaborate baby-sitting arrangements, even to dash to the store for some forgotten item.

The disadvantages of sharing your home can outweigh the advantages if you are careless about whom you invite to live with you. Be sure you and your children like her, that you and the other person share similar values and tastes, and that she is financially independent and emotionally stable. Pick someone you know or who is known by your friends. Do not risk having a stranger move in who would be a bad influence on your children or who is likely to become too involved in your personal life. Though you will be sharing the same living quarters, you must maintain some distance and a respect for one another's privacy.

If you decide to rent a house with another divorced mother, make specific rules in advance about children, expenses, a housekeeper, baby-sitting, cooking and household chores, guests, weekends. This could be a convenient, happy arrangement profitable to all involved, or a real nightmare. I know one divorcee who tried it some years ago—she rented a house with another divorced mother whose children were quite disturbed. My friend was stuck with most of the housework, cooking, and child-tending because her roommate drank heavily, worked sporadically, and had boyfriends in all hours of the day and night. My friend's children were abused by the other mother's children, their toys were used without permission and often broken, and daily life was pure chaos. The arrangement did not last long, and the women ended up enemies.

Another woman found a novel solution to her problem. She was divorced after about twenty years of marriage and left with a large home and a swimming pool which she could not maintain alone. She found two male boarders—they paid well for their comfortable rooms and her excellent home cooking and also helped her with the maintenance of her home and property. After about three months of this, one of the boarders fell so madly in love with his "landlady" that he married her!

Perhaps you might consider a male boarder instead of a female, if you'd like to take a page from *that* woman's book instead of mine! (She remarried after three months—I did after six years!)

IT'S TIME TO FOCUS ON GETTING ORGANIZED

If your furnace breaks down, your washer and dryer go on the fritz, your basement drains back up for the fourth time in three months, your $125 gold crown falls out and needs replacing, your son breaks a picture window your insurance does not cover, your dog bites someone, your best friend thinks you're after her husband and has excluded you from her party list for the second time in a year, you get one ticket for speeding and two for parking, you just noticed your insurance has lapsed (any insurance—car, health, life, fire and theft), you run out of flour, sugar, coffee, tea, vinegar, potatoes, and salt—all in one week—and you wail "Everything happens to me," hold it! These may not all be unfortunate "accidents."

Maybe you're so zeroed in on your misery that you're forgetting to maintain your expensive equipment properly; you empty ashtrays into the toilet bowl and you neglect to stop your children from dropping banana peels, apple cores, dirty socks, and leftover airplane parts in the same place; you absent-mindedly crack nuts with your teeth while watching TV because you're too dead-tired to search for the nutcracker (When are you going to organize your kitchen drawers?); you're not supervising and disciplining your children properly; you've forgotten for three days in a row to buy dog food and your pet is tired of skimpy leftover meals; you're crying on your best friend's husband's shoulder a bit too much. Your mind is not on driving—you're so out of it you don't notice No-Parking signs; when you remembered the insurance premium was due, you were out of checks—when the bank finally sent the checks, there wasn't enough money in your checking account so you shoved the final insurance notice under the other bills and said "To hell with it." You never have time to make a list when you go shopping and your cupboards are such a mess you never know where things are. . . .

What you need is *organization*. No one is going to do all these things for you. If you keep this up, you'll lose your mind and waste much time and money in the process. I ran into some of these problems (not all in one week) and realized I was using my divorce as an excuse to evade reality. My experience with psychotherapy taught me to face reality, no matter how unpleasant. Perhaps you don't need therapy or can't afford just now the time or money it takes. How can you get organized? You must face that you now have a double load of responsibility; being efficiently organized will help you more than letting things slide indefinitely.

One of my answers was making lists of what had to be done. I usually have a daily list of chores and appointments, and I also prepare a yearly list. My lists work because I make myself take care of everything on them. The yearly list is indispensable. I make a schedule of what must be done each month—jobs inside and outside the house, medical and dental checkups for myself and my sons, birthdays, income-tax-return preparation, car tune-ups, dates on which certain large bills fall due (such as car and other insurance), college registration dates, and so on. My schedule serves as a reminder and I don't feel so overwhelmed by all that must be done.

Jobs won't sneak up on you if you anticipate them. The woman alone has no one to remind her that her car needs winterizing, the furnace needs cleaning, the grass needs to be fertilized and the trees and shrubs pruned. Make plans in advance to hire a teenager to help with your yard work, arrange your children's doctor and dentist appointments in advance, plan your own and also family vacations, and perhaps a stay at summer camp for your children, ahead of time.

Read the owner's manual carefully and learn to properly maintain your own car. Learn to change a flat tire, find out what kind of oil your car requires, be sure you have antifreeze put in when necessary. When you must buy a new car, consider the following: how much can you afford per month (include monthly payment, insurance, maintenance, gas and oil), what your personal and family needs are, how much driving you do in a year. Remember that a small new car is a more economical buy than a large used car because maintenance is cheaper; you will have warranty coverage; insurance, gasoline, oil, and tires will cost less. Don't overload your budget with unnecessary optional equipment when you buy a new car (such as air-conditioning and white-wall tires). Shop for the best deal, and if you are in doubt about what car to buy, ask a man who knows about cars to help you make a choice. A new car is probably the biggest purchase you'll make—be well informed when you make your choice and keep your budget in mind. You may be tempted to buy an expensive sports car, but in a one-car family, where will you carry groceries, children, and equipment when going on trips? Be certain your car insurance protects you adequately, and take your car in for regular warranty inspections. You can't enjoy the freedom and independence your car can offer you and your children if it is a constant drain on your budget.

Now that you'll be the number-one family driver, here are some suggestions for safe driving: have seatbelts in your car, front and back, and *use* them—be sure your children use them, even if you are only driving five miles; know how much air should be in your tires; learn to recognize when little things go wrong with your car and have them fixed immediately; carry a first-aid kit, a flashlight, and a nighttime warning signal. If your car stalls at night, put up the hood and tie a piece of cloth to the radio aerial and use your warning signal. Don't carry a lot of junk or sharp objects in your car. Make rules about behavior in the car when taking trips with your children, and enforce them. If you are not a good, safe driver, perhaps you should take some instruction. A book you might read is *Are You a "Woman Driver"?* by Denise McCluggage (Grosset & Dunlap).

THE DIVORCEE AND HER MONEY

In America, five million women head their own families. Many of these breadwinners are divorced mothers. Something you'll have in common with other divorced mothers is uncertainty about money. If you don't know how to handle your funds and if you don't have a reliable income, you'll feel insecure and depressed about money. If you've been handling your family's finances for years, you may have a complete understanding of your now-broken family's financial picture. You should know how to control your financial situation.

If you were like many young married women I know, money was something your husband doled out or that you both earned and put into the family kitty. You didn't worry much about it because your husband was there to do the worrying. One of the biggest revelations I've had in my life came shortly after my divorce when I realized I was in *full* charge—I was the sole breadwinner and head of the household. I learned the real value of money (and my ability to earn it) when there was no child support for four months after the separation.

After divorce, my financial picture changed several times. I know what it is to have surplus cash and to be able to pay cash for anything, to buy stock, to take vacations. I also know what it is to operate in the red because of illness and inability to work, irregular child-support payments, too many emergencies, and poor planning for those emergencies. The former gives one a marvelous sense of independence and security; the latter gives one insomnia, wrinkles, gray hair, and a shrill voice. One gets tired of saying at least six times a day "No, we can't afford it." Is there anything you can do to avoid this? I have one quick suggestion. If you don't have much money now for extras, educate your children to that fact *immediately* and tell them not to ask you for anything that costs over a nickel because it will make Mommy cry.

But you don't want to go on that way forever—one of your goals as an independent human being is to be solvent and financially responsible. How can you accomplish this? If you are going to live without a man around for any length of time, and you've never handled the money, you must educate yourself quickly and properly regarding money management. This section will give you a few pointers, but you ought to read one of the excellent books available on the matter. Here are the names of three:

> *How to Manage Your Money* by John Kirk (Essandess Paperbacks), available in most banks.
> *Managing Your Money* by J. K. Lasser and Sylvia Porter (Doubleday & Company, Inc., 1963).
> *How to Make the Most of Your Money* by Sidney Margolius (Meredith, 1966).

You should know the answers to the following questions:

> What will your weekly net income be?
> How much money do you have in savings accounts?
> Do you own stock? What is it worth?
> How much in government bonds do you have?
> How large is the mortgage on your house and what is the yearly tax bill?
> What is your house worth in the present market?
> Do you have adequate life insurance?
> Does your children's father have life insurance with them as irrevocable beneficiaries?
> Are you entitled to Social Security retirement income?
> Are you covered by disability income insurance?
> How much do you owe?
> Does anyone owe you money? How much?
> What was your income tax last year?
> Where are your valuable papers kept?

You should know what your net monthly income will be from

your job, child support and alimony, other sources such as rent, trust funds, securities. Make a list of all your fixed monthly expenses, your once-a-year expenses (car insurance, car license plates, Christmas, and so on), your future needs for the next year, and any luxuries you'd like to have. This will give you an estimate of where you are financially. While you're at it, make a list of your assets and liabilities. You may be in better shape than you think. For help with assets and liabilities, ask your local banker to help you compute your net worth. If you'd like to do it yourself, simply list everything you *own:* automobile, house and furnishings, personal property, real estate, life insurance (cash value), pension and profit-sharing funds (cash value), stocks and bonds, money due from others, and cash, savings accounts, checking account. Then list everything you *owe*—on your house mortgage, your car, any charge accounts, loans, debts. Subtract what you owe from what you own—the difference is your net worth.

The day my husband moved, I purchased a journal in which to enter my daily expenditures. Since then I have kept track of everything I spend—this habit has helped immensely for computing income tax, for determining business expenses as a model, and for seeing where I overspend. It also helped when I had to prove in court that I needed more child support. Make a daily record of what you spend for car, groceries, children, lunches; keep a monthly list of all expenses so that you can see where you are being extravagant. It's a good idea to keep separate records of your children's expenses in case you go to court for a modification in child support.

Most banks offer a variety of services—acquaint yourself with what your local bank has to offer, and if you need help with handling your funds, ask for a book on money management and perhaps another book in which to keep financial records. You can write checks free if you maintain a certain monthly balance in your regular checking account (I'm not going to help you balance your checking account because I *still* have trouble with mine!); you can keep your valuables in a safe deposit box at the bank for as little as 2 cents a day; * you can save automatically in some banks by trans-

* Keep these in a safe place: savings bonds, stocks and bonds, insurance policies, deed to your home, title to your car, your will, birth certificates, divorce papers, tax receipts, social security card, contracts and business papers, letters of reference, valuable jewelry, legal papers, adoption papers, passports, notes, trust agreements.

ferring a regular amount from your checking to your savings account—the bank does it for you; you can bank by mail or use the night depository if you're too busy to go in person; you can get a loan, using your savings account as collateral. At my bank, if one opens a savings account with $500 dollars or more, one can earn 5 per cent interest and have a free checking account. Your bank might also assist with your will, estate planning, and a trust fund for your children. You can buy savings bonds at your local bank and get some counsel about investments while you're at it.

Get to know one of the officers at your local bank, in case you ever need a loan in an emergency.

A few years ago I decided to get a personal loan on my signature only. When I went for an interview at the bank, I was asked questions about my marital status, how long divorced, how much child support I received, was it regular, how long had I been making the mortgage payment, my average annual income, what I owed to various creditors, the amount of debts I wished to pay, my future financial obligations, how much money did I have in various accounts, how much stock and property I owned, and would I be able to get a co-signer if necessary. At that time we also computed my net worth, and I was suprised to see how good I looked on paper (I thought, as I went home, "If I'm worth so much, why do I need a loan?").

I was asked how regular I am at paying bills. I left the bank wondering if I would qualify for that loan and was surprised when I got it on my signature alone. But it was to my advantage that I had been making mortgage and car payments regularly for years, that I had a good credit rating and few outstanding debts. I was told by the bank officer that, in general, divorcees are considered poor credit risks. A divorcee's income is unreliable—her ex-husband may default on child support or alimony; if her children are ill she must take time off from her job, and she is considered generally less stable financially than married or never-married women.

How do you get a good credit rating? First you must establish yourself as a good credit risk—you must prove you are competent enough to handle ordinary financial responsibility. In the majority of marriages, the husband earns and handles the money, pays the bills, has his name on charge accounts, and the wife is usually the chief purchasing agent but nothing more. If she tries to get credit in her own name, it is usually denied without the husband's okay. I

learned this when I went to purchase a new car several months after
my separation, when my $50 heap collapsed in the driveway. I had
not had any charge accounts in my own name, although I had been
earning a better-than-average income (for a woman) for several
years. I was able to make a one-third down payment and the bank
decided I did not need a co-signer for my car loan.

To establish a good credit rating, pay your bills regularly. Perhaps you can get a small loan and pay it off on time just to establish
good credit. If you're going to be late paying any bill, a simple note
of explanation or a phone call before the bill is due is appreciated
by your creditors. Perhaps they'll revise the terms of your obligation
and take a partial payment. They'll be patient with you if you
convince them you are making a sincere effort to meet your obligations. If you run into trouble paying your bills, you might want to
consolidate by getting a loan and paying off everything you owe so
that you have just one monthly payment.

Beware of traps set by bill collectors. I once received a mysterious postcard that said "Your papers are ready—Urgent—call 341-
3558." I couldn't remember if I had applied for any special papers,
and my curiosity won out. I called the number and it was a collec-
tion agency after me for a delinquent account of $10 I forgot I owed
a doctor! I felt dumb and sent them a check that very day.

How can you stay out of financial difficulty? I've talked to a
variety of divorcees about their problems; most of them have ex-
husbands who default regularly on child support. How can you
manage if your children's father does not hold up his end of the
bargain?

This is one reason it is essential for you to be financially solvent.
Don't overcommit yourself, know your income and outgo, have an
emergency fund of at least three months' income in the bank, know
your net worth, and have a regular savings program. My habit was
to save 10 per cent of everything I earned. I had a good-sized
emergency account that I used when I became too ill to work regularly.

According to Sidney Margolius, there are ten ways most families
dribble their money away:

1. Constant payment of large finance charges on installment
purchases (can eat up 5 per cent of your annual income).

2. Overspending for food (you can feed your family nutri-

tiously for about $1.10 per person per day—somewhat higher now because of inflation).

3. High household and household operating costs.

4. Heavy car and car operating expenses (your car should cost no more than 12 per cent of your after-tax income).

5. Larger than necessary expenditure for insurance.

6. Heavy spending for commercial recreation.

7. Overpayment of income tax.

8. Failure to take advantages of sales and clearances.

9. Random spending for toiletries, cosmetics, household drugs, and other miscellaneous items.

10. Failure to make savings produce maximum yield.

Here are some things women in charge should avoid:

1. *Impulse buying and nonessential purchases.* You probably spend about $10 a week on items such as coffee and a sweet roll, candy bars, trinkets, and attractive junk you or the kids don't actually need; greeting cards (try a personal note—it's much nicer and costs the price of a stamp and a sheet of paper instead of a quarter); cabs when you could walk or take a bus; snacks and nonfood you or the kids toss into the shopping cart at the supermarket; extra cocktails at lunch or dinner (Don't ever get into the habit of always paying for your own lunch or dinner!); weekly trips to the beauty shop (why not once every two weeks if you can't bear to give up this luxury?).

2. *Unnecessary items purchased on "sale"* that you never use, don't need, but couldn't resist.

3. *Cost of services*—delivery of milk, dry cleaning of items you could wash or clean yourself, haircuts for your children (my sons' father trims their hair and this saves me $2.50 per head; fortunately, longer hair for boys is "in").

4. *Installment payments.* Did you know you pay 18 per cent annually on department store revolving charge accounts? Save your money *first,* then make your purchase to avoid that high interest rate. Remember that it costs *you* money to use someone else's money. Loans at commercial banks cost 12 per cent interest; the cheapest loan you can get is a collateral loan at 5 per cent interest (although it may be higher by the time you read this).

5. *Driving an expensive car.* Your original cost, gas and oil, service and maintenance, and insurance are all much higher for a lux-

ury model than for an economy car. The jazzier car may give your ego a boost, but wouldn't you rather have the extra money in the bank?

6. *Not taking all your rightful income tax deductions.* If you qualify as head of the household and pay more than 50 per cent of your children's expenses (including housekeepers and baby-sitters), you can claim them as a deduction. If you receive alimony, you must pay income tax on it, but you are not required to pay income tax on child support. Read the instruction booklet that comes with your tax forms so you are certain to take all the deductions to which you're entitled. It might be a good idea to have your attorney help you compute your tax after your divorce so you don't make expensive mistakes.

Also, wash your car yourself or have your children do it in warm weather; bulk oil for your car is 50 per cent cheaper; prepared foods, frozen dinners, cake mixes, and the like add dollars to your food bills; save from 50 to 75 per cent on items you sew at home, if you have the time. Consider resale shops for some clothing—also when possible buy secondhand goods such as bicycles, sporting equipment, appliances, furniture, musical instruments.

Additional ways to stretch dollars: take advantage of white sales, buy basic clothing after the season at sales; tell relatives and friends to buy clothing for your children for Christmas and birthdays; shop at discount stores whenever possible; buy day-old baked goods (you can hardly tell the difference when day-old bread has been frozen and warmed in the oven). If you read a certain magazine regularly and buy it at the newsstand, subscribe to it instead—you'll save at least half the price. Avoid first-run movies—wait until they come to your local theatre; use the public library for books, records, movies; go to free concerts, museums, art galleries, and the like.

Saving money becomes a fascinating challenge if you have a definite goal in mind, such as a year in another country, owning stock, higher education for your children. You need not become a miser—all that is required is to learn the best way to handle your funds, stay within your limitations, and be certain you don't dribble your hard-earned money away. Build up an emergency fund of at least two to six months' income in case you become disabled.

What's the best way to save your money? Most commercial banks pay 4 per cent or more interest on regular passbook accounts;

they also issue savings certificates that pay as much as 5 per cent interest (on initial amounts from $500 to $2500)—the longer the maturity, the higher the interest. Develop an *interest* in interest. Did you know that you can save $1000 in five years by putting aside just $3.50 per week at 4 per cent compound interest? (You probably can cut that much from your weekly grocery bill and not miss it.)

The table below gives you a better idea of how 4 per cent compound interest works:

WEEKLY DEPOSIT	HERE'S THE AMOUNT YOU'LL HAVE IN			
	5 YEARS	10 YEARS	15 YEARS	20 YEARS
$ 5	$1,433	$ 3,182	$ 5,316	$ 7,920
$10	2,866	6,364	10,633	15,841
$15	4,299	9,547	15,949	23,762
$20	5,733	12,729	21,266	31,682
$25	7,166	15,911	26,583	39,603

Savings and loan associations pay 4 to 4.75 per cent interest on passbook accounts, and up to 5¼ per cent on certificates. Be sure your money is insured by the Federal Savings and Loan Insurance Corporation. Mutual Savings Banks pay 4¼ to 4½ per cent on savings, some as high as 5 per cent.* If you want to save through payroll deductions, you can buy Savings Bonds which pay 4.15 per cent interest if held to maturity (Series E bonds mature in seven years, Series H bonds mature in ten). Shop around for the method of saving that suits you best—try to develop the habit of saving a specific amount regularly, *before* paying monthly bills and spending for recreation.

What about investments? If you have surplus cash (after building up an emergency fund and a good bank account), you might want to begin a regular investment program. Do consider an investment club or mutual funds. Female shareholders outnumber male shareholders 51 per cent to 49 per cent; at the present time, almost ten million adult women own more than $100 billion in shares of publicly held corporations. Get good advice before you invest, and don't take risks—they can be expensive! I have a divorced friend who

* Interest rates on savings will probably have risen by the time you read this.

gives her children a share of stock every Christmas and has their grandparents do likewise.

Review your entire insurance program with your attorney and your insurance agent. Be certain your present policies cover your family's needs, but that you are not "insurance-poor." I cashed in a $2000 life insurance policy several years ago and bought instead $10,000 worth of term insurance, which ought to help my sons through college in case I'm not around to do so. The new policy gives us five times the amount of protection but of course, has no cash value.

I've mentioned several times that two out of three divorced mothers do not remarry. Plan for your old age now, and take into consideration that if you never remarry you will not get any widow's benefits.* If you divorced after more than twenty years of marriage, you are eligible for Social Security benefits. Assuming you don't remarry, will your savings, insurance, Social Security, pension, stock and other holdings provide enough money when you retire? Do you have adequate accident and health protection for yourself and your children?

Perhaps your children can take part-time jobs to pay for part of their expenses and to save for their college educations. In 1965, teenage allowances and earnings in the United States amounted to $14 billion—seven million youngsters worked in the summer of 1965, and one in five U.S. automobiles is owned by a teenager. As a divorced mother, you need all the help you can get, so encourage your teenagers to pay part of their own way. Many high school juniors and seniors earn an average of $500 annually. If you teach your child the value of money and inspire him through your own good habits, he'll soon learn to be financially independent.

The cost of putting a son or daughter through college can range from $1500 per year (if he lives at home) to more than $3000 a year if he goes to school away from home. The cost can be defrayed if your child earns part of his way, if he learns to save *now* by working summers and part-time, if he is able to get a scholarship, loan, or federal grant. Start a college fund now for your children—don't make the mistake of putting it off "until things get better"—and save regularly from your child support checks even if all you can presently manage is $5 or $10 monthly. Get the Public Affairs Pam-

* The average wife outlives her husband by seven years.

phlet by Sidney Margolius, "Paying for a College Education," for 25 cents by writing to Public Affairs Committee, 381 Park Avenue South, New York, N.Y. 10016. Incidentally, if child support is to stop at age eighteen but your ex-husband earns enough to send your children through college, this can be arranged legally.

Do you have a will? People who die without leaving a will risk having their estates divided up in a way contrary to their wishes by a court-appointed administrator not of their choosing. They also risk having the estate reduced by lack of tax planning. Consult your attorney about this. You will need an executor, and your children may need a guardian in the event of their father's death. Be certain that your children are beneficiaries on any insurance policies you have.

Another extremely valuable book to assist you with financial planning is *What Every Woman Doesn't Know,* by attorney Gustave Simons. The book covers in detail everything a woman needs to know to be financially secure: insurance, income tax, investment programs (stock market and real estate); employee benefit programs, banks, bank accounts, contracts, careers for women (he goes into considerable detail about opportunities in real estate, insurance, investment consulting, interior decorating, landscaping, public relations); estate planning, wills, trust funds, and there is a section on divorce and widowhood. Mr. Simons tells women how to find competent professional advice, and he believes that every woman— married or single—needs a competent attorney.

Here is some advice from a divorced mother I know. She's been husbandless for five years, and hospitalized several times with a seriously disabling illness that prevented her from working for a whole year. She is never in debt, receives a modest amount of child support, and received very little money or property at the time of her divorce. She has a substantial savings account, attends night school regularly (she's working on an advanced degree), both she and her children take weekly music lessons, she is able to send her children to summer camp, and she takes an occasional vacation. Currently she is working part-time because of illness. Her main advice for the divorced mother is "Pay cash for everything! Avoid installment buying—that 18 per cent interest will kill you." She has charged things occasionally, but only if she knows she can pay the bill in thirty days to avoid interest charges. In five years the one item she purchased on an installment plan was a new piano, and she feels the

$60 interest was worth the pleasure she and her children derived from their new purchase.

"No woman can afford to spend money she doesn't have," she says.—"It's a mistake for the working mother to think like a man. Even though you're the breadwinner now, if your kids get sick, *you* have to stay home with them. What if you get sick and need help in the house? A man doesn't have these problems."

She tells her relatives to give her two children clothes for gifts, and she's not ashamed to take hand-me-downs for herself or her children ("If you can't use it, sell it"). She shops for specials, avoids stores that give trading stamps because their prices are higher, buys quality meat at a good meat market ("It's worth ten or twenty cents more a pound to have a good cut of meat—I can economize somewhere else"); she does not operate on a cut-and-dried budget, tries to use her own earnings for basic living expenses and child support for "extras" and savings ("My ex-husband is so irrational that he might stop sending the money any time—I've had him in court twice for arrearage and we've learned not to count on him"); she believes it's better to buy two good dresses that she does not have to iron for her daughter than five cheap ones that fall apart after a few washings. She drives a six-year-old car, sews many of her own clothes, carries her lunch, and tries to buy what she needs at a discount. She occasionally trades a day or a weekend of baby-sitting with a friend to save on the cost of baby-sitters. Her large flat costs $95 a month and is pleasantly furnished. When she finishes her education, she will be able to do work that is less physically taxing. "My financial security gives me emotional security," she remarked.

She is a woman with a goal for the future and the means to attain it.

Chapter 8

Stress, Divorce, and Psychotherapy

STRESS has been defined as the rate of all the wear and tear caused by life. Physiologist Dr. Hans Selye says in *The Stress of Life* that the same stress which makes one person sick can be an invigorating experience for another, and that one's health and happiness lie in being able to adjust to ever-changing conditions of one's life. Many common diseases are caused by errors in our body's adaptive responses to stress rather than by direct damage by germs, poisons, or other external agents. Says Dr. Selye: "In this sense many nervous and emotional disturbances, high blood pressure, gastric and duodenal ulcers, certain types of rheumatic, allergic, cardiovascular, and renal diseases appear to be essentially diseases of adaptation."

How adaptable are you? Divorce, a major crisis in any individual's life, is sure to bring emotional and physical changes, and may change your existence more than you expect or desire. Your divorce and the conditions that have led to it have no doubt put your under considerable stress.

If you understand what is happening to you physically and psychologically, you may be able to minimize the many damaging effects of the stress of divorce. Though you may feel completely out of balance for a time, there are things you can do to make your life less stressful. Protect and preserve your mental and physical health by treating yourself properly (eating a balanced diet, getting adequate rest and exercise), avoiding additional stress-producing situations, learning to relax, organizing your life efficiently.

Is there a correlation between the stress of divorce and serious physical ailments? While in the hospital for major surgery several years ago, I had the opportunity to think about the state of my physical health since my separation and divorce compared to my health during the first twenty-nine years of my life. I also thought about the health of other divorced women I knew compared to that of women who were still married (I am not saying "happily" because I am not trying to measure happiness here). I compared eight divorced mothers I knew with eight women who were still married to their first husbands. The divorcees as a group had many more physical ailments, of a much more serious nature than the ailments of any of the married women, and had been hospitalized many more times in connection with these ailments. The married women went to the hospital, but usually to have more babies, not for sicknesses.

You may be saying by now "Women who end up divorced are probably more disturbed or neurotic than women who stay with their husbands, and that's why they are sick more often." Not necessarily. I was hardly ever seriously ill during my marriage—the only times I went to the hospital in almost ten years of marriage were for pregnancies, plus for a tonsillectomy three months after being married. Though I was not particularly serene or happy during the last half of my marriage, my physical health was better than average—because I did not have to do everything alone. I have been a happier person since my divorce but have been hospitalized four times (once from an automobile accident), and my health generally is not as good as it used to be. Shortly after my former husband and I separated, I learned I had an ulcer (they don't pop up overnight), which was cured after nine months of dieting and a change in attitude. Recently I learned I have hypoglycemia,* which if not treated properly can cause unbearable fatigue and other unpleasant symptoms. I've endured much more serious physical illness than most women my age, though nothing totally debilitating, and I believe most of it—perhaps all—has been a reaction to the stresses I've coped with as a divorced mother.

In the hospital I compared notes with a thirty-seven-year-old

* The opposite of diabetes—a condition in which the pancreas over-produces insulin, causing low blood sugar and fatigue.

nurse who was the divorced mother of four. Her own health was not too good, she felt overworked and overwrought, and she agreed that her divorced friends and acquaintances with children all had more ailments than her married friends. For several years I've been conducting my own informal survey and the answers are usually the same: the divorced mother had average or better-than-average health during her marriage, but soon after her divorce she developed serious new ailments. I don't mean the minor psychosomatic ailments we all tend to develop during short periods of minor stress or crisis—headaches, acne and skin disturbances, insomnia, stomachaches, and so on. I mean rush-you-to-the-hospital kinds of sickness like cancer, heart ailments, Addison's disease, and bleeding ulcers.

The mother alone with her children must work and worry much more than the married mother; we generally put in longer harder hours and have no one to relieve or comfort us most of the time. There is no one to share the adult responsibility of managing a family. Combine this with our psychological problems, the stigma of divorce, our uncertain future, our new and enormous responsibilities, and our unfulfilled needs—all terrific stress-producers! This may sound like a contradiction, but women *can* be happy while leading stressful lives—they simply wear out faster than women facing less stress.

Some stress is required for normal human development. Without it we wouldn't grow and develop. The three kinds of stress—physical, mental, and emotional—can come from external circumstances or situations which make sudden, extraordinary demands upon an individual. How you react to the stress in your life depends on your motivations, your life situation, and how you learned to deal with stress in your early life. Divorce can be considerably more painful for the woman who has not learned adequate rational methods of control. If too many situations arise that you cannot handle, you'll begin to think you're a failure and may then fall into a pattern of behaving like a failure. If you haven't learned healthy ways of dealing with life's problems, you'll resort to immature defense mechanisms instead of reasonable solutions.

Improperly handled stress causes wear and tear to the organs of the body, interferes with your life goals, reduces energy, causes you to become neurotic and withdrawn and to develop psychosomatic ailments. If you can't struggle with life, can't come to terms with pressures, and consistently distort reality, you'll limit your life experiences by being afraid to take risks, making yourself vulnerable to even more stress! You may not be able to progress to healthy, high-level solutions to your problems. Too much stress may lead to regression and eventually to a total breakdown into a psychotic state, requiring hospitalization.

If your problem after divorce is what psychologists refer to as "transient reaction to acute stress," you may benefit greatly from some sessions with a psychotherapist. If your problems are more deeply rooted—if they are caused by a serious personality disorder —you may require and desire a rather long period of psychotherapy to reconstruct your personality.

You as a divorced mother face the same common human problems others do: getting enough love and approval from significant individuals, gaining social acceptance, conflict between dependency needs and striving to be independent, handling aggressive impulses, achieving social and occupational success in the face of your limitations, and expressing and controlling your sexual impulses—but you face all these problems alone, while you are probably depressed, anxious, feeling like a failure, and responsible for the care of one or more children!

Most of us today are hypersensitive to mental illness—perhaps we unrealistically expect constant happiness and find it too hard to cope with the occasional anxiety and depression that are a normal part of life. The woman burdened with unbearable anxiety, tension, anger, and depression will certainly benefit from professional help. You may be asking "Do I need this kind of help?" If your problems are not too severe, you might possibly gain the necessary insight by talking with your minister, your family doctor, or with any wise older person who has known you a long time.

Not all divorcees are neurotic, but those of us who make and break unhappy marriages have many ungratified needs—for safety, love, respect, prestige, a feeling of belonging and of identification with others. The divorced mother certainly does not feel "safe"; her security is usually shattered by the events which led up to the divorce, whether it was she or her husband who wanted to end the marriage. She has loved and lost, and she probably is not especially respected by others because she resorted to divorce. Often the divorcee experiences a feeling of alienation after the first euphoric taste of freedom wears off. If you have had psychotherapy before your divorce, you will still encounter the practical problems, but you probably will not have all the psychological hang-ups that can accompany them.

Psychologist Abraham Maslow says in *Toward a Psychology of Being:* "The absence of love certainly stifles potentialities and even kills them. Personal growth demands courage, self-confidence, even daring, and non-love from the parent or the mate produces the opposite, self-doubt, anxiety, and feelings of worthlessness and expectations of ridicule, all inhibitors of growth and of self-actualization."

A prerequisite of healthy human growth is having your basic needs gratified. The ideal way to become a mentally healthy adult is to have been born into a sane, loving family who provided you an environment in which your basic needs were satisfied—but we have no control over that!

What about the divorced mother whose basic needs have never been gratified? Now she must rear her children alone while handling a host of other problems. Must she go through the rest of her life feeling psychologically uncomfortable, looking for something but not knowing what it is or how to find it? Must she live with a feeling of emptiness, a lack of identity, with shame, guilt, and aimlessness? If this is the state she's in, the horror is that she will surely pass on the same attitudes to her children.

The person who is unable to enjoy anything, who lives with anxiety, despair, boredom, and fear, needs help. Psychotherapy is no panacea for all human problems, but it can and usually does lead to improved self-knowledge and self-acceptance. It *is* possible for an individual to become more strong, creative, kind, loving, and actually improve and change her human nature. Therapy also can lead to an improved knowledge of others and of reality in general.

After divorce, one trades security for growth. Often the psychological pain we experience after a disappointment in love and marriage can lead us to greater insight, better values, real happiness. The search for an identity and more meaningful values is worthwhile, but while one lives through the process, there is much frustration, anguish, self-doubt. You must know the difference between neurotic pseudo-problems and the real, unavoidable problems of human life.

Can you do anything on your own to cope with the stress of divorce? If you are fairly mature, in good physical health, and not handicapped in too many ways, you can probably reduce or tolerate the confused emotional state that accompanies your divorce. However, if you *always* have had trouble facing troublesome situations, you may resort to defense mechanisms that make it difficult or impossible for you to approach your problems realistically, which will make you still more anxious. Unresolved conflicts cause us to be highly emotional and generally out of control, and the horrible cycle continues.

Emotional tension is not always bad, but intense and persistent anger, fear, frustration, and worry will threaten your health and make it impossible for your body to relax. Although our hormones work for us to handle stress, *we* must help by knowing how to handle our tensions, and knowing and accepting our emotional and physical limitations.

These are some suggestions by Dr. Peter J. Steincrohn to help overcome tension and fatigue: have a complete physical to make sure you do not have organic disease; relax regularly and don't lead an overactive life; remember that chronic fatigue magnifies all problems; learn to take short naps—if possible, take a short nap in the afternoon, perhaps at lunchtime; get up earlier than usual so you do not rush all day to catch up; don't eat at your desk; learn to rest while you work; learn to stop working before you are exhausted—rest a while, and you can work more efficiently later; don't try to pack thirty-four hours of living into twenty-four hours; cut down on socializing; try to get an extra hour of sleep at night—you may find you have more energy; cut down on smoking and drinking; relax on weekends, and get away from your children occasionally; don't waste your spirit and energy on vague fears—get help if you need it from your family doctor, psychiatrist, preacher, or lawyer; fill your hours with good literature, good music, good talk; never take sedatives or sleeping pills on your own.

When I am tense, a good brisk walk or a bicycle ride helps. Sometimes I relax by doing fifteen or twenty minutes of yoga (on an empty stomach). Occasionally what I need is a hot bath or shower and a short nap to relax. I have learned to stay "unkinked" both physically and mentally by following a regular program of physical exercise and stopping in the middle of any kind of work to relax completely. If you work a forty-hour week, you may find it makes sense to take a fifteen-minute nap during one of your coffee breaks every day and go outdoors during your lunch hour for a walk.

Some women respond to the stresses of divorce by avoiding or ignoring their real problems. There is a desire to escape from reality, which some do by indulging in ultimately self-defeating and self-destructive activities such as:

1. Dating "wrong" kinds of men, who are bad for them psychologically, perhaps unsuitable and impossible as potential marriage partners, having indiscriminate sexual affairs; spending most of their free time dating and searching for the "right man." It is all too easy to fool yourself into believing that this or that new man is in love with you, thereby justifying the love affair you're having. I've heard it said that women give sex to get love and men give love to get sex. If you learn to resolve your conflicts, you won't have the *need* or the desire to search desperately for a man. The more you search and the more you cling when you find him the harder he will try to get away (see the next chapter).

2. Spending money recklessly—on trips, new clothes, and expensive new car, entertaining, new furniture. Perhaps the divorcee receives a cash settlement after it's over; instead of using the money constructively and wisely, she may dissipate her funds on utter nonsense and leave herself with little or no financial security. I heard of one divorced mother who went through $6000 in a year—she bought a wreck of a house and decorated it—after seven months she sold the house at a loss of $2000; she was talked into a bad business investment and lost about $1500; she decided to change her looks (which were actually better than average) by having complete plastic surgery. She dribbled away the rest on clothes and trips.

3. Socializing too much; finding escape in drinking; use of drugs, such as pep pills, tranquilizers, or sleeping pills, to help escape emotional pain.

4. The newly divorced mother may throw herself into her work, spending too much time away from home, almost as much as a man does. She may feel justified about this now that she is the family breadwinner and find it easier to turn her children over to a relative or housekeeper. Perhaps she must be out of town frequently on

business, or she wants to socialize with persons who can further her career. None of this is beneficial to her children, and, of course, it's not good for her if her children are being harmed.

Psychologists feel that behavior disturbance results from severe frustration, emotional deprivation, and conflict. Let's look at another definition of stress, this time from a psychology textbook:

Stress—biological or psychological—may be defined broadly as the external or internal stimulus conditions, noxious or depriving, which demand very difficult adjustments. Stress may consist of emotional trauma and emotional deprivation as well as biological conditions. A stress reaction is a severe disturbance of the balance and regulation of functioning that results from exposure to stress stimuli. The organism must always adjust to changing stimuli, but under stress the adjustment is onerous or even impossible.*

Shouldn't you learn about your own weaknesses and distortions of reality, if there are any, before you take on the full responsibility of running a family or marrying another time? Love is a response to values. If you loved and married a man with inferior, inadequate values or no values at all, shouldn't you now examine your *own* values?

If you grew up in an unhappy or broken home, it is likely your own needs have never been gratified. You thought they would be gratified in marriage, but that failed. Now what? You must learn a method of dealing with internal and external pressures, to learn to assess reality accurately, become emotionally healthy, come to terms with your environment and learn to master it, and use your abilities for your own good. You owe this much to yourself, and you also owe it to your children. *You* are the primary model for their behavior.

What can psychotherapy do for you? Psychotherapy is based on the theory that personality structure can be altered, and its purpose is to teach the patient to develop resources to solve *any* emotion-producing problem—in other words, to be able to handle any stressful circumstance that occurs in a lifetime. Psychotherapy is literally treatment of the psyche—a direct verbal method of approach to personality change.

* *Abnormal Psychology,* by Ephraim Rosen and Ian Gregory, W. B. Saunders Company, Philadelphia, 1965.

Most persons are driven into therapy by pain. But the trouble must not be so severe that the individual has lost all contact with reality. The essence of therapy is re-education through talking. The patient must be intelligent enough to be able to communicate experiences and feelings at a high level of abstraction. The brighter you are, the better you can understand the dynamics of your own personality. You'll need to be able to verbalize your problems and have enough ego strength to stick with the therapeutic process until you reach the point of gaining insight. You must also be introspective, motivated, not too old, and of course able to afford it.

Does therapy really produce personality change? That depends on whether the person gets supportive therapy or insight therapy. In supportive therapy, the patient gets help that will pull him through a temporary crisis, but no attempt is made to reconstruct the personality in a major way. (There are two kinds of patients who get this type of therapy: one whose general mental health is good but must face a crisis in his life, and one who is too disturbed to face a really deep probing of his personality disorders.) Insight therapy takes longer, goes considerably deeper, and is intended to lead to an examination of the patient's values and defenses and effect a major change in the personality.

What follows is a brief description of the therapeutic process. Bear in mind that there are more than three dozen systems of psychotherapy; many psychotherapists are eclectic and draw from several systems, or change their methods to suit a particular patient.

The first part of therapy is *catharsis,* the venting of feelings and problems. The patient is usually relieved to let it all out. After a while in therapy, the patient protects himself from painful insights; this is called *resistance.* When the patient becomes a little more ready to face the truth about himself, *transference* begins to take place. The therapist becomes extremely important to the patient as the patient transfers emotions he has experienced with significant adults in his life (such as his parents). When the patient is ready to conclude his therapy, he is also ready to give up this transference. He sees the significance of his own behavior, he understands that certain actions or inactions are defense mechanisms he unconsciously uses to avoid facing reality—he is gaining *insight* (in other words, he is experiencing and observing simultaneously). The next process is *working through*—this is the re-education that therapy was intended to bring about, and the patient applies the insights and learns rational ways of handling his conflict and life problems.

The term *defense mechanism* is also called *ego defense* and is a way of protecting one's self-esteem and reducing anxiety and fear by concealing or disguising feelings from oneself and from others. You may have heard of some of the following defense mechanisms: suppression, repression, regression, projection, rationalization, fixation, sublimation, reaction formation. They are all unconscious processes: you are not aware that you are doing or *not* doing something when faced with a conflict-producing situation. Defense mechanisms prevent us from facing life squarely. Through the therapeutic process you can learn to recognize your own defense mechanisms and those of others, and consequently change your behavior so that you do not continually thwart your own goals and needs.

According to Dr. Albert Ellis, a neurotic is an individual who consistently acts illogically, irrationally, inappropriately, and childishly. He does not reach goals and harms his potential; is more unhappy, inefficient, fearful than he needs be—he may have the talent, health, looks, intelligence, but somehow he does not get along successfully. Neurosis is an inner contradiction, a discord between what the individual wants to do for himself and the means he uses to achieve his own goals. In *How to Live with a Neurotic,* Dr. Ellis lists these symptoms of emotional disturbance: indecision, doubt, conflict, fear, anxiety, feelings of inadequacy, guilt and self-blame, supersensitivity, oversuspiciousness, hostility and resentment, inefficiency and stupidity, self-deceit, lack of realism, defensiveness, rigidity, compulsiveness, shyness, withdrawal, antisocial and psychopathic behavior, psychosomatic symptoms, hypochondria, bizarre behavior, constant unhappiness and depression, self-centeredness, inability to love, tenseness, inability to relax, overexcitability, manic tendencies, inertia, lack of direction, overambitiousness, compulsive striving, escapism, avoidance of responsibility, alcoholism, use of drugs, self-abasement, self punishment.

If you're thinking by now "No wonder I couldn't live with my husband, he had all those neurotic symptoms," you've missed my point. Look for *your own* symptoms.

I'd like to briefly discuss my own experience in psychotherapy, for the benefit of any readers who do not know persons who have had psychotherapy.

I was driven into therapy by pain—physical pain (the ulcer) as well as psychological pain. Each time I tried to communicate with my husband about the problems we were having in our marriage he shifted the burden to me; one of his favorite defenses was saying that it was all the woman's job to make the marriage work. I believed then and I believe today that marriage is a *cooperative* enterprise. We were neither communicating nor cooperating, and finally I decided the only solution was a divorce. It took me three years to make the decision to see a lawyer. After filing for divorce I was vastly relieved—at least I had made a decision. But I discovered six or seven months later that I did not have enough personal resources to live with that decision. I knew I was intelligent, reasonably talented at earning money, getting along with people, loving my children, but still something was wrong. About six months after my husband moved out of our home, I was having a conversation with a friend who was going through therapy. She pointed out to me that I said "I can't stand it" about four times in our talk, and she suggested I see her psychologist. I resisted the idea, saying I could not afford it, I was really not that disturbed, and gave several other weak excuses. She ended the conversation by saying "You can't afford *not* to go."

For about five days I thought hard about myself and where I was going. I was thirty years old and had a few vague ideas of what I wanted to do with myself, and I was very upset about the prospect of facing life alone. I came to three conclusions before making an appointment with the psychologist:

1. I was ill physically and it was apparent to me that my ulcer was caused by the stress of my unhappy marriage, my impending divorce, and my vague fears about the future.

2. Psychologically, I was more uncomfortable than I had admitted or realized—my saying "I can't stand it" was not a joke.

3. I could not think clearly enough to formulate rational plans. I did want to rearrange my life, to be in control of my existence, but I did not know how or where to begin.

I *did* have problems, they were all mine, and somehow I had to solve them. I began to work seriously on those problems the day I called for an appointment with the psychologist.

A few days later I walked into his office. I appraised him and decided after a few minutes that I could trust him. The session lasted forty-five minutes. I felt somewhat better after leaving—in fact, I was relieved. That evening I thought about the challenging statements he made to some of my "neurotic" remarks and read a book he had given me.

I had individual sessions once a week for about three months, and then about seven months of group therapy with an occasional individual session once every four or five weeks. In three months I was functioning much better. My psychosomatic ailments were leaving me, my skin was improving, I was sleeping much better than I had in years. After about six months I felt sublimely happy (the ulcer was completely healed by then) and I thought "I can quit now; I've got it all figured out." I told the doctor some of my new ideas and actions and he explained that I was over-reacting. But I had a new power and felt a new kind of freedom. I enjoyed rebelling against everything and everyone. After a few months I learned to be more moderate; I did not have to be so outspoken about these new insights and I learned to think clearly about myself and my goals. Life had become a stimulating challenge and I was equal to it.

I was ready to stop therapy after ten months—the two clues were I did not need to make an individual appointment every time something went wrong in my life because I could handle the situation myself, and I resented paying that money for forty-five minutes of another human being's time. I had learned an efficient method of thinking through my life problems, and I was able to act upon conclusions I had reached. In short, I learned to be my own therapist.

I would like to discuss briefly the views of philosopher and psychologist Nathaniel Branden, who has done outstanding work in providing definitions of mental health and mental illness. A number of experts think that mental health is relative to the culture, and that a basic, universally applicable concept of mental health is impossible. Therefore, a person is considered mentally healthy if he conforms to cultural norms. But what if the values and norms of his culture are irrational? (Take Nazi Germany for example.) What *is* the essence of mental health? Branden says, "The health of a man's mind must be judged by how well that mind performs its biological function."

Medicine has a universal concept of the physical health of man:

A healthy body is one whose organs function efficiently in maintaining the life of the organism; a diseased body is one whose organs do not. The health or disease of any part of a man's body is judged by the standard of how well or poorly it performs its survival-function. *Life* is the standard of judgment. . . . It is only the alternative of life or death that makes the concept of health or of disease meaningful or possible.*

The science of psychology must use the same standard in judging the health or disease of a man's mind: how well does his mind perform its biological function?

What is the biological function of mind? Cognition—evaluation—and the regulation of action . . . survival requires that the evaluative function of consciousness be ruled by the cognitive function—i.e., that values and goals be chosen in the full context of rational knowledge and understanding.†

Man is not infallible, and mental health does not consist of never making an error of knowledge or judgment. The concept of mental health pertains to *the method by which a mind functions.*†

Because we can reason, we can think abstractly and in principles. Our capacity to reason can be improved. A psychological disorder is caused by a blocked consciousness—a mind which works to avoid reality through evasion, repression, rationalization and the like. To quote Branden again, "A consciousness dissociated from reality is unhealthy. . . . Irrational beliefs, emotions and actions are the symptoms by which we detect the presence of mental illness."

Without free will, one cannot change one's self psychologically. An individual can *choose* to evade and pretend certain facts of reality do not exist.

There is a direct correlation between self-esteem—the reputation you have with yourself—and mental health. The person with adequate self-esteem is able to think rationally, cope with reality, and control his existence. Anxiety, a common neurosis, is a result of the loss or lack of self-esteem. Your evaluation of yourself depends upon your worthiness and efficacy. Your happiness and survival depend upon making right choices. You are free to act in your own interest,

* "The Concept of Mental Health," by Nathaniel Branden, *The Objectivist,* February, 1967, p. 8.
† *Ibid.*

or you can surrender to the authority of others. A passive person avoids challenge; his constant safety-seeking causes anxiety when he realizes he is selling himself short. Sometimes a person mistakenly has a low estimate of himself. Not *all* competent persons are fully aware of their true worth; it is quite possible to be outstanding in many ways and yet have a poor self-image because of what one has been conditioned to believe. Therapy would help such a person see himself as he is and learn to take pride in his own value.

If one acts better in general, the result will be increased self-esteem. Neurotic symptoms will diminish in frequency and intensity and one can begin to think realistically, efficiently, and develop a realistic estimate of the self. The patient in therapy must be able to translate insight into action; first he must realize that he *can* change. His new knowledge, received from the psychotherapist, must be integrated into his system of values and premises, and he must disintegrate and replace his old associations and connections. To effect a change of emotions, the ideas of the individual must be changed. He must learn to base his actions on reason, not feelings alone; in this way he will learn to remain in conscious control.

Mental health is unobstructed cognitive efficacy. Unobstructed cognitive efficacy requires and entails intellectual independence. A doctrine that is subversive of intellectual independence is subversive of mental health.*

What do you see and how do you see it? What do you think and understand about it? What do you do about it? *You* must be able to decide if something is good for you, or if it goes against your goals and best interests.

And now, to discuss briefly Dr. Abraham Maslow's concept of a psychologically healthy person, or the self-actualizing personality. Following are five characteristics of such a personality:

1. A self-actualizing person is able to use fully and exploit his own talents, capacities, and potentialities.
2. He seems to be fulfilling himself and is doing the best he can, and his past and present basic emotional needs are being gratified.
3. He seems to be loving and is being loved; he is unanxious, has self-respect, and respects others.

* *Ibid.*

4. His cognitive needs for knowledge and understanding are being met.
5. He seems to have worked out for himself his own philosophical and religious bearings.

According to Dr. Maslow, there are twelve basic ingredients of the self-actualizing personality:

1. A superior perception of reality: is comfortable with reality, can detect fakery, dishonesty.
2. Increased acceptance of self, of others, and of nature: accepts—both physiologically and psychologically—sexuality, menopause, aging, etc.; no pretense, hypocrisy, or artificiality; has a good appetite and sleeps well; does not accept improvable shortcomings in others, such as excessive jealousy, laziness, hurting others, etc.
3. Increased spontaneity: feels free, has an easy naturalness about him; is not too unconventional, and is able to go through the motions of conformity when necessary but does not compromise his values.
4. Problem-centered rather than self-centered: is not a problem for himself and is able to make worthwhile contributions to solving problems of the world, outside himself.
5. A desire for privacy: not afraid to be alone.
6. Increased autonomy: is able to live effectively in society, feeling no need to withdraw from a "sinful" world; is not a slavish follower of a modal style of life.
7. Greater freshness of appreciation and richness of emotional reaction.
8. Higher frequency of peak experiences: capable of self-transcendence, losing himself in a religious experience, love, music, art, etc.
9. Increased identification with the human species and capable of great, profound love for a few people; able to surrender himself totally to another in love.
10. More democratic preferences for others, based upon performance and ability.
11. Changed and improved interpersonal relations.
12. A sense of humor devoid of hostility.

Dr. Maslow believes that tragedy can sometimes be therapeutic and that therapy often seems to work best when people are driven into it by pain. In his book, *Toward a Psychology of Being,* he says:

> Only the flexibly creative person can really manage the future—only the one who can face novelty with confidence and without fear. I am convinced that much of what we now call psychology is the study of the tricks we use to avoid the anxiety of absolute novelty by making believe the future will be like the past.

SELECTING A PSYCHOTHERAPIST

How does one find a good therapist? Should you consult a lawyer, doctor, clergyman, or should you see a social worker, psychiatrist, or a psychologist? Lawyers, doctors, and clergymen can be of some assistance, but they are not always professionally trained to deal with all psychological problems. What you require is someone formally trained to deal with neuroses, psychoses, and personality disorders. There are several things you can do to prepare yourself to find an effective, well-qualified therapist you can trust and like.

When you have a physical problem, you probably call a doctor, who will examine you, diagnose your physical condition, and prescribe treatment. If surgery seems to be required, you may decide to get opinions of several other doctors first. You check around to locate the best doctor you can find for your type of physical problem; after some more investigation and deliberation, you make arrangements to have your operation. You want your doctor to be competent, but you don't necessarily have to like his personality.

Unfortunately we are not always this sensible when we deal with our psychological problems. We either ignore them completely or go to the wrong persons and places for help. It is almost impossible for the person with an unhealthy consciousness to make good, right choices when he is desperate and uninformed.

You can get maximum effectiveness from psychotherapy if you like and respect the person who is attempting to re-educate you, and if you can respond to him positively. You must also be willing to work and discipline yourself.

The first essential is to learn everything you can about therapy. Read about the different methods; talk to persons who have undergone therapy and ask them as many questions as they'll answer. What would you do if you needed heart surgery? Wouldn't you read everything you could find on the subject and talk to persons you know with heart trouble? You'd be cautious before choosing a doctor—your heart is too precious to take chances with. Well, so is your mind!

Next, get names of therapists from friends, relatives, your lawyer, your physician. You can also get names of qualified therapists from the American Association of Marriage Counselors, and the Academy of Psychologists in Marital Counseling. If you have a minister, he might be able to give you some temporary help with your problems and refer you to a trained psychologist later.

Last, shop around. Pick several therapists from your list. Call them, ask as many questions as they will answer over the telephone, then make appointments to see the ones who have impressed you most. Keep the appointments. If you are not certain about their credentials, check their diplomas (which should be displayed on the walls of their offices). Don't be embarrassed about this. If you've never heard of the schools, write down the names and check later. Be critical and observant when you go for that first visit. Select one you like after you have "interviewed" several, and then begin your therapy.

You're probably asking now, "How can I learn about therapy?" It's important to be reasonably well informed because you're going to invest valuable time and perhaps a considerable amount of money in this. An excellent book for the average person to read to get a general picture of the kinds of therapeutic methods available is *Psychoanalysis and Psychotherapy* by Robert A. Harper. Dr. Harper is an eclectic psychologist who practices in Washington, D.C. His book describes thirty-six different therapeutic systems, is available in paperback, and is published by Prentice-Hall. Dr. Harper gives listings of selected readings if you are interested in learning more about psychology, and his book contains a glossary of technical terms.

What are the educational requirements for a psychotherapist? A psychologist should have a doctoral degree in psychology, which means he has approximately eight or nine years of college-level training in his field; he should have the technical experience of actual clinical work under supervision, and he should also have undergone intensive psychotherapy himself so he is free of serious emotional problems.

A psychiatrist has a medical degree in addition to a specialization in psychiatry. Some social workers holding master's degrees in sociology can be effective therapists.

What are the personality characteristics of a skilled psychotherapist? He should be objective, intelligent, empathic, emotionally stable, and flexible.

Do not be content with the information about psychotherapy you have gleaned from newspapers, magazines, and mass communications in general. Don't waste your time on "self-help" books, don't try to analyze yourself, and above all don't let a friend who has been through therapy "work" on you. Psychotherapy is not a parlor game, nor is it limited to movie stars and the very rich. All kinds of persons in all occupations, at all social levels, can and do have serious psychological problems that often cause more pain than many physical ailments. (And remember that many physical ailments are caused by psychological problems.)

If you have friends or relatives who have successfully undergone therapy, ask them about their therapists. Perhaps you will find your therapist through a personal reference, as I did. Does the therapist have the required formal education, does he offer group therapy as well as individual therapy; what method does he use—is he directive or nondirective? Is he a Freudian analyst? Do his patients spend a lot of time talking about dreams and early childhood, or does the therapist get his patients to concentrate on their present problems and help them cope with their immediate difficulties? You do not have to spend four or five years (and five to ten thousand dollars) on the couch. One of the best ways to determine if someone's therapist is effective is to take a critical look at that person after he has completed his therapy. Is he different than he was when he began his treatment? Is he more stable, effective, rational, happy? Incidentally, if someone you know has been unsuccessful in therapy, perhaps it was because of his or her lack, not a lack in the psychotherapist, or there may have been a personality clash.

Ask your lawyer about counseling services available in your town. He is sure to know social workers, psychiatrists, psychologists, and others. Perhaps your local court offers some kind of counseling—either marriage counseling or post-divorce counseling. Ask about outpatient clinics, welfare services, and the like. Your family doctor will also be able to give you the names of various therapists. If money is your problem, perhaps your doctor or attorney will help you find free or low-cost help.

Do not overlook the possibility of using the services of your local clergyman. Today many more ministers and priests receive advanced training in marriage and psychological counseling. You may benefit from regular counseling with your own clergyman if he is specially trained or if he works in conjunction with a psychotherapist. If your problems are not too severe or too deeply rooted, this may be all your require to get your life moving in a better direction. Your clergyman should be able to evaluate your state of mind well enough to know if you need more help than he can give you.

Many persons are afraid of becoming involved with someone who is not professionally qualified and, consequently, may stay away from psychotherapy altogether. Admittedly there are some quacks, but there are also highly skilled men and women who are able to help many emotionally disturbed individuals become more rational. Unfortunately, there are not enough trained therapists to go around. However, if you are serious, determined, and diligent, you can locate one.

After you have compiled a list of several therapists and know what their training is, and whether they are psychologists or social workers, you must determine which one you want. Call each one on the telephone. Ask about his method; ask how long each session is, what he charges; inquire about individual and group therapy (group therapy sessions are usually cheaper, last longer, and can be highly effective for some persons); ask about professional qualifications if you do not already know (did he teach at a university, did he work in a clinic, social agency; how long has he been in private practice?). Do not make your phone call too long. The therapist is very busy and will no doubt have a client in the office when you call. If he's too busy to talk, ask him to call you back. He will not resent your questions. He'll probably be glad to know someone has taken the time and effort to learn something about him and his field and that you are informed enough to ask intelligent questions. If he *does* mind and becomes irritated, that's his problem! Scratch him from your list, because such a person would not be a very effective therapist for you.

After you have made an appointment for your first visit, write out the problems which are disturbing you. Often a person goes to a psychotherapist's office and cannot think of anything specific to say. A prepared list of your specific problems (or what you think your specific problems are) may help. The therapist is skilled enough to ask you questions that enable him to determine how he can best help you. However, if you sit there like a lump with nothing to say, nothing will happen. He is not a mind-reader.

While you're talking to him, notice his attitude. Is he objective; does he seem kind, sincere, reasonable; do you like him? Do you think you could establish a good rapport with him? Most of the persons doing this work are humane and dedicated to helping others solve the problems of living—the philosophical and psychological problems as well as the seemingly ordinary problems of daily life. They are scientists and can view you with great objectivity. Don't be ashamed or embarrassed about anything that is bothering you or any aspect of your own behavior. It is extremely difficult to shock psychotherapists—they are familiar with every kind of peculiar or abnormal human behavior. This is undoubtedly the one time and place you will not be blamed or judged.

After you have seen and "interviewed" several therapists, you must make a value judgment. Think about each person you have seen and talked to and decide which one is best qualified to help you with your psychological problems. Then make another appointment with that person and start the real work of psychotherapy.

What about the cost of therapy? The rate I paid about six years ago was $15 for forty-five minutes for individual sessions, and $8 for an hour-and-a-half group session. As I recall, the total cost of my therapy was $600 or $700. Rates are generally somewhat higher today, and I think the average for an individual session is $20 to $30 per forty-five minutes if your therapist is a psychiatrist or psychologist; social workers generally charge less.

Suppose you go to one individual therapy session a week for fifty-two weeks at a cost of $20 each time. The total cost to you will be $1040. It is possible to have some of this cost defrayed by health insurance (if you go to a psychiatrist) and all of it is income-tax deductible. You cannot make a better investment. Don't use the excuse "I can't afford it." As my friend told me, if you feel that *you can't stand it,* you cannot afford *not* to go.

If you live in an area that has no psychiatrists or psychologists, what can you do? I think sound psychotherapeutic counseling is important enough to warrant traveling a good distance once a week, or even moving to another location if necessary. It is worth any kind of temporary "sacrifice" to get what you need most—the ability to control your existence. If you must give up some creature comforts, hobbies, or doubtful pleasures, or move to another state or city to make yourself fit to live in reality, do you think it's worth it?

It is your choice—you can face it or not face it. You can go on as you are, psychologically (and no doubt physically) uncomfortable, beset by fears and anxieties for the rest of your life. Or you can make yourself fit to live now in this world.

Chapter 9

The Divorcee and the Men in Her Life

As A divorcee you will be more involved in the world of men than you were as a wife, so you'll need to examine and evaluate your attitudes about men. Because you don't wish to marry impulsively or prevent yourself from falling in love again, you must also re-evaluate your attitudes and expectations regarding romantic love. This chapter will touch on the problems of the divorcee who must now confront all males directly, without benefit of a male go-between or protector, and the divorced mother's serious romantic relationships.

Nobody can tell you how to get a second (or third) husband; I know of no special formula or technique which could work for all women. Be comforted with the knowledge that if one man found you desirable enough to marry, perhaps another will too. A larger problem may be *finding* a man you'd like to marry. You will soon learn as a divorcee that there is not that much to choose from.

If you're thinking you can use sex as a weapon to land another husband, forget it. Your competition is keen—there are many eager younger women looking for husbands too, and they will be dating many of the same men you'll meet. You'll need more to offer than mere physical charm, and this is where your age and experience can be assets.

I know three women who got their second husbands three different ways: one refused to sleep with the man she loved, and he mar-

214

ried her because she was a "woman of principle." Today they are most contented and have a houseful of children—hers and theirs. Another slept with her man on the first date, he moved in on the second, and two years later they were married. Today they are happy and contented together. The third fell in love with a married man who had a mistress. She had a short but intense affair with him to let him know how wonderful she was, then said "You'll have to get rid of the mistress and your wife if you want me." He did, and they have been one of the most happily married couples I've ever seen.

These three divorcees were too smart to use sex as a weapon. They did what seemed right and natural to them, and their men married them in spite of sex, not because of it. The significant factors in all three marriages were mutual love and similar values.

Sex may pull teenagers and young adults into early marriage, but love and marriage between adult men and women must be based on many values other than sex. After you find the man of your choice, you must get him to think and feel "Because of what you are, you are essential to my happiness." Once this happens, marriage is usually not far off.

To prepare myself for this chapter I've read countless articles and books on the subject of love, and also on man, woman, sexuality, role confusion, motherhood, the battle of the sexes, homosexuality, the psychology of love, and so on. I've watched many television programs covering these subjects, and I've listened to a number of excellent interviews and panel discussions. I've talked to many men and women at great length and in depth above love, their emotional and physical needs, their successes in and out of marriage. I've studied married couples I know, trying to determine why the happy ones are happy and the miserable ones miserable; I attended a series of ten outstanding illuminating lectures on the psychology of romantic love by Nathaniel Branden, in Detroit. I've participated in a church coping group and have also sat in on many group therapy sessions dealing primarily with marital problems. In addition to the reading, talking, listening, and watching, I've dated many men and have had several romantic relationships of my own (the field work was the most fun), and as a divorcee I was more involved in the world of men socially and in business than I was as a wife.

As part of my research for this chapter, I dug out some old love letters, which provided unusual, unexpected insights. A sentence in one letter from a twenty-six-year-old attorney who was smitten with me when I was eighteen stands out. In his last letter to me, after he realized there would not be a real romance between us, he wrote: "I had hoped that you could make a human being out of me."

I've thought about that statement many times, and have come up with various interpretations. I've finally concluded some things that I wish had been possible for me when I was eighteen.

Women in our culture have been conditioned to believe that men are the stronger sex, that they are self-sufficient, independent, and that they really don't need or want a deep, lasting emotional relationship with a woman. We have also been conditioned to believe that if we try to achieve any goals of our own while we are married, separate from home and family, we are aggressive, dissatisfied to be women, threatening our men and competing with them, and even emasculating them! As a result of this conditioning, men and women have serious problems in love and marriage. Women have been generally sexually repressed and some find it difficult if not impossible to be as warm and loving in marriage as men would like. The symbols of blatant sexuality we see around us do little to help individuals in their own romantic lives. Some men become overstimulated and preoccupied with gorgeous paper dolls, thinking the flesh-and-blood women around them are lacking. Many women, in an attempt to "hook" or "trap" a man (words generally associated with fish and animals, and certainly not appropriate for human beings), develop a surface sexiness. We enter marriage totally confused about our identity—what is it to be masculine, what is it to be feminine?

Some men think that being masculine means you are physically strong, have much hair all over your body, and would never wash the kitchen floor. Some women think that being feminine simply requires producing babies and being helpless when men are around. Some think all that is required of them in marriage is that the man "bring home the bacon" and the woman be a good little mother and housewife. With such a limited view of what we can be to one another, it is not surprising so many of us fail.

As a woman of thirty-seven, I know without a doubt that men need and want women just as much as women need and want men. Not just for sex, not just to exist together in a house in a suburb, not just to reproduce. And certainly not to "make human beings" out of one another, as my friend thought. We should be *human beings* when we enter marriage. There is the sad idea in our culture that it is all right for men to be "animals" until some woman "traps" them and spends the next thirty or forty years domesticating and civilizing her animal.

No doubt you are just as personally affected by our high divorce rate as I have been. You probably are tired of "games" between men and women, and would like to dispense with the battle of the sexes. Myths and misinformation about romantic love and marriage have probably caused you much suffering. What shaped your attitudes? If you're divorced or planning to be divorced soon, you have had serious difficulties with one man, and it's possible you have some questions about masculinity and femininity.

EVALUATING YOUR ATTITUDES ABOUT MEN

Have you ever used a microscope? If you have, you know something about the importance of perfect focus. Before you can evaluate your attitudes about men, and make value judgments, you must be in focus. In marriage you were very close to one man. How clear was the focus?

How did you form your ideas about men? Do you like most men? Do most men seem to like you? Have you ever been called a man-hater? Do you believe that most of the world's problems are caused by men? Do you have the reputation for being a flirt, tease, nag, bitch, shrew? Or do most men think you are a grand person? Are you satisfied with the interaction between you and the men you know?

Now that you are alone, men are going to be more important to you than ever before. You will directly confront males in your environment as a single, independent woman. How you relate to these men and how each of them relates to you is of great significance.

Consider all your dealings with all males, not just romantic relationships. What about your dentist, milkman, employer, and colleagues? How well do you get on with male relatives, your doctor, lawyer, minister, the principal of your children's school, your friends' husbands, and so on? Do you find it easy to meet and talk to men, either socially or for business purposes? Did you meet many boys and men, or were you sheltered from them early in life? Your answers may help explain some of your behavior, and should bring you some insight about what you want from them and what you think of them. A negative, destructive, and hostile attitude can't be covered with sugary words and sweet smiles. How would you like to relate to *one specific man?* How realistic are you about men? Are men always letting you down? What do you think a man has a right to expect from you? Would you be able to distinguish a psychologically healthy male from a disturbed one?

Were you told irrational, untrue things as a child which have made it difficult for you to relax with men, trust them, respect them, and like them? Were you told they are all animals who are interested primarily in sex and a woman's body? I have a friend whose parents drummed this into her. She is attractive, well-educated, sensitive, and a confirmed man-hater. Were you told to "get all you can" from a man? Did you know that men bitterly resent the materialistic, gold-digging attitude of some women? Most hard-working men are delighted by a woman who wants to work for what she gets; though they like to provide for us and protect us, they respect a woman who can pull her own weight.

We women are taught many myths about men through the mass media, our traditions, and various institutions. Your mother and other significant females in your life gave you their ideas and opinions about men. Perhaps you've accepted most of what you heard without evidence. The men around you—your father, brothers, teachers, boyfriends—helped form your attitudes, not so much by what they said as by what they did.

My own association with the opposite sex was quite limited until after my divorce. I had a tendency to judge all men by what I knew about a few—my former husband, my father, a few employers, and what other women told me. After I started to check out the situation, I was surprised to learn that many men are insecure and have worries about their jobs, their masculinity, their health, their physical attractiveness. They were not so perfect or formidable as I'd believed. I learned in a hurry that men are people too.

Though we don't segregate the sexes in our country, many young women grow up in what is primarily a female environment. We get little chance to learn what healthy maleness is and have slight opportunity to interact with males of any age. The young divorced mother who had been reared with a younger sister by a widowed

mother who never dated or remarried, who went to a girls' school
and saw very few males of any age during her childhood and had
limited social contacts, taught school, and married the first shy
young man who proposed is much different from the woman who
lived with both parents and four brothers in a noisy, active family in
which many males of all ages came and went, who attended co-
educational schools, dated and had several affairs before marriage,
and worked in an otherwise all-male office.

A woman who has been unhappy in marriage may resent men
and feel generally hostile toward them all. Who is to say she had
that attitude before marriage or that her marriage to a particularly
undesirable man fostered her attitude? She is the one to judge, and if
she can't judge alone, she may need help.

Man is not your natural enemy. Although women are still sub-
jected to injustices and inequalities in all parts of the world, the
situation is gradually improving. The woman who genuinely wants
to, *can* grow to full maturity. She can have her own achievements, a
career, a husband and family, though perhaps not all at the same
time. Sometimes women who do not have the kind of lives they
want behave as though there has been a big conspiracy—as though
all the men in this country sat down one day and said "Let's make it
tough for women—let's keep them subject to our will, let's deny
them the vote, equal rights, education, and while we're at it, let's
keep 'em barefoot and pregnant. Let's never let them forget that
they're the second sex."

It never happened! *Men* are the ones who helped us get the vote,
who worked hard every day in office, factory, and laboratory to invent and produce the goods we enjoy and consume every day (and
would not want to live without), who invented the Pill so we would
not have to be barefoot and pregnant all our life, and who are teaching females in colleges and universities to use their minds so they
can have worthwhile goals.

A healthy, rational, strong *man* does not want an incompetent,
dependent, lazy, and helpless female. He wants a woman who can
face life's challenge with him. He knows that modern technology
has released woman from much drudgery, and he is happy to see her
fulfill herself, and have worthwhile, productive goals. He knows that
if she has genuine self-esteem (which can come only from her own
achievements, not through him), she will be that much more valuable and stimulating to him.

Men have their problems. They die seven years sooner than we do; they get ulcers and heart disease four times as often as we do; many of them are driven to drink not by us, but by the strain and pressure of living in a technological society where the competition is literally killing them. Some of them are worried because women are starting to compete with them, too.

Men have many more personal and social problems than we do: the male crime rate is eight times the female crime rate; men have a much higher rate of deviant behavior than women, including homosexuality and drug addiction; they have a higher rate of mental illness, a sucide rate four times as high, more personality disorders, and so on. In general, males are more a problem to themselves and others around them than females are.

Of the some 15,000 books in the New York public library dealing with the so-called woman problem, most were written by men. There are only about 1,000 books written about men. It seems by pointing the finger at *us,* by trying to analyze us, dissect us, discover why *we* are so illogical, emotional, in need of love and affection, and so forth, men have tried to keep the spotlight off themselves!

Men are in trouble. They need reasonable, loving women—not to control or guide them, but to understand them, to love them, to work with them, and to judge them when necessary. The last thing men need today is to be pampered by women who neurotically want to remain parasitical dependents. We should judge them with love and reason. We will have the right to do so *only* when we are actively working to change what we know to be evil, harmful, and unfair—in ourselves, in our men, and in our society.

A RATIONAL ATTITUDE TOWARD MEN

The psychologically healthy female looks for strength of character in men. A man who is respected and admired by women has rational control of himself, but he is not inhibited or repressed. He is ruled by his own judgment, loyal to his own values, and has the self-confidence necessary to assert himself. Though he has control of his emotions and does not base his decisions on feelings alone, he knows what his emotions are and is not afraid to show them. He has no desire to seduce every woman he meets; what he is seeking in a woman is a spiritual equal who shares similar values.

Unfortunately, many men have been conditioned to believe that a "real" man does not feel anything, does not communicate emotion, does not need love, and does not need a dynamic, enduring relationship with just one woman. The truth is that men need and desire love and emotional closeness and intimacy as much as women do.

A woman who feels superior to men, who thinks they are all little boys who must be manipulated and deviously controlled through feminine wiles and coquetry, is not psychologically mature. Because she feels men are a threat and has no respect for them in general, she wants to emasculate them. She may have an aggressive desire to be "pals" with men and is often fault-finding, sarcastic, and patronizing. She fails to recognize that femininity is a psychological characteristic and is not defined only in terms of motherhood. She fails to understand that nothing is required to produce babies, because nature provides the equipment, but that rearing a child properly takes intelligence and character. Some females are infants in women's bodies—the weak, clinging-vine type who depends upon a man to think for her and would never dare contradict him or judge him and thinks her man is wonderful no matter *what* he does has little respect for her man or herself.

The *"femme fatale"* who manipulates men ends up despising them and is basically afraid of them. The woman who changes radically when she is with men has profound self-doubts and feels her natural self is not good enough for them.

A worthwhile, psychologically healthy woman desires and expects admiration and respect from men. She has an identity, is able to think independently, form values, choose goals, and act upon them. She is glad to be a woman, she likes sex, and her own body; she likes men and finds the male body attractive. She is confident enough to express admiration for her man openly and enthusiastically.

Before you can love a man, you must like men. Before you can like men, you must like yourself. Before you can like yourself, you must have self-esteem.

YOU AND YOUR EX-HUSBAND

The relationship between ex-mates is sensitive and peculiar. Usually a man and woman who have been married and divorced have little in common other than their children. They have seen and participated in the mutual destruction of a mutual dream. They are not enemies and they are not friends. It may take years for some couples who are divorced to fall completely out of love. They may think they are out of love because they hate one another. But the opposite of love is indifference, not hate. They must fall out of hate and learn to be neutral. When this happens, they stop feeling the sting of one another's disapproval.

Many divorced mothers believe their troubles with "that man" will end with divorce. Your ex-husband isn't going to be any better as an ex-husband than he was as a husband; in fact, he may be somewhat worse! I have never heard any divorced mother say she was completely satisfied with the way her ex handled things—child support, visits, gifts to the children, other things. And every divorced father I've discussed this with has a gripe or two about his former wife. There is a way to control this—through self-control. The less you do to antagonize your former spouse, the smoother your post-divorce relationship will be.

Many ex-husbands expect their ex-wives to be saints. An ex-husband may unrealistically criticize the way his former wife spends the child support; he may make nasty remarks about her new social activities and the men she dates. He may openly resent her new sexual freedom so much that he runs her down to mutual friends or even to their children. You can have healthy, happy, beautifully "adjusted" children who get straight A's, are talented, popular, active in sports, play musical instruments, are kind to animals, babies, smaller children, and old folks, yet your ex may tell you that you're a bad mother if they need haircuts or have holes in their socks or a button off a dress, or swear in the bathroom.

It is difficult if not impossible for most men to be chivalrous toward their former wives. Some men lose completely any protective feelings they may have had toward the mother of their children. Part of their bitterness is created by our divorce laws—it is hard to see how a man can feel protective towards a woman who has proved him "guilty" of a marital offense.

If couples could be divorced by mutual consent, there would be much less resentment afterward. The degree of bitterness accompanying any divorce depends upon the maturity of the individuals, and the laws should be changed to make the aftermath as painless as possible. Many individuals are still threatened by the very idea of divorce, even after the marriage contract has been dissolved.

If you requested and obtained the divorce, your former husband may heap blame and abuse on you. Your morality will be attacked, and at times he may even question your sanity. The best way to communicate with a suspicious, angry, or frightened man is to show a persistent, calm willingness to listen to his side. Avoid provoking him. If he abuses you verbally, ignore it. If you try to communicate and he rebuffs you, don't be discouraged. Keep trying if the issues are worth communicating about. If he is deeply suspicious, don't be too friendly. He may be convinced you're up to no good, and if you're overly friendly it may come across as condescension or an attempt to put something over on him. Firmly defend yourself against physical attack, and be certain you do not invite it. Remember that most murders occur during marital or other family quarrels. When there is a problem about visits or child support, be firm, reserved (*don't nag*), and consistent. If you have difficulty talking to him, try writing a short, businesslike note, but don't be too cold. Remember, you were once man and wife.

Get legal help with problems you cannot handle. In Michigan, the Friend of the Court assists divorced mothers and fathers. There is often a huge backlog of cases, and it usually takes several months to have a case reviewed. I was told by a Friend of the Court employee that the greatest burden of their work is caused by fathers who default on support and alimony payments.

You have no right to ask your former mate for anything for yourself—his legal and moral obligations are to your children. Whatever extra help he offers you or them will have to be his idea. Some men may do peculiar things to punish their former wives. A man's ego is tender and can be brutally bruised by the ultimate rejection of divorce. Your former husband may try to get even in dreadful little ways you don't understand at all, particularly if you threw him over for a new love.

Give yourselves time to become unemotional. Remember that he owes you nothing except common courtesy. It may be some time before he can give that.

Many men feel they have been cheated after a divorce. They are required to share perhaps one-fourth to one-half of their property

with their wives; they lose custody of their children; they are sometimes required to pay alimony to women they no longer love. They
may angrily question whether their wives are entitled to all this.
Small wonder some of them are resentful and uncooperative.

There is usually a considerable psychological difference between
the man who seeks divorce and the man who is divorced by his wife.
The man who seeks the divorce may have fallen in love with another, and because he feels guilty may try to compensate by being
financially generous, spending extra time with his children and helping his former family adjust to their new realities.

On the other hand, the man whose wife wanted the divorce usually feels no need to be chivalrous. When she calls on him for help
of any kind, he may say "You wanted the divorce, it's all your problem now." He may complain to friends about what she did to him,
and play on the sympathy of his children.

The women are usually quite different types too. The wife who is
divorced by her husband may be dependent and unable to adjust to
being head of the household. Perhaps she became a drudge and a
drag who couldn't keep up with him during the marriage. Perhaps
she became overdomestic, lost her charm and looks, and became
dull and boring. The wife who divorced her husband may be *too* independent. Perhaps she refused to tolerate any of his faults, perhaps
she had other interests that became more important than her husband, or perhaps she turned to other pursuits because he left her unfulfilled. Or she may have fallen in love with someone else. An
exceptionally independent woman would not consider turning to her
former husband for help of any kind.

Some immature ex-husbands play a peculiar game after divorce:
they tend to dissociate themselves from their children if they do
poorly in school, behave badly, or get into any kind of trouble.
There may be a perverse satisfaction in saying "She's a rotten
mother. It's all her fault—let her worry about them. She wanted the
divorce, I didn't." He may try to exonerate himself from all responsibility and may think his wife's faults, real or imagined, relieve him
of the burden of child support. After all, *he* wanted to stay married,
he wanted to continue the game, and he is frustrated because she
refused to play. Maybe she matured enough to say "I've taken all I
can. Now you must grow up and treat us properly, or leave." He
refuses to change, she files for divorce, and he spends years trying to

continue the game. I've heard this type of man say in group therapy: "If she thinks I'm going to send any child support so she can date other men and use my money for baby-sitters, she's crazy. Let her get a job and support the kids."

One divorced woman has been married to a kind, loving second husband for six years. Her first husband comes around about once a month to visit his two teenage children and has fallen several thousand dollars behind in child support. He is a bad influence on his son: the boy is disturbed for days after a visit. At times his daughter refuses to leave with him. He neglects his children in many ways, but does love them and care about them in his own fashion—but it's not enough. He thinks he has a right to be called "father"—but the title belongs to the man who lives with them, worries about them, guides them, helps them with their homework, and loves and supports them.

WHEN YOUR EX-HUSBAND REMARRIES

A man may praise his second wife, himself, and his new marriage, hoping to vindicate himself for sins and mistakes in the first marriage. He may suggest to his children that something is wrong with their mother because no one wants her or she hasn't fallen in love yet. Perhaps as proof of love for the new wife, he may treat his former wife more poorly than before. The second wife is inclined to regard the first wife as a threat. She may encourage her new husband to cut the child support or alimony, she may complain about the established visiting schedule he has with his children. You cannot force his second wife to recognize the moral and legal rights of your children—she should have faced all this before she married a divorced father.

Perhaps she is a divorced mother herself and understands his and your problems. Or perhaps you two women are jealous of one another. She may subtly or vigorously, depending upon her style, try to push you out of the picture. He'll soon cut down on visiting—perhaps every other week instead of regularly on Sunday; he may try to lower the support or alimony. He may stop communicating with you altogether because of pressure from her. One divorced mother told me she had reasonably good communication with her ex-husband until he remarried and returned from his honeymoon. He came to pick up his children for a visit and seemed embarrassed when they asked about his trip. She invited him to have the usual cup of coffee and he said "I can't, Helen is waiting to use the car," nervously collected the children, and rushed out. He never again set foot in the house. Their friendly communication about the children's progress came to a halt; when he came to pick them up, he tooted the horn and waited for them to come to the car. After three or four months, he saw his children about half as much and their visits were not too pleasant because of his second wife's insecurity.

A man and woman who have been married a long time have difficulty breaking the emotional bonds. Some couples may continue a relationship that is unwise and unhealthy, particularly if one or both of them have remarried. After divorce, try to forget him. Do whatever is necessary to make your life rich and full so you have no need to invent excuses to see or call your former husband except of course to discuss your children.

To summarize the best ways to co-exist with a former husband:

1. Be realistic in your expectations. Don't demand that he be better to you now than he was as your husband.

2. Encourage and help him to meet his responsibility to your children.

3. Don't be upset by his criticisms. Analyze what he says. If it is objectively valid, make the necessary changes. Don't ignore good advice simply because it comes from him.

4. Maintain a rational distance. Don't become involved in his personal problems and don't invite him to become involved in yours.

You are now legally divorced—the emotional divorce may take somewhat longer to be final.

ON MEN AS FRIENDS

According to C. S. Lewis in *The Four Loves,* a friend is someone who sees the same truth you do. Friendship has been called that relationship between human beings in which each dispassionately seeks the welfare of the other. Erich Fromm says friends find themselves in each other, and gain greater self-possession and self-knowledge through their friendship.

Is it possible for a man and a woman to be just friends? It is—I've had male friends all my life, and my six years as a divorced woman were enriched by the advice, companionship, solace, and even criticisms I received from my men friends. I agree it is difficult for men and women to be friends because we have been conditioned to see one another not as human beings first, but as male and female and therefore as sexual beings and possible mates.

A man once told me he would never have for a friend a woman he would not want to sleep with if he ever had the opportunity. I can't imagine any woman I know feeling that a prerequisite for friendship with a man would be finding him sexually desirable. Several men have told me they've never had women as friends—they are interested in women only as love or sex objects. However, there *are* men who can be friends with women, who do not base the relationship on sexual attraction. I've noticed that men who have not had sisters have a *need* for women friends, although they might not be as relaxed around women as men who grew up with sisters. Having a friend of the opposite sex definitely increases your understanding of human behavior. Perhaps your male friend is someone you know through community work or politics. Or perhaps you share a business or intellectual pursuit, or love of a particular sport. Whatever you do together and wherever you find him, he can be almost as indispensable as a good woman friend.

A male friend can take you to a lecture or a movie when you don't have a date. He may advise or console you about your romantic affairs, and you may do the same for him. He'll help you move, or go with you when you select a new home or car. Perhaps he'll help you paint the ceiling and in turn you'll sew curtains for his apartment. He may know your children well enough to be a good friend to them too, and perhaps he'll take them to football games or the zoo. He can warn you when they seem to be getting out of hand; he can also tactfully tell you when you are wrong. He may help you find a good job, or even give you a good job. Perhaps you are colleagues. Or maybe he lives in another city now, someone you can call when you are depressed or lonely.

You can endear yourself to your men friends by introducing them to single women. Of course, you run the risk of losing your friend! I introduced two of my dearest friends to one another, and now they are so busy together that neither of them has much time for me. Incidentally, I think only the rarest kinds of individuals can be close friends with men who are in love with their closest female friends. This is one type of triangle I avoid. If you introduce a close male friend to a dear female friend, do your best to stay out of their quarrels. Listen when they need to talk, but don't make comments that could be misconstrued or repeated later.

What about married men as friends? For one thing, they're too busy with their wives and familes to dash over on a Saturday afternoon to help you with a problem or a project. Perhaps you can enjoy a business relationship or a limited social relationship, but it is difficult to carry on a *real* friendship with a married man without some kind of strain. Of course, this depends upon the customs of your social circle. It is not unusual for married upper-class men to escort divorced or widowed upper-class women to various functions, or to dine with them occasionally.

Don't be alarmed if your friends' husbands become cool to you after your divorce. They may regard you as a threat to the security of their own marriages. A friend's husband became openly hostile to me after my divorce, not so much because he liked my former husband as because he thought I might encourage his wife to be independent and "sassy" to him. Some men resent the divorcee's sexual freedom and may think their wives' ears are being filled with tales of sensational romantic liaisons. Or perhaps a man is suddenly attracted to his wife's friend and he fights it by being distant or even rude. Whatever the reasons, don't be too hurt or alarmed if this happens. I've observed that men who are insecure about their masculinity are threatened by divorcees. Most men in your group will probably be protective and kind.

I don't believe for one moment that the majority of men are waiting to pounce on lonely, frustrated divorcees, *unless they are somehow invited to do so.* Make it clear you're not interested in anyone's husband or lover, and don't spend all your free time hanging out at a married couple's house, crying on their shoulders (especially *his*), asking for advice and consolation.

Men usually like to do favors for women, and your men friends often turn out to be more dependable and helpful than men you have had romances with. One of my long-time friends and former colleagues advised me well when I started to write this book; another man I have known for years read parts of the manuscript and offered useful suggestions and criticisms; still another male friend loaned me money so I could continue to work on it.

What must you do to have a good male friend? It helps to see the same truth, to have similar values and an interest or two in common. Look for the same elements you do in friendships with women: honesty, mutual respect and trust, shared experiences, concern for one another's welfare and happiness, approval and acceptance. One man I know says a primary requirement in the woman he'll marry is that she can be his friend.

There are some men of such excellent character, with such rich personalities, that one cannot pass the opportunity to know them better. Men teach us different things about life and ourselves; they can broaden our perspective, add to our insight, challenge us to learn and grow. Sometimes there can be greater objectivity between you and your friend than between you and your lover. It is foolish to discard all members of the opposite sex simply because they cannot be potential lovers or husbands. A sensitive woman can easily convey to a potential male friend that she respects him and would like to know him better, but she is not interested in a romantic relationship. You have undoubtedly heard many times that the male ego refuses to accept this, but that is part of the unreasonable idea that men are animals first and human beings second.

I participated in a discussion about this once in a therapy group, and there was present a lovely, intelligent, but sexually frustrated and unhappy woman whom all the men claimed they wished to "protect"; the majority of the men also admitted they wanted to take her to bed. As we discussed differences among women, the men in the group decided I was aloof and sexually cool compared to this woman. One man said to me "Why, you're like Joan of Arc, so how could a man think of making a pass at you?" But that was the way I wanted to be sensed by the men there—as a woman who was impervious to a pass because I was deeply in love and not sexually available.

I know a rather plain woman who got her second husband by being his closest friend. She realized she would not be able to attract him as a sweetheart because she was not very attractive physically, but she knew he would like her if they had time together. She concentrated on developing a warm, close friendship with him. After several years he realized her virtues and charm had so completely disarmed him that he was in love with her. Once he saw the beauty of her soul, she had become essential to his happiness. They are now married and still friends.

What about more casual relationships with men? Don't overlook the need to remain on friendly terms with neighbors, gas-station attendants, owners of hardware stores, your insurance agent, gardeners, delivery men, and others of similar status.

You may not think of yourself as a damsel in distress after your divorce, but many men will. They will offer help of one kind or another, and their intentions will be honorable. But there will be those few who suddenly behave in new and peculiar ways. Perhaps one day you'll ask a neighbor to look at your broken-down furnace. Somehow he gets the idea that you want more from him than help with that furnace, so he says something completely out of character— and out of line. You always thought he was decent and happily married and you feel outraged because he's offering his "services." Don't be coy or cute. Firmly but gently let him know you are not interested in anything but his knowledge about furnaces. Be certain you are not overtly inviting advances. Some divorced women naïvely complain about passes, but these attentions are usually solicited by a woman's manner of dress, behavior, or speech. True, some men feel a pass is expected of them; others behave much differently than we would like them to. If you do not think of yourself as fair game, you'll be treated with courtesy and respect. Whenever I have asked a male neighbor for help, I've made a point to have my children present when he came to our home. If I've offered a drink, it has been coffee or a soft drink or a beer, but I have not made a practice of inviting someone's husband to have a martini with me. It's possible to have good friendly relations with men after divorce if your behavior is above reproach and you govern yourself with good sense.

One well-built, pretty divorced mother I know told me how she handles these situations. When she suns in her yard she wears rollers in her hair or a patch of zinc oxide on her nose so the impact of her bikini is a little less stunning to her male neighbors. If she pops in to borrow a hammer, she tries to look messy if the husbands are home because she knows her female neighbors now consider her a threat. When she visits married friends, she cuts her visits short when the husband appears, because she recognizes that very few women want to share their husband's precious time with divorcees. She has plenty of friends of both sexes.

Some men are jerks—face it. If a jerky neighbor makes a pass, ignore it. If he does it repeatedly, let him know in no uncertain terms that you are neither available nor interested. Your genuine male friends will not insult you or risk embarrassing themselves by making offers or propositons you are neither ready for nor interested in.

One jerk told me that he kept close track of the women he knew who were going through divorce because they were sexually frustrated and easy to engage in affairs. Yes, there are plenty of men (if you want to call them men) around who will try to exploit you because they think you are desperate and not in control emotionally. Recognize them as jerks and don't be flattered by their attentions. Fortunately, at last count, they appear to be in the minority.

THE DIVORCEE'S BUSINESS RELATIONSHIPS

You'll now be in complete charge of the business end of your life. There's no one but you to take care of car, life, health, and other kinds of insurance; income tax; stocks and bonds; property improvements and major purchases for your home, and so forth. You'll deal directly with men in a number of professions, depending upon your style of life. You'll need competent advice and efficient service more than ever because you have neither time nor money for costly mistakes. Be sure to pay your bills promptly to the plumber, tax man, landscape service, repair men, and so forth so they'll serve you again when you need them. If you must delay a payment, call or send a note of explanation. Most men will be lenient with you for the first year or so after your divorce, but after that, you'd better be organized.

Know what you need and want, ask intelligent questions, and don't go around waving your arms, saying "Oh, I'm so dumb—I just don't know what to do." If you don't know, *find out*. Most men are not especially charmed by incompetence or stupidity. Don't expect free advice. At times the professional men you deal with may be willing to discuss a particular problem without charging a fee. They know you're adjusting to being alone. Read books or articles that will help answer your questions.

My insurance agent has always given me excellent advice and service regarding my family's insurance needs. I try to save his time by preparing myself in advance when I have a question.

A competent attorney is indispensable. If you had good rapport with the one who handled your divorce, you may wish to retain him for future problems. He can prevent you from making serious, expensive mistakes. The woman alone should *always* get informed advice before making major decisions that involve large sums of money. As a new divorcee, you may be inclined to make impulsive decisions based on emotion instead of reason. A smart lawyer can protect you from yourself until you're in better control.

It pays to have smooth relations with your landlord if you must rent. You'll need service and repairs to your living quarters, and if you and your children are exemplary tenants, you'll get what you need promptly. Keep the youngsters under control so that they do not damage property or disturb your neighbors. You probably had a hard time finding a place that would accept children, so you don't want to go through all *that* again. It also pays to have cordial relations with the others in your apartment building. Most apartment dwellers I have talked to think of their living quarters as temporary; the ones with children plan to own their own homes, and the ones without children plan to marry or move on soon. Even though you may think you will live in your apartment for a year or two and no more, you could end up there a long time. You don't have the same rights when you rent as when you own. If you are forced to be late with your rent, offer an explanation and be sure it doesn't happen habitually.

The other men in your community you and your children will come in contact with—the pharmacist, their scoutmasters and music teachers, baseball coaches, and the like—all can help you in small ways. Be aware that some will try to exploit you because you're alone. They may think you don't know what's happening. At times you may be overcharged for goods and services. The worst offenders seem to be appliance-repair men, so when you need something overhauled, do your best to be knowledgeable about what's wrong. Ask a male friend to look at the washing machine or television before you call a service man so that you can say "It needs a new tube" or "The gasket is shot." Find a car mechanic you can trust (usually a man can tell you where to get excellent service) and keep your car in top condition.

When a man repairs something for you, ask how it's done, watch so you can do it yourself the next time, and *do it* the next time. Keep a notebook in the kitchen and list all the things you should know as you learn them—what type of fuses to buy, what size washers to use in faucets, what brand of fertilizer to use on your lawn, whom to call when the septic tank overflows or how you can prevent it from happening again.

Don't expect the men you date to help with the maintenance of your home. That is your problem. Any job that takes more than five minutes is not the responsibility of a casual date. If you mention that something is broken and you don't know how to repair it, you may embarrass your date if he is not the fix-it type. Perhaps he has never been married and lives in an apartment; perhaps he's never seen a wrench. I dated one marvelously mechanical man who loved to repair broken storm doors and window latches, and almost every time he came to my home he spent ten minutes or so repairing something. If you have such a friend, treat him well—serve him the best steak available; after all, it's cheaper than hiring repair men!

THE DIVORCEE ON THE JOB

A new stimulus in your life, if you have never worked outside the home, will undoubtedly be working with or for men. Work provides excellent opportunities to meet all kinds of men—you may even meet your next husband on the job. If you've been employed right along, your employer is more likely to tolerate any temporary inefficiency caused by your broken marriage. But the woman going through a divorce will run into trouble on a new job unless she keeps regular hours and is on time, alert, and efficient. Leave your personal problems at home. The woman with children to support can be an excellent employee, once she has come to terms with herself about her emotional problems. A book that might be helpful is *380 Part-Time Jobs for Women* by Ruth Lembech (Dell Publishing Co.), available in paperback.

The men you work with will be sympathetic and friendly at first, but they do expect you to be competent. You may be discriminated against occasionally for a variety of reasons—perhaps your male co-workers know your husband and side with him; perhaps they think you are after their higher-paying jobs; perhaps some of them are becoming a little too frisky to suit you. Several women have told me that hard work was excellent therapy after divorce. If you are lucky enough to have a job which is a challenge and offers a future, do your best. You may surprise yourself and your boss.

ROMANTIC RELATIONSHIPS

You, as a mature woman with a child or several children and a marriage and divorce behind you, undoubtedly have new questions about love. What sort of love and marriage partner can you be now; what are your chances to find happiness in love? Because a romantic love relationship is the most important and intimate relationship that can exist between two persons, it is vitally important you have a realistic guide to test those relationships. It's far too dangerous to let feelings alone determine if you are in love.

Love today is a matter of individual choice, but you must be *free* to make that choice. After divorce, you're legally free, but you must also be free in other ways. One of the poorest reasons to choose a second husband is because of dire economic need, yet a great many divorced mothers marry again because of money problems. Another danger is to need someone because you are psychologically dependent; many women who cannot bear to be alone grab the first man who asks or succumbs and spend years regretting their haste. Still another danger is to marry because of sexual need. Our divorce rate is high because of the persons who marry and divorce two and three and four times; they feel forced into impulsive choices because of inner pressures.

Romantic love today, with its great emphasis on the value of the individual, could not have existed for primitive man; the group was more important than the individual, and close emotional ties between two persons then would have been impossible. One's mate had to be physically strong for survival purposes, and persons were more interchangeable because of the few differences between individuals.

As suggested earlier in this book, the primary cause of divorce is value conflicts. By the same reasoning, the primary basis for love is similar values. Two individuals meet and feel some kind of "mysterious" attraction; they find pleasure in one another's company, they wish to share certain aspects of life together, and they feel mutual sexual desire. Each feels that the loved one is of great value, and they learn to value one another more and more. They are motivated by a desire for happiness in their relationship. Upon close examination, they discover the attraction between them is not so mysterious after all. There are many good reasons for them to be in love.

This is part of an essay titled "Philosophy and Sense of Life" by Ayn Rand:

Love is a response to values. It is with a person's sense of life that one falls in love—with that essential sum, that fundamental stand or way of facing existence, which illuminates an entire personality. One falls in love with the embodiment of the values that formed a person's character which are reflected in his widest goals or smallest gestures, which create the *style* of his soul—the individual style of a unique, unrepeatable, irreplaceable consciousness. It is one's own sense of life that acts as the selector, and responds to what it recognizes as one's own basic values in the person of another. It is not a matter of professed convictions (though these are not irrelevant); it is a matter of much more profound, conscious and *subconscious* harmony.*

What are the basic elements of a good romantic relationship? What sort of woman is capable of achieving the heights of emotional, intellectual, physical, and spiritual love; what sort of man? What is ideal femininity? Ideal masculinity? What can one expect in a rewarding romantic relationship? What about sex and the divorced mother? These are some of the questions to be explored in the rest of this chapter.

The majority of divorcees (especially those with young children) hope to remarry, and so most of my comments are directed to those women. All women have some problems in common regarding their love relationships, but there are special conflicts for the divorced mother because she must always consider the needs of her children as well as her own.

* *The Objectivist Magazine,* February, 1966.

There are undoubtedly many divorced women who have no intention of remarrying for one reason or another, including career demands, negative feelings about marriage, advanced age or poor health, financial status—some women may find it advantageous to remain single because of generous alimony payments, desire to travel and meet many men rather than become attached to one, or the wish to avoid all men except for business purposes.

If you enjoy your single style of life, be aware that many persons who are not so happy will regularly question you. Comments such as "You sure do look tired—you need a husband to take over" or "When are you going to settle down?" or "Your children need a father—why don't you marry again?" or, the cruelest of all, "You don't have many good years left—you'd better find a husband before it's too late," and many more will upset and irritate you. Don't even bother to reply or be defensive. If you've decided that marriage is not for you, that it isn't the be-all and end-all of your existence, just go on enjoying your life in your chosen way. Most people will attempt to show concern, but occasionally you'll run into a clod who is motivated by envy rather than pure concern for your welfare. Consider the source.

In the meantime, whether you plan to stay single or hope to remarry as soon as possible, you no doubt will meet a variety of men. Let us therefore explore the problems and delights of dating.

DATING AND THE DIVORCED MOTHER

Your best protection against hasty remarriage is to meet and date a number of men. Statistics show an alarmingly high divorce rate for second marriages: two out of five. This should serve as warning that it would be wise to take your time before you remarry. You may feel you're too busy with other demands and don't have much time for dating; or perhaps you want to get into another marriage immediately.

The years you spend between your first and second marriage will probably be your only real opportunity to form your character and clarify your values if you have not done so before your first marriage. Recognize your need to grow, learn, and develop as an individual, not as part of a couple. You need the opportunity to interact with a variety of men in a variety of situations. Several years of dating and even several love affairs are far less traumatic than a second marriage failure.

When my children were curious about my dating practices right after my divorce, I said: "I would like to marry again some time, but first I must meet and know different types of men so that I can pick the one best for me." I explained that I met their father when I was a mere eighteen, dated him for two years, married at twenty, and lived with him until I was almost thirty. They could understand that I wished to avoid another mistake. Neither boy developed the habit of nagging me about remarriage. I have been honest with them and have included them in many of my activities whenever possible, although it was difficult to duplicate anything like the family life that can exist in a marriage which is going well. If your children seem especially interested in your romantic life, it is primarily because they want to be part of a united family and hope to see you remarry. Be sure they don't rush you!

The way you handle dating depends upon your age, the number of children you have, your background, financial status, the kind of work you do, your geographical location, among other factors. If you live in an area where there are not many single men, consider moving. As mentioned earlier, there are apartment complexes springing up all over the country which cater to single men and women. Perhaps you live in a state in which the females outnumber the males.

The men you date will teach you much you did not know before about life, love, different occupations, and styles of life. If you think of this as a continuation of your education, you'll enjoy yourself a lot more.

For me, meeting eligible men was not a problem; finding *desirable* men was. *Eligible* simply means available. I soon learned that many men were available primarily because they were undesirable. Many eligible men like to think of themselves as highly desirable because so many women compete for their attention. But women are sometimes forced to compete because we outnumber men and also outlive them! Many more men are homosexuals than are women, many of them are in the service or off to war, and a good number of them are locked away in various institutions. Many more men become "skid-row" dropouts from society than do women. All these factors decrease the supply, thereby increasing the demand.

My two best sources for dates were close friends and large parties. I have never looked for men in bars, nor did I find it necessary to join "singles" clubs, but I see nothing wrong with either. Men are everywhere, but since *you* can't be everywhere, you must choose places and activities that appeal to you most so you're likely to find an appealing man. One man I dated steadily for more than a year I met in group therapy—we were both interested in becoming more stable and had much in common.

Condition your children in a relaxed way that you're going to date. Let them participate occasionally so there will not be so much mystery about your new social life. However, do not include them in everything, or they'll get the idea your dates are actually *theirs* and you may end up sitting alone in the kitchen with a magazine while your friend plays darts with your son.

A man will be favorably impressed by your maternal qualities, but don't go overboard. Remember that he is more interested in you than he is in your children; he'll take them as part of the bargain after he has made up his mind about you. Protect him from them until he demonstrates genuine interest.

Some men just naturally adore kids. If you find such a gem, he'll no doubt suggest many activities for all of you. However, the average man you'll date will be either an older, unmarried bachelor who knows little about children and may even be afraid of them, or else he's a divorced father who feels guilty about any time he spends with another man's children. Beware the man who's more interested in your children than he is in you. He may be a frustrated camp-director or scout-leader type who never had any of his own and may not be interested in being a lover, husband, or father—he just wants to be a pal to kids. Also watch out for the man who constantly teams up with your children against you, so that you always look like an old meanie because you won't let them sip your martini or stay up until two watching the Late Show. Be on the lookout for all such signs of arrested development; they could cause acute problems for your children.

Look for good masculine qualities in the men you date. If you want to be mother to a grown man, that's your problem. If you become involved with a man who dislikes children, don't consider him marriage material (unless your children are grown and you don't plan to have any more). You need a man who can be a real help rather than a hindrance in your family, so look for one who can make daily life sweet.

Consider these points:

1. *Be selective about the men you spend time with.* Learn what the man's values are, on the first date if possible. If they clash too violently with yours, drop him. Don't be fooled by what you think is "great chemistry" if you can't agree about anything. His friends will undoubtedly be much like he is, and you won't gain anything by using him to meet other men (although if men are in short supply, try it—there are exceptions to all rules).

2. *Don't limit yourself to one man at first.* Meet as many new and different men as you have time for, but don't spread youself too thin. You're not trying to run a relay race. In my first year of dating, I counted the dates I'd had after one exhausting week: four lunch dates, two coffee dates, one cocktail date, three evening dates, and one Sunday-afternoon date. Eleven different men, and not one I cared to see a second time. The woman who works full-time had better not try such a schedule or she'll drop dead in a month. I limited myself to about two or three dates a week after that.

3. *Don't anticipate that each new man who calls will be "the one."* A deep, appealing telephone voice too often belongs to an unappealing man. (But don't be put off by a voice that doesn't turn you on. My second husband did not interest me the first time we talked on the telephone. I had corresponded with him for about a year before we met. When he returned to Michigan, he called, and after talking to him I had no special desire to meet him other than mild curiosity. That all changed after we met two weeks later.)

If you anxiously expect the next man you meet or talk to to be "him," you'll set yourself up for countless disappointments. There are few—too few—Prince Charmings around; the less up-tight you are, the more relaxed you can be when you meet a man. A woman who is too obviously man-hunting scares off desirable men. The word gets out that you're desperate and you lessen your chances to meet a man you can respect, admire, and eventually love. You *will* attract jerks and creeps—the ones who are after sex but not a deep emotional involvement. A worthwhile man is careful about whom he gives himself to—not just physically, but emotionally, intellectually, and spiritually as well.

4. *Don't use sex as a weapon or as bait.* Recognize that you're probably sexually frustrated because of your unhappy marriage. Try not to confuse sexual gratification with genuine love. As a woman you need both—be sure you are equipped to give as well as get both. If you seem to have enormous tension and unfulfilled needs, trouble sleeping and relaxing, and so forth, take your problems to a competent psychotherapist rather than play musical beds. I almost fell for a man who said, right after my divorce, "I'll bet no one has ever made love to you properly" until I realized it was just another line jerks use on newly divorced women. Remember: You're vulnerable. Become strong so that *you* can choose. Don't allow any man to use you.

5. *Don't limit yourself to any special age group, profession, or type of man.* Stay open-minded and as flexible as possible, and you'll have a better chance of letting love come into your life.

LOVE, SEX, AND THE DIVORCED MOTHER

You should know the difference between infatuation (or neurotic love) and authentic love. If you are infatuated, you respond to a particular characteristic of a person, but not to the *whole* person. You're caught in irrational responses and motives, and there is a good deal of fear, anxiety, and game-playing in neurotic love. I think this is where the idea of pain and suffering as an adjunct to love comes in. But in authentic love between two mature individuals, there is a minimum of suffering and anguish because the lovers want to make each other happy and are reasonable enough to be able to do so. In infatuation, the involved individuals are not in control of their existence and consequently are unable to do much to make each other happy. Because the individual who falls into neurotic love is not thinking clearly, he lives in a whirlpool of disturbing, sometimes overwhelmingly frightening emotions.

Authentic romantic love is for adults—there is no room for deception, game-playing, or illusion, and the lovers experience a profound emotional response based on each other's sense of life. The loved one becomes important to your happiness and is responsible for your heightened self-awareness. You wish to interact in every way, and give to one another. According to psychologist-philosopher Nathaniel Branden, there are three crucial characteristics of a good love relationship: (1) Each partner has a good effect on the other; (2) one feels an enhanced sense of one's value as a human being; (3) if the relationship is good, one does not need to fight to preserve one's self-esteem and sense of self.

In an essay Mr. Branden writes:

Of the various pleasures that man can offer himself, the greatest is *pride* —the pleasure he takes in his own achievements and in the creation of his own character. The pleasure he takes in the character and achievements of another human being is that of *admiration*. The highest expression of the most intense union of these two responses—pride and admiration—is romantic love. Its celebration is sex.

It is in this sphere above all—in a man's romantic-sexual responses— that his view of himself and of existence stands eloquently revealed. A man falls in love with and sexually desires the person who reflects his own deepest values. . . . A man of self-esteem, a man in love with himself and with life, feels an intense need to find human beings he can admire—to find a spiritual equal whom he can love. The quality that will attract him most is self-esteem—self-esteem and an unclouded sense of the value of existence. To such a man, sex is an act of celebration, its meaning is a tribute to himself and to the woman he has chosen, the ultimate form of experiencing concretely and in his own person the value and joy of being alive.*

If your values regarding love and sex are confused, your behavior will conflict with your thoughts and emotions. One of the big questions you must answer as a divorced mother is "What do I think about sex outside marriage?" You must decide whether you think it is moral and proper for a responsible adult to participate in sexual intimacy without the legal and social sanction of a marriage contract. If your romantic life becomes something you feel you must lie about to your children and perhaps others, you must stop to evaluate *what* you are doing and *why*.

* "The Psychology of Pleasure", by Nathaniel Branden, page 65, from *The Virtue of Selfishness*, by Ayn Rand, New American Library, 1964.

It is not my intention to advise any woman to have or not to have a sex life after divorce and before another marriage. Such a decision is determined by many factors: your philosophy of life, your code of ethics, your values and standards, your physical and mental health, age, needs, and sex temperament.

Though the expression of sexuality is often a serious problem for both sexes in our society, it is usually more a problem for women than for men. Most divorcees I've talked to have had some sexual difficulty in and out of marriage. Attorney Louis Nizer goes so far as to say: ". . . the greatest single cause for family unit destruction and divorce in this country is a fundamental sexual inadequacy within the marital unit." * Poor sex relations are the rule rather than the exception, it seems. It is beyond the scope of this book to present a thorough exploration of this, and discussion is limited to some of the sex problems of the divorced mother.

There can be as many risks in participating in sex without marriage for the older divorced woman as there are for the inexperienced young woman: guilt, anxiety, risk of unwanted pregnancy, possibility of contracting a venereal disease and of ruining one's chances to bear children, loss of one's good reputation. The divorced mother has an additional problem: her children.

Yes, there are risks. Many more for you than for the man you sleep with. If this sounds as though I'm saying "No matter what, don't do it," read me again. If you are a mature woman, you should be emotionally equipped to handle a responsible romantic relationship and choose a man with whom you can have such a relationship. You should know what you think and why you think it. If you are clear in your own mind about this, you need never defend your actions to anyone. It is a matter of personal choice, as it has always been for all women, regardless of what various institutions have demanded of us.

Here is part of an interview with philosopher and writer Ayn Rand:

QUESTION: You have denounced the puritan notion that physical love is ugly or evil; yet you have written that "Indiscriminate desire and unselective indulgence are possible only to those who regard sex and them-

* From the introduction to *Human Sexual Response,* by William H. Masters and Virginia E. Johnson, Boston: Little, Brown and Co., 1966.

selves as evil." Would you say that discriminate and selective indulgence in sex *is* moral?

RAND: I would say that a selective and discriminate sex life is not an indulgence. The term indulgence implies that it is an action taken lightly and casually. I say that sex is one of the most important aspects of man's life and, therefore, must never be approached lightly or casually. A sexual relationship is proper only on the ground of the highest values one can find in a human being. Sex must not be anything other than a response to values. And that is why I consider promiscuity immoral. Not because sex is evil but because sex is too good and too important.

QUESTION: Does this mean, in your view, that sex should involve only married partners?

RAND: Not necessarily. What sex should involve is a very serious relationship. Whether that relationship should or should not become a marriage is a question which depends on the circumstances and the context of the two persons' lives. I consider marriage a very important institution, but it is important *when* and *if* two people have found the person with whom they wish to spend the rest of their lives—a question of which no man or woman can be automatically certain. When one is certain that one's choice is final, then marriage is, of course, a desirable state. But this does *not* mean that any relationship based on less than total certainty is improper. I think the question of an affair or a marriage depends on the knowledge and the position of the two persons involved and should be left up to them. Either is moral, provided only that both parties take the relationship seriously and that it is based on values.*

Any discussion of sex and the divorced mother must include also a discussion of the love needs of women. Most women who have been unhappily married dream of having a tender, considerate lover who will be the "great love" of their lives. I think most women who divorce their husbands, whether or not they have another man selected for the next marriage, do so because they believe a great love is possible for them. According to Havelock Ellis:

A woman may have been married once, she may have been married twice, she may have had children by both husbands, and yet it may not be until she is past the age of thirty and is united to a third man that she attains the development of erotic personality and all that it involves in the full flowering of her whole nature . . . and it is often the lover more than the husband that the modern woman needs. . . . Of woman as a real human being, with sexual needs and sexual responsibilities, morality has often known nothing.†

* *Playboy* magazine.
† *On Life and Sex* (New York: Mentor Books, 1957), p. 85.

Perhaps the divorcee's husband was impotent or a grossly poor, inconsiderate lover. Kinsey found that about 45 per cent of all married men interviewed felt their sexual performance inadequate. According to findings of various sexologists, perhaps 25 per cent of all men are impotent or inadequate. Dr. Albert Ellis says, in *Sex and the Single Man:* "Literally millions of American males today are sex perverts or deviants." It appears we are in short supply of men who can be tender, considerate, strong lovers and husbands.

Both men and women have been tragically cheated in their love lives for countless reasons too complex to cover in this book. Although I am told there is a sexual revolution going on, that so-called revolution has done little to change the effects of repression, inhibition, hypocrisy, and the thwarting of normal sexual desires, at least for many members of my generation. It is not sufficient just to *want* a rewarding love and sex life—a considerable amount of thought, pain, change of attitude, and rational action is necessary.

It is impossible to write about this without turning to my own experiences and training. I've wondered what things actually shaped my early attitudes about love. As a former Catholic, I was struck by these words in an article by John Ciardi in the September 21, 1968, *Saturday Review:*

For there is a fundamental anti-sexual bias in all Christianity, and though some latter day sects have become possibly more anti-sexual than the Catholic church, church doctrine and church practice still think of sex as an evil to be tolerated only within the sacramental dispensation of matrimony and then only for the specific purpose of begetting children for God's harvest of souls.

If you have good reason to believe your marriage failed because of misinformation or sexual inadequacy, get the most competent help available and move on to a new and more satisfying phase of your life. You may have been a frigid, unloving wife, or you may have had a repressed, impotent husband, but with the proper changes in your own attitude and personality, and with the right partner, love is possible.

Psychoanalyst Theodor Reik says, in *Of Love and Lust,* that "Only the brave can struggle to love." The search for authentic love is certainly worth the effort. But sometimes one is also foolhardy while learning to be brave. Don't be afraid to be hurt. If you are overcautious and unable to trust yourself or another enough to love again, love will elude you. You must be strong enough to take the risk.

I am willing to bet that nine out of ten newly divorced persons are not ready for a *great* love. You may desire it intensely, but being capable of achieving it may take several years and perhaps several attempts which end in neither love nor marriage. Sick, unhappy marriages cripple, stunt, or warp some individuals—but not necessarily for a lifetime.

As one who has been changed by divorce, I have many opinions about love and sex that I did not hold while unhappily married. I believe genuine love is impossible for the woman who lacks self-esteem. Perhaps your biggest problem during marriage was that you did not think yourself a worthwhile human being (you may be very worthy indeed, but if you *think* you are inadequate and worthless, more often than not you will be treated as if you were—by husband, children, friends, and others). If you considered yourself not worthwhile, it follows that you would not expect anything so wonderful as romantic love and sexual ecstasy to happen to poor worthless you. The woman with self-esteem is probably going to succeed in love for these reasons:

1. She recognizes her own worth and wants others to recognize it as well.

2. Knowing she is worthy of love, she chooses the most desirable, worthwhile man she can find.

3. She is strong enough (sure enough of herself) to expect and get good treatment from her man. If and when he fails to treat her properly, she is not afraid to inform him of her needs and desires. She values herself and feels she deserves to be happy; she values him and wants to make him happy too.

4. If she finds it necessary to criticize the man she loves, he is able to accept her criticism because he realizes she is a worthy judge of his actions.

A great love consists of having superb communication on four levels: emotional, intellectual, physical, and spiritual. Some of us live a whole lifetime without ever having all four. Perhaps you're willing to settle for three out of four, or two out of four. If you're holding out for all four, you may end up alone, or you just could meet him and have the most rewarding love experience possible. I know several women who waited; they claim it was well worth it. One said of her third husband: "A day with him was worth the eight years of waiting."

Philosopher Max Scheler sees the essence of love as the capacity to grasp the gist, the central value of a personality, in a single perception. Love disregards manifest qualities and sees right through them down to the true essential value.* If you have had the thrilling experience of "love at first sight" and wonder if you've gone somewhat daffy, don't be too suspicious of your perceptions. It *is* possible to see into someone's soul in one full perception and know that you could love that person. If it happens to you but not to the other person, don't run from it. Pursue it as gracefully as you can. I've talked to several women who have had this happen to them; they were confident and persevering and today they are with their men. One was a patient in a hospital when she met her future husband— he was an intern who examined her, and she knew he was the man for her, though it took her some months to convince him.

The stress and misery of an unhappy marriage can shred a woman's ego. Any new liaison must be entered into with a spirit of hope and optimism, but at the same time a woman must try to remain objective. Simone de Beauvoir says in *The Second Sex:*

But a new lover who is respectful, amorous, and sensitive can best transform the despitefully used woman into a happy mistress or wife; if he frees her from her inferiority complex, she will give herself with ardor.

It takes much more than a respectful, amorous, sensitive lover to repair a woman's ego. She must change her life and her behavior so that she has reasons, *real* reasons, to shed her inferiority complex. One does not shed it in bed. A good lover cannot make a woman feel what she is not. If she is ill-equipped to handle her life's problems, no amount of good sex and tender love scenes will transform her into the woman she dreams of being. Any such change in her behavior will be only temporary and will end when the love affair does, unless she learns to feel authentically proud about who she is for authentic reasons.

* A. M. Krich (ed.), *Women: The Variety and Meaning of Their Sexual Experience* (New York: Dell Publishing Co., 1953), p. 292.

LOVE, SEX, AND MORALITY

As a divorced mother you must clarify your thoughts about love, sex, and morality because you pass on values that will shape your children's lives for good or ill. The woman who decides that sex is evil, ugly, and degrading, that men are not worth loving, that true love cannot exist between a man and woman will convey these attitudes to her children either explicitly or implicitly. You must demonstrate that romantic love is a value worth struggling to achieve.

I believe that the sex lives of consenting adults are their private business unless their actions harm others. You will not derive much comfort from the knowledge that if you, as an unmarried female, participate in sexual intercourse (or almost any other sexual activity), you are breaking one or more laws, however unenforceable and antiquated they may be. Very few individuals are caught and prosecuted, and the fact that laws exist prohibiting and inhibiting the love lives of consenting adults in the twentieth century is appalling. I hope this book brings about additional discussion regarding divorce, sex and the law, because only through intelligent discussion and dissent can we change irrelevant and outdated laws.

Supposing an author of a book of this nature wanted to use a personal experience to illustrate a point about love and sex—she would have to admit in print that she as a single divorced mother had broken a law, for which, technically, she could be convicted. Also, such a person could possibly face a custody battle on the ground of being "morally unfit" (although it is difficult to prove that women are "unfit" mothers because of their illegal sexual activities).

Our children are begging us for honesty and reason. They hear parents saying many things in public and doing just the opposite in private. They see that much of what we call morality is not moral at all, and they resent the hypocrisy and irrationality of many adults in power.

If what you do is moral, it is also moral for your child someday to emulate your behavior. If what you do is immoral, it is immoral whether or not you have children.

The divorced childless woman is free to pursue any kind of love life she chooses. The divorced mother is not so free. A Caucasian divorced mother who falls in love with and marries a Negro man could possibly lose custody of her children (there is evidence of such a case, although the judge claimed the child was taken away from her mother for reasons other than interracial marriage). Even though you are a mother, you are also an adult female with intense, unfulfilled sexual and romantic needs. Your divorce does not change that. You are responsible for the moral training of your children. If you feel that your actions are so shameful that you would be mortified if your children ever learned you have a sex and love life, it is time to rethink things. You may even benefit from psychotherapy. The only problems your children should present to your romantic life are simple, practical problems. Don't use their existence as the reason for your psychological problems about sex.

The divorced mother who is shamed by the question "Did you and Mr. Brown make love last night?" must examine her emotions and values regarding love and sex. If your answer is "yes" and you feel guilty, you have not resolved your own conflict. Why do you continue to do something you think is wrong? Is it really wrong? Have you thought about your own moral position on this, or have you unquestioningly accepted what was taught to you? One divorced mother told me her teenage son asked her that very question. She responded vehemently: "I do not feel it necessary to discuss my private life with a child." But he was not just any child, he was *her* child, and his question indicated his attempt to understand what goes on between adults in romantic relationships—the boy was aware, curious, and ready to form values. He showed remarkable insight when he replied "That means yes you did. If you had said 'no' right out, then I'd think well, *maybe* you did." What followed was an honest and intense discussion about human sexuality and morality.

Because there is no father present in a divorced home, the mother must be equipped to teach her children about love and male-female relationships. Be sure your values are clear so you can face the issues squarely. Your child must feel free to ask *any* question (even those which appear to invade your privacy) and know he will get a reasonable answer.

Whether you decide to have a sex life without marriage or not is not the issue here: the real issue is that you are consistently honest with yourself as well as your child, that your values are rational and clear to you both and are based on what *you know* to be moral, not on cloudy premises foisted on you by others.

If you decide to have a sex life openly and not try to hide it from your children, be aware that they may talk about it when you least expect them to. You can't expect them to lie or cover for you, but you can teach them the meaning of discretion and privacy.

Of the many divorcees I have met, I know of just one woman who refrained from all sexual contact after her divorce. She remarried about five years later, without having had sexual intercourse with her second husband until their honeymoon. She is the exception rather than the rule.

The divorced woman becomes sexually involved for many reasons. For one thing, it is difficult to turn off one's hormones and sex drive after having lived as a married person. Second, some women may have had such enormously ego-shattering sexual experiences in marriage that they are determined to find out if they actually *are* as inept or undesirable as their marriages would have indicated. Third, there are women desperate enough for affection to allow themselves to be used sexually by men they casually date. Fourth, there are many women who simply think sex is a great thing—that it's fun, exciting, healthy, and not to be taken very seriously. Then of course there are women with serious emotional disturbances who use sex for escape from reality. How do *you* choose to express yourself sexually?

The sexually active female of any age will not lose her responsiveness. Masters and Johnson say in their book *Human Sexual Response:*

Regardless of involutional changes in the reproductive organs, the aging human female is fully capable of sexual performance at orgasmic response levels, particularly if she is exposed to regularity of effective sexual stimulation.

Perhaps you are one of millions of women who experience orgasm rarely or not at all, and you wonder if the fault was in your husband. Perhaps you think you'll have a better love life after changing partners. You may have a number of misconceptions about sex ability in both male and female, all of which may have contributed to your unhappiness in marriage. You may have read somewhere that there is only one kind of *legitimate* orgasm—that which is obtained vaginally during intercourse—and the woman who does not experience vaginal orgasm is frigid. Perhaps you have reached climax another way and mistakenly think you have not been having "real" orgasms. But, according to Masters and Johnson, "There may be great variation in duration and intensity of orgasmic experience, varying from individual to individual and within the same woman from time to time. However, when any woman experiences orgasmic response to effective sexual stimulation, the vagina and clitoris react in consistent physiologic patterns. Thus, clitoral and vaginal orgasms are not separate biologic entities." *

Seek professional help if you have any doubts about your sexual ability. A thorough examination by a gynecologist should be first on your list. If you feel the need to discuss a sex problem, consult your doctor, and if he decides your trouble is deep-rooted, he will refer you to a psychiatrist or psychologist.

For readers who are interested in increasing their knowledge, here is a list of recommended readings suggested at the lectures I attended on "The Psychology of Romantic Love." These books can be obtained at the public library, although some of them are inexpensive enough to add to your personal library. *Human Sexual Response* is a highly technical book, and you might want to read instead *An Analysis of Human Sexual Response,* by Edward and Ruth Brecher, available in paperback.

The Natural History of Love by Morton Hunt

Encyclopedia of Sexual Behavior (2 volumes), edited by Albert Ellis and Albert Abarbanel

Human Sexual Response by William Howard Masters and Virginia E. Johnson

The Marriage Art by John E. Eichenlaub

Modern Sex Techniques by Robert Street

---

* Other experts, among them psychologists Dr. Albert Ellis and Nathaniel Branden, agree with this.

It has been estimated that possibly three-fourths of all married couples suffer from serious sexual problems. A new and dramatic treatment for problems such as impotence, inability to achieve orgasm, premature ejaculation, has been developed by Dr. William Masters and Mrs. Virginia Johnson, authors of *Human Sexual Response.* The method is a two-week intensive seven-day-a-week therapy conducted by a male and female therapist with both husband and wife. So far their method has helped 80 percent of their patients. See the August 1968 *Ladies' Home Journal,* page 54.

The Art and Science of Love by Albert Ellis
The Feminine Mystique by Betty Friedan
The American Male by Myron Brenton

If sex was a problem in your marriage, you will probably seek information and facts to help you understand why. You may be interested to know that monogamy in sex appears to reduce the risk of cancer of the cervix.* Women with cervical cancer on the average started having intercourse at an earlier age and had a greater number of sex partners. A history of early marriage ending in divorce were factors in women with cervical cancer, possibly because multiple partners increase the likelihood of passage of an unknown cancer-causing agent. Readers approaching menopause may be interested to know that there is a general loss of muscle tone and tissue elasticity after menopause, and vaginal lubrication diminishes considerably after menopause (about five years later) unless the woman has regular sexual intercourse.

If your divorce can be the catalyst for new thinking and action, you could be pleasantly surprised by the exciting changes in your attitude and life. Perhaps you will experience what many divorcees do—a complete change and rebirth. I hardly need to tell any woman who has been married how to attract a man—the biggest problem seems to be finding desirable men in your age group. Why not consider dating younger men? Biologically it makes great sense. We outlive men by an average seven years, and with all the commercial aids available plus sensible habits about diet, exercise, and rest, a woman can stay and feel young-looking well into her sixties. The male in his twenties is usually a good match sexually for the woman in her thirties.

I have dated men younger than myself and confess that a younger man encourages you to stay young. He can stimulate your thinking because he is still idealistic and energetic—he does not have middle-age spread of the mind or body. If you have the health and vitality to keep up with him, your relationship could even lead to marriage.

The younger man is somewhat awed by the wiser, older woman. If you are young-looking and like the feeling of being "worshiped," a younger man may be for you. There is one danger—the more experienced woman may try to dominate the relationship. Don't try to be his mother: forget your ages. If your love is based on values

* *McCall's*, April 1967.

other than physical appearances, a few years' difference should present no problem. It is extremely flattering and gratifying to have the love and attention of a man five or six, even ten, years younger. If you are the type who cries over each new wrinkle and grey hair, this definitely is not for you. If a marriage proposal comes up, be sure to discuss the issue of children and family. How does he feel about yours (how old are they compared to him—if you have a fourteen-year-old son and are dating a twenty-three-year-old, there could be some awkward problems—a young stepfather would have trouble asserting himself unless he is exceptionally mature). Does your love want children of his own and do you feel too old to have more? I talked to one lovely divorcee whose eldest child was seventeen—she was thirty-seven and was engaged to a man of twenty-eight who claimed he did not want to have children, but she felt he was "just saying that" because of her age.

Men and women often seem to be miles apart in their emotional and physical needs and most of the time don't even know what they want from one another. Men have complained to me that women are "generally dishonest" and "devious" and interested only in a meal ticket; women have complained that men are fickle, also dishonest, more interested in sex than anything else, or more interested in making money than in making love. Each sex accuses the other of playing games.

What *do* men want from women? One man I dated years ago gave me the best answer I have heard. He said he wanted joy and significance from the woman he loved. But I doubt that a woman can give this unless she loves life and loves herself—only then is she free to love *him*. Terms men use when talking about their ideal woman include earthy, honest, uninhibited, sense of humor, vital, sensitive, intelligent. I think that most men want their woman to be a mind-reader—they somehow expect us to *know* without being told, to be able to sense their moods and needs. I've heard again and again that women talk too much and often have nothing to say. Men would like us to be intelligent enough to know when to stop *talking* and communicate in other ways. Some men have said to me that their ex-wives were too materialistic, cold, selfish. I believe that men need more than they've been getting from us: more love, more encouragement, more inspiration, more physical intimacy, more communication on a deeper level, more compassion.

A man wants a woman to respond to *him*. If you're alarmed because your man always seems to be after sexual intimacy, remember that men are basically less complex than we are and measure love in much simpler terms. The way you respond to a man sexually is to him the clearest indication of your love; more than anything, men *want* to be loved by their women. Don't get the idea that *all* you need be is an exciting sex partner to attract and keep a man, but do remember that men like us to be uninhibited, expressive, assertive and even sassy at times!

ROMANTIC LOVE AND TRIAL MARRIAGES

The majority of divorced mothers have a love affair or two before remarrying. Some of us have more than one or two romances which look as though they might lead to marriage.* Contrary to what you may have read or heard, several romances do not necessarily mean you are fickle or unstable. Perhaps you have not become the right woman yet, or the right man for you simply has not appeared.

But suppose you have found the man you love. You become involved in a serious romance but you want to know more about one another before committing yourselves to marriage. You soon find that dating is unsatisfactory and in time you end up half-living together. This happens usually by accident rather than design. Perhaps it begins the first time your children are with their father for the night, and your man spends the night with you or invites you to his place. Then maybe he spends a whole weekend with you and your children, either at your place or his, or in a vacation setting. Or he sleeps in a guest room or on the couch, but one night you end up together in your room, and your children discover you together. Will they be emotionally disturbed as a result? There is no one answer that applies to every situation. If you're upset or feel guilty or ashamed, your children will sense it. If you feel that what has happened is right and natural, they'll sense that too.

I've talked to a number of divorced women who lived with their second husbands before marrying them. One twenty-seven-year-old childless career girl told me she would not risk making a second mistake—she was interested in learning how well they lived together

* See Morton Hunt's *World of the Formerly Married* for a more complete discussion.

because dating was too "phony": "People who criticize unmarried couples who try living together before marriage usually think we do it only for sex. But that's not the real reason. I want to know about his disposition in the morning, what he's like under pressure, what his general temperament is. When you date a guy, you see him in the evening after he has showered and shaved. Perhaps he's had a drink or two and he's considerably relaxed. Then you see him on Sunday, maybe Saturday. But how can you tell what it will be to live with him? What is his real character, what kind of moods does he have? If I had lived with my first husband before marriage, there would not have *been* a marriage. I think everyone should be able to get a license for a trial marriage if they want one." She and her lover married after a year of living together and now have a family. "If I'd had children," she said, "I'm sure I would have done the same— in fact, with children I think it's even more important to be sure."

Not everyone can handle such a situation. If you attempt to live with a man without the benefit of marriage, you and your children could be harassed and insulted, and you might find yourself ostracized in many social circles. There could be pressure from neighbors, relatives, your ex-husband. Don't slide into such a relationship without considering all the ramifications, pro and con. In the end, it is a matter of values. Yours.

SECOND TIME ROUND

The affair isn't over. You're engaged to be married and you both are so happy! He wants you to meet his family and you're understandably nervous.

What's in store for you? Well, you'll have to learn to field and answer some questions. How much has he told his parents about you? Do they somehow know "sordid" details of your past life? Remember that many members of the older generation are shocked by the high divorce rate and are predisposed to think negatively of *any* divorced person. If you are rejected outright because of your divorce, this could either end your relationship with him or cause him to have a serious, even permanent rift with his family. These are possibilities you must face. I'm not trying to set you up to think of his parents as "the Enemy," just trying to prepare you for the fact that they may consider *you* the enemy and not good enough for their son.

If you can show that you are a fine person, a good mother, a woman with values and virtue, they will not be completely against you for their son. He must be proud of himself and of you, *his choice*. If he is apologetic about you to his parents and does not protect and defend you if they should happen to attack you, expect serious problems if you marry him. The man who would let his parents decide whom he should marry is best forgotten.

You would like your first meeting with members of his family to go well, and subsequent visits to be relaxed and friendly. As one who has been looked over by prospective in-laws several times, I offer these suggestions: Agree in advance with him how much he is to tell them about you—he should do this as preparation for all of you. He knows his parents best—if they are against divorce because of a religious belief, they may resist you sight unseen because of your status, so perhaps he prefers to have them meet you first, then tell them later that you are divorced.

A first meeting on neutral ground is sometimes less taxing for all concerned, especially the prospective bride. Suggest to your fiancé that you all go out to dinner if possible rather than go to his parents' home for your first meeting. Let me explain why: his mother's home is *her* territory and if she is not the most open-minded person, you could be at an extreme disadvantage being on display for the first time on *her* stage. Undercurrents of tension could make you all nervous for that initial visit. Perhaps she is worried too about what impression she makes on you, how her home appears, and so forth. If you've been invited to dinner, she may be tired and cranky from spending time in the kitchen making preparations. Subsequent meetings and visits can be at their home or your home, but for the first one, pick neutral ground, even someone else's home (another relative perhaps, or a close friend who knows his family too). This puts you on equal footing. You are *not* a shy twenty-year-old virgin who must bow and show supreme respect for age and position—there is no need to act humble or insignificant around his mother and father. You've been married, had children, and are a woman. Many older persons make the serious mistake of treating young adults as though they were still little children.

Because you love him, you want his family to like you. Unless his parents are out-and-out swingers, it's best to underplay everything the first time you meet. Be cool, understated, don't expect the worst or the best, and remember they are only human beings. Most older persons—especially future in-laws, it seems—think all divorcees are gay and wild. How would they know that you spend all day Saturday working in the yard and on Sunday after church you cook for the following week? (Perhaps *he* could do some advance publicity for you.) They probably picture you slinking around in a low-cut dress and black net stockings, with a long cigarette holder between your fingers rather than a potato peeler. And they are *sure* you're going to break his heart. This all fits in with the stigma attached to divorce. The father will probably like you, but if he says too many nice things about you, his wife will look even harder for your flaws.

I would say a single man of thirty or so who still thinks he owes something to his mother is a poor marriage choice. He should respect her, remember her at the appropriate times, but *never* should he put his mother before you, or think he needs to explain you or apologize to her for anything about you, including your divorce.

This is all most important and not to be glossed over. The man who is still single after thirty or so is likely to have a problem *with* and *because of* his mother or even his father; if he still lives at home and seems tied to his parents, you may have to forget him. How can he be your protector and a father figure to your children if he is still a little boy at home? The man who has been married and divorced may also have a problem with his parents; he may bend over backward to please them because he failed at marriage, and now, above all, he wants their approval. Perhaps if they bad-mouth you often enough, he himself starts to wonder what it is he admires about you.

It's a shame some men must be put through this test. If it happens to you and your beloved, don't make a point of bitterly complaining about his parents to him. He knows they are being narrow-minded and is no doubt saddened by and even ashamed of their attitude. Be as calm and as gracious as possible. If he is the man you need him to be, he will firmly let his parents know that you are the woman he wants. The one main point that will eventually sell them on you is that you make him happy. If they can still resist you after that, stay away, but do your best to maintain an "open door" policy in case they change their minds and hearts.

Epilogue

As a divorced mother, you will move out of the world married women inhabit. Your biggest concern will no longer be what kind of wallpaper would look best in the hallway or how to keep up with the Joneses. Your biggest concern now is *survival*. You'll have to use everything you possess to make it. It's a challenge that may turn you into a courageous, adventurous risk-taker with many formerly undiscovered talents and abilities.

Use this time in your life to learn new approaches to everything. Crack the mold completely if you must. I have not wanted to make divorce sound too glamorous or exciting, but there *is* a certain element of excitement and glamour in it. Of course, if you're the type of woman who cannot bear emergencies and surprises, you'll have a difficult time as a divorcee. When you learn to count on yourself for almost everything, life will be easier.

I've talked a lot in this book about avoiding a hasty second marriage that could lead to another divorce, or more misery. Let me emphasize that there is no magic time or turning point that makes you ready to try again. *You* may be ready on the day your divorce is final. I was ready after six years of living as a divorced mother. As I finish this book, I'm in another phase of my life—that of a second marriage. I remarried in December, 1968, and looked forward to my new life as eagerly as any prospective bride, but this time I know much more about myself and marriage!

Divorce does not have to be a total disaster for you or your children. My sons' father and I have gone through a series of changes in our post-divorce relationship, and today we are both far more mature about how to handle our children and ourselves than we were seven years ago. Because we humans are so resilient and dynamic, we *can* live through near-disasters and not be permanently harmed by our negative experiences. Soon after my divorce, I carefully picked my way through entirely new territory (I often felt I was groping in a dark cave studded with daggers and shards of broken glass). There were many upsetting changes and events for us all, but we eventually learned to handle each new phase of our lives. I think my former husband would have to agree with me that it's too tiring and inconvenient to continue the battle after the divorce is final. We've buried the hatchet, so to speak, but not in one another's neck.

My sons love and respect their father, and their high regard for him is a result of his own good treatment of them as well as my ability to accord him the respect he deserves as their father. Whatever your feelings are toward your former mate, *do* make it possible for your children to form their own good working relationship with him.

One especially sad aspect for divorced parents is that they cannot share the growing up of their children. Oh, you can show your former mate their school- and artwork and swap little anecdotes, but it's not the same as being there, in it together. You simply cannot truly share the many funny, dear, beautiful, brilliant, or horrible things your children do. However, it could be worse—your children's father could be *dead*. When you start to feel sorry for them or yourself, remember this; then start to think about how to make things better. You will also be hurt knowing your children will grow up missing all this, yet many children grow up without either parent and somehow survive.

Another sad thing for you is that you don't receive praise from your child's father for doing a good job as a mother. Our way of divorce usually helps make the breach between mother and father final. The man usually does not want to say "I think you're doing a glorious job with our kids." The result is usually that neither of you praises the other for one of the *most significant, important jobs you do in your lifetime*. What often happens is that the divorced father develops his own way of complaining about his children, and he phrases his remarks so that you are mostly or entirely to blame. He somehow does not want to admit that the woman he could not or did not love properly might be an excellent human being and a superb mother. And of course, it may be difficult for you to approve completely of him as a father too.

I don't actually *know* what kind of father my former husband is these days—is he compassionate, firm, loving, understanding, just? I'm not around to see, and of course the children are too young to evaluate this. Nor does he know precisely how I'm functioning as a mother because he usually sees his sons in a rather holiday mood and atmosphere—they're all spiffed up and on their good behavior. It's almost impossible to think of each other as the real parents of real children. The system of checks and balances between man and woman, father and mother, is gone.

I don't think a woman ever can completely forget the father of her children. It is difficult to think of an ex-mate as *just another human being*—he will always be to you that particular person who was part of your young dream, who failed you and himself and your children. You no doubt are the same to him.

Many studies show that two things are vital to a child's later independence: warmly firm parents who admire each other and on whom he can model himself while learning to break away from them, and opportunities to prove his competence in work and love. The first requirement is extremely difficult where there has been divorce, but if you try hard, very hard, you can find things to admire about your former mate. Concentrate on them instead of his flaws when you discuss him with your children.

Many divorced persons have insomnia for a few months after it is over. The insomnia one has when one is alone is much less difficult to bear than the kind one has when one's hated mate is there, snoring and hogging the bed. On sleepless nights, get out of bed. Create something. Read, write, compose music, sew a new garment, paint a chair. Walk, run, exercise, dance by yourself, take a hot bath, eat something. But don't just lie there and fret. Eventually your insomnia will go away. It's a signal that you can't let go enough, that you have a serious unresolved conflict. Act on the conflict and the insomnia will stop. If it persists, consult your doctor. A highly tense woman may need a sedative to help her through this tough time in her life. But don't develop the habit of using drugs to solve your problems.

One possibility you must face is that you just might not marry again. Make a master plan for yourself that gives you something important and worthwhile to accomplish—select a goal and work toward it. I have seen that one of the best ways to find or be discovered by the right man is to be busy doing something else besides desperately searching for him.

Remember that women have a deep-seated need for legitimacy—don't sloppily become involved in casual affairs that make you ashamed of yourself. You no doubt ended your marriage or want to because you believe something better is possible for you. It is, but not without enormous effort. Learn to savor the freedom you and so many other women have struggled for, but learn also to bear the responsibility that necessarily goes with that freedom.

This book has been tough to write. I'm not an "expert" or an "authority" on anything but my own life. I have dedicated myself to telling the truth as I have discovered it, and have tried to pass on my insights about men, women, children, divorce, and love. Not everything I have said will apply to you because you have different attitudes, different values, different aspirations. But perhaps my words will lead you to insights of your own, and perhaps you will try again when you were ready to give up, or perhaps you will gain courage and go on, somewhat stronger in your struggle.

If you do end your marriage and find yourself back in circulation, dating and seeking a new love, take this into consideration: each man must be seen as a unique individual. You cheat yourself and narrow your thinking when you say "All men are alike" or "Who can trust men? They're all after just one thing from a woman" or any other variations of the same theme. You noticed that I did not make a list of the types of men one meets when dating, such as you find in some books or articles. I despise labels for human beings. I do not believe it is possible to put men (or women) into six or eight or ten readily recognizable categories such as "the playboy," the "domestic type," the "mama's boy," the "sportsman," and so on. Each of us is a unique, dynamic entity. We are constantly evolving. We face or do *not* face problems. We learn and try out new attitudes. Don't think of yourself in negative terms that may have been outlined for you by others, and don't judge *all* men by the experiences you've had with one.

Some men love to tell women that we are overemotional, illogical, impractical, sentimental. But it appears these men often project onto us the very attitudes they hold in abundance! Many men are more romantic, idealistic, impractical, illogical, and sentimental than women. Avoid labels for individuals and avoid them for groups too.

What *do* men want from women? I think they need and want us to be competent individuals with strength of character—not so that they can lean on us, but so that we are a source of inspiration. A man wants his woman to have a beautiful soul. He wants to believe that she is incorruptible, that she has the necessary virtue and integrity to demand the best of herself, and that she expects him to demand the best of himself also. Don't think you have the right to demand the best of a man unless you give *your* best.

When you start to date again, you may be alarmed to find men of all ages who run from woman to woman, trying to make conquest after conquest. Men like this are afraid—they sense they are weak, but can't admit they're in trouble. They don't yet have what it takes to commit themselves to another human being. A man who is so involved in "the chase" appears to be searching for a special woman to help him snap out of his fog—he does not seem to realize that he must help himself, that there is no magic woman waiting to turn him on to the meaning of life. If, however, you meet a man who has many wonderful qualities but seems to be busy chasing women, don't shut him out of your life forever. Perhaps he's recently divorced and afraid to marry or become emotionally involved again just now. Or there may be another good reason why he cannot commit himself. Go on with your life, meet other men, but do stay in contact. He may have some growing and learning to do, and when he's ready for one woman, perhaps he'll decide on you. But don't pin all your hopes on him!

We're all attempting to answer the same question: What is the meaning of life? The asking of that question gives us a common bond, but the way each individual answers is what makes each of us different. How do *you* answer the question and how would you like the man you love to answer it?

One cannot experience a divorce without significant changes in values and attitudes. I am free not only of a marriage I found disagreeable, but free of a self I did not enjoy. I am free enough to let my sons know *me*—not just as a mother who admonishes them to "do your homework–make your bed–say your prayers–write to your grandmother" but as a woman who does not always know the answer but is willing to try to find it with them; as one they can trust even though I am over thirty; as one who has made serious mistakes but learned from them. They have seen me laugh, cry, play, work, set a bad example, set a good example; they've seen me ardent, lazy, depressed, energetic, idealistic, petty. They've learned that they too can be all those things and more—and survive. They've discovered that the world won't cave in when they make a mistake or when someone they love and depend on makes a mistake.

Many of us have terrible problems about love—perhaps because we were not allowed to *know,* really know, a human being during our formative years. I'm thinking now of a friend who never saw either of his parents lose their tempers or show warm affection to anyone. His greatest problem was expressing the emotions he felt. He felt guilty and blocked half of the time and confused the other half; he learned to be *human* after the pain of divorce sent him to therapy. Far too many of us did not see or feel real love while we were forming our values—so how could we love as adults, or recognize love when it was presented to us by another?

The very first time I observed and sensed authentic romantic love, I was about eighteen years old. A friend and I went to visit a newly married couple. During the course of the evening, I realized I was in the presence of something almost holy, something I had never seen or felt before. I recall thinking as I went home, *I want that for myself someday.* For some reason, I could not hold out for it. Now, many years later, I have found it.

I have been asked "Are you sorry you're divorced?" This is impossible to answer without making several qualifications. I am sorry that, in order to survive and pursue values I knew were right for me, I had to end a marriage begun in hope and good faith. I am sorry the marriage did not provide what I had hoped it could, and I am sorry that I did not know then how to effect a small miracle. The miracle was love. It might have been easier, less a strain in many, many ways, to have continued on safely and securely as a wife, but neither of us wanted that. To this day my former husband and I do not agree about most significant issues, but we *do* agree that we want to give our sons the best that is in each of us. Yes, I am sorry that we could not stay together to do this, but I am glad that we were able to part and not live out our daily conflict in front of our sons. They have learned to know each of us in different ways—far more constructive ways than would have been possible if we had stayed together.

Every reader must know at least one married couple who, "for the sake of the children," stayed together but should not have, because they expose their offspring to vicious arguments, sullen moods, pettiness, endless bickering, or whatever happens to be their particular style of non-love. We have not done that.

Divorce need not shatter children. It is too soon for me to determine if my sons are going to be free, productive, happy and successful *adults*—but they're on the right path because that's the kind of children they are. Children can adjust to almost anything if they receive enough love.

It may be some time before you feel completely divorced. Occasionally, for no apparent reason, I feel a vague nostalgia when my sons' father comes to pick them up. At times I even wonder what might have been, but what *might* have been could have been ugly. Either one of us could have turned into an alcoholic or become seriously disturbed in other ways, trying to evade the reality of unhappy marriage.

My sons' father has remarried and appears to be finding happiness; I have just remarried but my life as a divorced mother was more happy than unhappy. Happiness is a direction, not a place. So to the question "Are you sorry you're divorced?" I must answer: No. I like myself and my life now, my sons are thriving, and all our lives are going on quite well. I am not completely sorry I married whom I did, when I did, because some good things did come out of that union, such as two beautiful boys. So it was not a total loss or a disaster.

I would say I've had a successful divorce.

Bibliography

Adler, Alfred. *What Life Should Mean to You.* New York: G. P. Putnam's Sons, 1958.

Armbruster, Dorothy M. *Pennies and Millions: A Woman's Guide to Saving and Investing Money.* Garden City, N.Y.: Doubleday and Co., Inc., 1962.

Arstein, Helen S. *What to Tell Your Child.* Indianapolis: The Bobbs-Merrill Co., Inc., 1962.

Beecher, Marguerite and Willard. *Parents on the Run.* New York: The Julian Press, 1955.

Bergler, Edmund. *Divorce Won't Help.* New York: Harper & Brothers, 1948.

Bernard, Jessie. *Remarriage: A Study of Marriage.* New York: The Dryden Press, 1956.

Berne, Eric. *Games People Play.* New York: Grove Press, Inc., 1967.

Bettelheim, Bruno. *Love Is Not Enough.* Glencoe, Ill.: The Free Press of Glencoe, 1950.

Blake, Nelson Manfred. *The Road to Reno.* New York: The Macmillan Co., 1962.

Blood, Robert O., Jr., and Donald M. Wolfe. *Husbands and Wives: The Dynamics of Married Living.* Glencoe, Ill.: The Free Press of Glencoe, 1960.

Brenton, Myron. *The American Male.* New York: Coward-McCann, 1966.

Brophy, Brigid. *Black Ship to Hell.* New York: Harcourt, Brace & World, 1962.

Brown, Helen Gurley. *Sex and the Single Girl.* New York: Bernard Geis Associates, 1962.

Brussel, James A. *The Layman's Guide to Psychiatry.* New York: Barnes and Noble, Inc., 1965.

Burgess, Ernest W., and Harvey J. Locke. *The Family.* New York: The American Book Co., 1953.

Caprio, Frank S. *Variations in Sexual Behavior*. New York: The Citadel Press, 1955.

Champagne, Marian. *Facing Life Alone*. Indianapolis: The Bobbs-Merrill Co., Inc., 1964.

Cotton, Dorothy Whyte. *The Case for the Working Mother*. New York: Stein and Day, 1965.

Coudert, Jo. *Advice from a Failure*. New York: Stein and Day, 1965.

de Beauvoir, Simone. *The Second Sex*. New York: Alfred A. Knopf, Inc., 1961.

de Rham, Edith. *The Love Fraud*. New York: Clarkson N. Potter, 1965.

Despert, Louise J. *Children of Divorce*. Garden City, N.Y.: Doubleday and Co., Inc., 1962.

Detroit Bank and Trust. *How to Manage Your Money*. New York: Benjamin Company, 1967.

Deutsch, Helene. *The Psychology of Women*. New York: Grune & Stratton, 1944.

Edwards, Morton. *Your Child From 2 to 5*. New York: Pocket Books, Inc., 1955.

Egleson, Jim, and Janet Frank Egleson. *Parents without Partners*. New York: Ace Star Books, Inc., 1961.

Ellis, Albert. *The Art and Science of Love*. New York: Lyle Stuart, 1960.

———. *The Intelligent Woman's Guide to Manhunting*. New York: Lyle Stuart, 1963.

———. *Sex and the Single Man*. New York: Lyle Stuart, 1963.

———. *Sex without Guilt*. New York: Lyle Stuart, 1958.

———. *How to Live with a Neurotic*. New York: Crown Publishers, 1957.

——— and Albert Abarbanel (eds.). *Encyclopedia of Sexual Behavior*. New York: Hawthorn Books, 1961.

Ellis, Havelock. *On Life and Sex*. New York: The New American Library, 1957.

Emerson, James G., Jr. *Divorce, the Church and Remarriage*. Philadelphia: The Westminster Press, 1961.

Friedan, Betty. *The Feminine Mystique*. New York: W. W. Norton & Company, 1963.

Fromm, Erich. *The Art of Loving*. New York: Harper and Row, 1956.

Golenpaul, Dan (ed.). *Information Please Almanac*. New York: Simon and Schuster, 1965.

Goodman, Paul. *Growing Up Absurd*. New York: Random House, 1960.

Ginott, Haim. *Between Parent and Child*. New York: Grove Press, Inc., 1962.

Goode, William J. *Women in Divorce*. New York: The Free Press (Macmillan), 1965.

Harper, Robert A. *Psychoanalysis and Psychotherapy—36 Systems*. Englewood Cliffs, N.J.: Prentice-Hall, Inc., 1959.

Havemann, Ernest. *Men, Women and Marriage*. Garden City, N.Y.: Doubleday and Co., Inc., 1962.

Hilgard, Ernest R. *Introduction to Psychology*. New York: Harcourt, Brace & World, 1962.

Hilliard, Marion. *Women and Fatigue*. Garden City, N.Y.: Doubleday and Co., Inc., 1960.

Hunt, Morton M. *Her Infinite Variety*. New York: Harper and Row, 1962.

——. *The World of the Formerly Married*. New York: McGraw-Hill, 1966.

——. *The Natural History of Love*. New York: Alfred P. Knopf, 1959.

Huxley, Julian S. *New Bottles for New Wine*. New York: Harper & Brothers, 1957.

——. *Religion without Revelation*. New York: Harper & Brothers, 1957.

Ilg, Frances L., and Louise Bates Ames. *Child Behavior*. New York: Dell Publishing Co., Inc., 1956.

Kendall, Elaine. *The Upper Hand*. Boston: Little, Brown and Co., 1965.

Kinsey, Alfred C., Wardell Pomeroy, and Clyde E. Martin. *Sexual Behavior in the Human Male*. Philadelphia: W. B. Saunders Co., 1948.

—— and Paul H. Gebhard. *Sexual Behavior in the Human Female*. Philadelphia: W. B. Saunders Co., 1953.

Kling, Samuel. *The Complete Guide to Divorce*. New York: Bernard Geis Associates, 1963.

Krich, A. M. (ed.). *Women: The Variety and Meaning of Their Sexual Experience*. New York: Dell Publishing Co., 1953.

Lasser, J. K., and Sylvia Porter. *Managing Your Money*. New York: Doubleday and Company, 1963.

Lazarus, Richard S. *Adjustment and Personality*. New York: McGraw-Hill, 1961.

Lefferts, George. *Special for Women*. New York: Avon Book Division, The Hearst Corporation, 1962.

Lerner, Max. *America as a Civilization*. New York: Simon and Schuster, 1957.

Lewinsohn, Richard. *A History of Sexual Customs*. New York: Harper & Brothers, 1958.

Lewis, C. S. *The Four Loves*. New York: Harcourt, Brace & World, 1960.

Lindbergh, Ann Morrow. *Gift From the Sea*. New York: Pantheon, 1955.

Lindesmith, Alfred R., and Anselm L. Strauss. *Social Psychology*. New York: Holt, Rinehart and Winston, 1956.

Locke, Harvey J. *Predicting Adjustment in Marriage*. New York: Henry Holt and Company, 1951.

Malinowski, Bronislaw. *Sex, Culture and Myth*. New York: Harcourt, Brace & World, Inc., 1962.

Maslow, Abraham H. *Motivation and Personality*. New York: Harper & Brothers, 1954.

——, *Toward a Psychology of Being*. Princeton, N.J.: D. Van Nostrand Co. Inc., 1962.

Masters, William H., and Johnson, Virginia E. *Human Sexual Response*. Boston: Little, Brown & Co., 1966.

Maxwell, Florida Scott. *Women and Sometimes Men*. New York: Alfred A. Knopf, Inc., 1957.

Mead, Margaret. *Male and Female*. New York: The New American Library, 1955.

Merton, Robert K., and Robert A. Nisbet (eds.). *Contemporary Social Problems.* New York: Harcourt, Brace & World, 1966.

Montagu, Ashley. *The Natural Superiority of Women.* New York: The Macmillan Company, 1952.

Moore, Marcia, and Mark Douglas. *Diet, Sex and Yoga.* York Cliffs, Me.: Arcane Publications, 1966.

Morgan, Douglas N. *Love: Plato, the Bible and Freud.* Englewood Cliffs, N.J.: Prentice-Hall, Inc., 1964.

Neill, A. S. *Summerhill: A Radical Approach to Child Rearing.* New York: Hart Publishing Co., 1960.

Rand, Ayn. *Atlas Shrugged.* New York: The New American Library, 1961.

————. *The Virtue of Selfishness.* New York: Grove Press, Inc., 1949.

Riesman, David, Nathan Glazer, and Reuel Denney. *The Lonely Crowd.* New Haven: Yale University Press, 1950.

Reik, Theodor. *Of Love and Lust.* New York: Farrar, Straus & Giroux, 1956.

Rosen, Ephraim, and Ian Gregory. *Abnormal Psychology.* Philadelphia: W. B. Saunders and Co., 1965.

Ruitenbeek, Hendrik M. *The Male Myth.* New York: Dell Publishing Co., Inc., 1967.

Schneider, Isidor (ed.). *The World of Love.* New York: George Braziller, 1964.

Schur, Edwin M. *Crimes without Victims.* Englewood Cliffs, N.J.: Prentice-Hall, Inc., 1965.

Selye, Hans. *The Stress of Life.* New York: McGraw-Hill, 1956.

Simon, Ann. *Stepchild in the Family.* New York: Odyssey, 1964.

Simons, Gustave. *What Every Woman Doesn't Know.* New York: The Macmillan Company, 1964.

Sinclair, Andrew. *The Better Half.* New York: Harper and Row, 1965.

Spock, Dr. Benjamin. *Baby and Child Care.* New York: Pocket Books, Inc., 1968.

Stein, Robert. *Why Young Mothers Feel Trapped.* New York: Pocket Books, Inc., 1966.

Sutherland, Edwin H., and Donald R. Cressey. *Principles of Criminology.* Philadelphia: J. B. Lippincott, 1966.

Taylor, G. Rattray. *Sex in History.* New York: The Vanguard Press, 1954.

Tillich, Paul. *The Eternal Now.* New York: Charles Scribner's Sons, 1963.

Van de Velde, T. H. *Ideal Marriage.* New York: Random House, 1965.

Watts, Alan W. *Psychotherapy East and West.* New York: The New American Library, 1961.

Wylie, Philip. *Generation of Vipers.* New York: Farrar & Rinehart, Inc., 1942.

American Jurisprudence (sections on Divorce). Lawyers Cooperative Publishing Co. of Rochester, N.Y., San Francisco: Bancroft-Whitney Co., 1965.

About the Author

CAROL MINDEY was born and grew up in Chicago. She first married at twenty, had two sons, and was divorced at thirty. She has recently remarried after six years as a divorcee. She lives in Bloomfield Hills, Michigan.